Global Justice and Desire

Employing feminist, queer, and postcolonial perspectives, *Global Justice and Desire* addresses economy as a key ingredient in the dynamic interplay between modes of subjectivity, signification and governance. Bringing together a range of international contributors, the book proposes that both analyzing justice through the lens of desire and considering desire through the lens of justice are vital for exploring economic processes. A variety of approaches for capturing the complex and dynamic interplay of justice and desire in socioeconomic processes are taken up. But, acknowledging a complexity of forces and relations of power, domination, and violence – sometimes cohering and sometimes contradictory – it is the relationship between hierarchical gender arrangements, relations of exploitation, and their colonial histories that is stressed. Therefore, queer, feminist, and postcolonial perspectives intersect as *Global Justice and Desire* explores their capacity to contribute to more just, and more desirable, economies.

Nikita Dhawan is Professor of Political Science at the Leopold-Franzen University Innsbruck.

Antke Engel is the director of the Institute for Queer Theory in Berlin, Germany.

Christoph F. E. Holzhey is the founding director of the ICI Berlin Institute for Cultural Inquiry, Germany.

Volker Woltersdorff is currently a fellow at the ICI Berlin Institute, Germany.

Social Justice

Series editors: Davina Cooper *University of Kent, UK*, Sarah Lamble *Birkbeck College, University of London, UK* and Sarah Keenan *Birkbeck College, University of London, UK.*

Social Justice is a new, theoretically engaged, interdisciplinary series exploring the changing values, politics and institutional forms through which claims for equality, democracy and liberation are expressed, manifested and fought over in the contemporary world. The series addresses a range of contexts from transnational political fora, to nation-state and regional controversies, to small-scale social experiments. At its heart is a concern, and inter-disciplinary engagement, with the present and future politics of power, as constituted through territory, gender, sexuality, ethnicity, economics, ecology and culture.

Foregrounding struggle, imagined alternatives and the embedding of new norms, *Social Justice* critically explores how change is wrought through law and governance, everyday social and bodily practices, dissident knowledge and movements for citizenship, belonging and reinvented community.

Titles in this series:

Intersectionality and Beyond: Law, Power and the Politics of Location
Emily Grabham, Davina Cooper, Jane Krishnadas and Didi Herman (eds), 2009

Regulating Sexuality: Legal Consciousness in Lesbian and Gay Lives
Rosie Harding, 2010

Rights of Passage: Sidewalks and the Regulation of Public Flow
Nicholas Blomley, 2010

Anarchism and Sexuality
Jamie Heckert and Richard Cleminson (eds), 2011

Queer Necropolitics
Jin Haritaworn, Adi Kuntsman and Silvia Posocco (eds), 2014

After Legal Equality
Robert Leckey (ed.), 2014

Subversive Property: Law and the Production of Spaces of Belonging
Sarah Keenan, 2015

Chronotopes of Law: Jurisdiction, Scale and Governance
Mariana Valverde, 2015

Law, Environmental Illness and Medical Uncertainty
Tarryn Phillips, 2015

Global Justice and Desire: Queering Economy
Nikita Dhawan, Antke Engel, Christoph F. E. Holzhey and Volker Woltersdorff (eds), 2015

Forthcoming:

Power, Politics and the Emotions: Impossible Governance?
Shona Hunter

Protest, Property and the Commons
Lucy Finchett-Maddock

Regulating Sex After Aids: Queer Risks and Contagion Politics
Neil Cobb

The Sexual Constitution of Political Authority
Aleardo Zanghellini

Law Unlimited
Margaret Davies

Global Justice and Desire

Queering Economy

Edited by Nikita Dhawan, Antke Engel, Christoph F. E. Holzhey and Volker Woltersdorff

Routledge
Taylor & Francis Group
LONDON AND NEW YORK

First published 2015
by Routledge
2 Park Square, Milton Park, Abingdon, Oxon, OX14 4RN

and by Routledge
711 Third Avenue, New York, NY 10017

a GlassHouse Book

Routledge is an imprint of the Taylor & Francis Group, an informa business

British Library Cataloguing in Publication Data
A catalogue record for this book is available from the British Library

Library of Congress Cataloging-in-Publication Data
A catalog record for this book has been requested

ISBN: 978-0-415-71225-5 (hbk)
ISBN: 978-1-315-88416-5 (ebk)

Typeset in Galliard
by Apex CoVantage, LLC

Contents

Notes on the contributors

Jon Binnie is Reader in Human Geography in the Division of Geography and Environmental Management in the School of Science and Environment at Manchester Metropolitan University in the UK. He is an urban, social, cultural and political geographer whose research interests concern the urban and transnational geographies of sexualities. His work focuses on the geographies of LGBTQ political claims and their connection to issues of social and economic justice. He is the author of *The Globalization of Sexuality* (Sage 2004) and co-author of *The Sexual Citizen: Queer Politics and Beyond* (Polity 2000), *Pleasure Zones: Bodies, Cities, Spaces* (Syracuse University Press 2001) and *Sexual Politics Beyond Borders: Transnational Activist Networks and LGBTQ Politics in Europe* (Manchester University Press, forthcoming). He is also co-editor of *Cosmopolitan Urbanism* (Routledge 2006).

S. Charusheela is Associate Dean and Associate Professor at the School of Interdisciplinary Arts and Sciences, University of Washington, Bothell. She is past editor and editorial board member of *Rethinking Marxism*, and member of the Governing Board of the Cultural Studies Association. Her co-edited volume (with Eiman Zein-Elabdin) *Postcolonialism Meets Economics* was published by Routledge in 2004. Recent publications include 'Response: History, Historiography, and Subjectivity' and 'Engendering Feudalism: Modes of Production Debates Revisited' (both in *Rethinking Marxism*) and 'Gender and the Stability of Consumption: A Feminist Contribution to Post-Keynesian Economics' (in the *Cambridge Journal of Economics*).

Nikita Dhawan is Professor of Political Science at the Leopold-Franzen University Innsbruck and Director of the Frankfurt Research Center for Postcolonial Studies, Cluster of Excellence 'The Formation of Normative Orders', Goethe University Frankfurt. She has held visiting fellowships at Universidad de Costa Rica (2013); Institute for International Law and the Humanities, University of Melbourne, Australia (2013); Program of Critical Theory, University of California, Berkeley, USA (2012); University of La Laguna, Tenerife, Spain (2011); Pusan National University, South Korea (2011); Columbia University, New York, USA (2008). Her publications include *Impossible Speech: On* *the Politics of Silence and Violence* (2007), *Decolonizing Enlightenment: Transnational Justice, Human Rights and Democracy in a Postcolonial World* (editor, 2014); *Postkoloniale Theorie: Eine kritische Einführung* (with Maria do Mar Castro Varela, 2014).

Antke Engel is Director of the Institute for Queer Theory in Berlin, a site where academic debate meets up with political activism and artistic/cultural practices (www.queer-institut.de). She received her PhD in Philosophy at Potsdam University and works as independent scholar in the fields of queer, feminist and poststructuralist theory, political philosophy and visual cultural studies. She held visiting professorships at Hamburg University (2003–2005) and at Vienna University (2011), and a research fellowship at the ICI Berlin Institute for Cultural Inquiry (2007–2009). She has published numerous essays and the two monographs *Wider die Eindeutigkeit* (2002) and *Bilder von Sexualität und Ökonomie* (2009).

Roderick A. Ferguson is faculty in the Departments of African American Studies and Gender and Women's Studies at the University of Illinois at Chicago. He is the co-director of the Racialized Body/Postcolonial Sexualities research cluster at UIC. He is the co-editor with Grace Hong of the University of Minnesota Press series *Difference Incorporated.* Also with Hong, he is the co-editor of the anthology *Strange Affinities: The Gender and Sexual Politics of Comparative Racialization* (2011). In addition, he is the author of *The Reorder of Things: The University and Its Pedagogies of Minority Difference* (2012), *Aberrations in Black: Toward a Queer of Color Critique* (2004) and numerous articles.

Jule Jakob Govrin is a PhD candidate in philosophy at Freie Universität Berlin and a research assistant at the Institute for Queer Theory, Berlin. After studying philosophy and comparative literature at Freie Universität and the University of Paris VIII, she published several articles, including *Widerspenstige Körper: Ein Vergleich körperkonzeptueller Widerstandsstrategien bei Judith Butler und Pierre Bourdieu* (2012). In her PhD project *Aufbegehren und Begierden: Zum Verhältnis von Begehren und Ökonomie*, she is focusing on the epistemological and socio-political entanglements of desire and economy in the light of neoliberalism. Her research interests include political and social philosophy, theories of desire, sexuality studies, body politics, poststructuralism, psychoanalysis and philosophy of economy.

Randi Gressgård is Professor of Gender Studies in the Social Sciences at the Centre for Women's and Gender Research (SKOK), and affiliated with the research unit International Migration and Ethnic Relations (IMER), University of Bergen. Her research interests include migration and minority studies, gender and sexuality studies, and urban studies. Among her recent publications is *Multicultural Dialogue: Dilemmas, Paradoxes, Conflicts* (New York and Oxford: Berghahn Books, 2010/2012).

Evangeline Heiliger is Visiting Assistant Professor of LGBT/Queer Studies at Oberlin College, Ohio. Her publications include 'Ado(red), Abhor(red), Disappea(red): Fashioning Race, Poverty, and Morality Under Product (Red)™' and 'Coffee "Tied With a Pink Ribbon": Transgender Phenomena and Transnational Feminisms in Twenty-First Century Ethical Consumer Movements'. She is writing *Sexy Sustainabilities*, a book-length feminist cultural study of racialized gender and sexualized nature in the green and queer economic bodies that comprise American ethical consumerism. Heiliger's research interests include: queer of color critique; gender, sexuality and feminism; feminist pedagogy; cultural studies; sustainability; feminist science; critical development; coffee; class; alternative economies; and environmental justice.

Christoph F. E. Holzhey is the founding director of the ICI Berlin Institute for Cultural Inquiry. He received a PhD in theoretical physics (1993) and another in German literature with a dissertation on the critical potential of paradoxical pleasures (2001). His edited volumes include *Tension/Spannung* (2011), *The Scandal of Self-Contradiction: Pasolini's Multistable Subjectivities, Traditions, Geographies* (with L. Di Blasi and M. Gragnolati, 2012), *Situiertes Wissen und regionale Epistemologie: Zur Aktualität Georges Canguilhems und Donna J. Haraways* (with A. Deuber-Mankowsky, 2013), *Multistable Figures: On the Critical Potentials of Ir/Reversible Aspect-Seeing* (2014) and Wendy Brown and Rainer Forst, *The Power of Tolerance: A Debate* (editor, with L. Di Blasi, 2014).

Ratna Kapur is Global Professor of Law at Jindal Global Law School, India. She is currently a Visiting Research Fellow at the Graduate Institute for International and Development Studies, Geneva. She is also on the core faculty of the Harvard Law School Institute for Global Law and Policy. She has been a Visiting Professor at a number of universities including Yale Law School, Zurich University, Georgetown University Law Centre, and New York University School of Law. Her major books include *Makeshift Migrants and Law: Gender, Belonging and Postcolonial Anxieties* (2010), *Erotic Justice: Law and the New Politics of Postcolonialism* (2005), *Secularism's Last Sigh?* (co-authored, 2001) *Subversive Sites: Feminist Engagements with Law in India* (co-authored Sage, 1996). Her recently published articles include, 'Battered Bodies and Sexy Dressing on the Indian Street' (*SIGNS* 2014), 'In the Aftermath of Critique We are not in Epistemic Free Fall: Human Rights, the Subaltern Subject, and the Non-Liberal Search for Freedom and Happiness' (*Law and Critique* 2014); 'Gender, Sovereignty, and the Rise of a Sexual Security Regime in International Law and Postcolonial India' (*Melbourne Journal of International Law* 2014).

Christine M. Klapeer holds a postdoctoral position at the Department of Development Studies at the University of Vienna. Her current research interests include intersections of queer/postcolonial/feminist approaches with theories of post/development. She is particularly focusing on the challenge of LGBTIQ-inclusive development agendas and she has also published on institutionalized forms of heteronormativity, (queer/ing) sexual citizenship and lesbian/queer theories. She received her doctorate in Political Science from the University of Innsbruck and has been working as a lecturer at several Austrian universities in the field of Gender, Queer and Postcolonial Studies.

Jamila M. H. Mascat is currently a postdoctoral researcher at Nosophi-University of Paris 1 Panthéon-Sorbonne and collaborates with the chair of Practical Philosophy at the Sapienza University of Rome. She received her PhD in Philosophy at the University of Siena in 2008 and has been a research fellow at the University of Paris VIII (2009), at the Jan Van Eyck Academie in Maastricht (2011–2012) and at the ICI Berlin (2013–2014). She is the author of *Hegel a Jena: La critica dell'astrazione* (2011). She has also co-edited *Femministe a Parole* (2012), a critical dictionary at the intersection of feminist, queer and postcolonial theories (2012) and *Il bisogno di filosofia*, an anthology of Hegel's Jena writings (2014). Her current research focus is on the French reception of Hegel.

Lyn Ossome has recently completed her doctorate in Political Studies at the University of the Witwatersrand (Wits), and currently holds a postdoctoral position at the Unit for the Humanities at Rhodes University (UHURU), South Africa. She is a researcher in feminist political economy and writes on land and agrarian issues, postcolonial queer feminist theory, labour sociology, social policy and political theory. Recent publications include 'Democracy's Subjections: Human Rights in Contexts of Scarcity' in N. Dhawan (ed.) *Decolonizing Enlightenment: Transitional Justice, Human Rights and Democracy in a Postcolonial World* (2015), and 'Feminist Organizing, Electoral Representation and Transformation in Africa' in A. Ampofo, C. Rodriguez and D. Tsikata (eds) *Transatlantic Feminisms: Women and Gender Studies in Africa and the African Diaspora* (2015).

Leticia Sabsay is a Lecturer in Psychosocial Studies at Birkbeck College, University of London. Until she left Argentina in 2002, she was Assistant Professor of Communications at the University of Buenos Aires. Since then, she has continued to collaborate with this university at the Gino Germani Research Institute for the Social Sciences, and carried out postdoctoral research at the Freie Universität (Germany) and the Open University (UK). Her publications include *Las normas del deseo: Imaginario Sexual y Comunicación* (Cátedra 2009), *Fronteras Sexuale: Espacio Urbano, Cuerpos y Ciudadanía* (Paidos 2011), and numerous articles in edited collections and journals such as *Citizenship Studies* and *Cultural Studies.*

Karin Schönpflug is an economist with a degree from the University of Vienna, Austria. She has worked in the Austrian Ministry of Finance and is now a researcher at the Institute for Higher Studies, where she is working in applied economics. She has been teaching economics and transdisciplinary studies at universities in Austria and in the US. Her academic interests involve radical feminist methodologies and elements of queer theories; she has been connecting feminist economics with utopian approaches. Lately she has been exploring how neoliberal rhetorics influence queer subjectivities and heterodox economics.

Eva von Redecker works as a research assistant at the Chair for Practical Philosophy and Social Philosophy at Humboldt University, Berlin. Her research interests are in the area of critical theory and social philosophy, both in the tradition of the Frankfurt School and from the perspectives of feminist and queer theory. She works on the following topics: revolution, history, gender, property, recognition and power. Eva has authored an introduction to the work of Judith Butler and a monography on Hannah Arendt's moral philosophy. She is also an editor at the mutualistic micro-publisher Peer Press.

Margot Weiss is Associate Professor of American Studies and Anthropology at Wesleyan University; her scholarship focuses on the sexual politics of late capitalism. Her book *Techniques of Pleasure: BDSM and the Circuits of Sexuality* (Duke University Press, 2011), awarded the Ruth Benedict Prize for outstanding monograph in queer anthropology, is a queer, feminist, and materialist analysis of BDSM. Her current book project, *Visions of Sexual Justice*, draws on multi-sited fieldwork with queer activists in North America to explore the possibilities and parameters of a radical political imagination at a time of economic precarity.

Volker Woltersdorff (aka Lore Logorrhöe) is an independent scholar and affiliated fellow at the ICI Berlin Institute for Cultural Inquiry. He received a PhD in Comparative Literature at the Freie Universität Berlin with a thesis on gay coming-out narrative and practice. From 1999 to 2010 he was research assistant at the Institute of Comparative Literature of Freie Universität Berlin and Member of the Collaborative Research Centre 'Kulturen des Performativen'. His main research interests lie in queer and feminist theories, studies in sadomasochism, subcultural aesthetics and the intersection of heteronormativity and capitalism. He has published numerous essays and the monograph *Coming out: Die Inszenierung schwuler Identitäten zwischen Auflehnung und Anpassung* (2005).

Foreword

Many people have contributed to the realization of this volume, the making of which started with a reading group and subsequently the conference 'Desiring Just Economies – Just Economies of Desire' at the ICI Berlin Institute for Cultural Inquiry in June 2010, which was co-organized by the Sonderforschungsbereich (Collaborative Research Centre) 'Kulturen des Performativen', Freie Universität Berlin, the Frankfurt Research Center for Postcolonial Studies, the Cluster of Excellence 'The Formation of Normative Orders', Goethe University Frankfurt, the Institute for Queer Theory, Berlin, and ICI Berlin Institute for Cultural Inquiry.

With scholars and political activists from five continents and a wonderful gathering of more than 200 participants, the conference inspired intense debates and was a resounding success. While our initial focus was on desire and economy, the notion of justice increasingly gained importance as we tried to link and explore questions of sexuality and economics.

In addition to the speakers and participants at the conference and the contributors to this volume, we want to especially thank the following individuals for their support: Johanna Leinius, Susanne Bernhart, Elisabeth Fink, Rirhandu Mageza-Barthel at the Frankfurt Research Center for Postcolonial Studies, the Cluster of Excellence 'The Formation of Normative Orders', Goethe University Frankfurt; Jule Jakob Govrin and Paula Alamillo at the SFB 'Kulturen des Performativen' Freie Universität, who skilfully managed organizational tasks as well as much of the correspondence; Claudia Peppel, Kirstin Müller and Florian Rosenbauer at the ICI Berlin Institute for Cultural Inquiry; and Jess Dorrance, assistant at the Institute for Queer Theory, who also curated the short film program 'Oh Economy, Up Yours!' for the conference.

Despite the growing interest in intersectional[1] approaches and postcolonial critique in both queer theory and economics, as well as in queer approaches in

1 The model of intersectionality explains how different forms of discrimination overlap and intersect transnationally to produce precarious subject positions. An intersectional approach unfolds how, for instance, justice in the realm of gender and queer politics is not just a question of equality between the diverse genders or different sexual orientations. It is also a question of how factors such as race, class, religion and able-bodiedness complexly interact with gender and sexuality to generate particular conjunctures of oppression as well as resistance.

postcolonial studies, these interventions remain undertheorized in the respective fields. The focus of this volume and its specific contribution lies in drawing connections between the approaches mentioned above and enriching these debates by bringing them together. Moreover, the effort is to provide a profound conceptual reconsideration of the notions of economy, desire and justice and how they relate to each other. These kinds of conceptual reconfigurations – particularly when experimenting with new theses or novel connections – do not necessarily take place in academia, but often in activist contexts, including through creative writing or artistic practices.

We are delighted that the multi-media artist Tejal Shah consented to contribute a cover image to the volume. The video still from 'Animation', channel III of the five-channel video installation *Between the Waves* (2012), shows a collage of golden paper and white chalk drawings on a black background. It represents a horned beast, which houses in its ripped-open belly the cogwheels of a machine and on its back a settlement of warped high-rise buildings. By mixing organic and technical forms, Shah makes it impossible to tell whether the body-like figures in the belly are digested or crunched by the wheels. The inside might also be the outside, and the act of incorporation oscillates between pleasurable consumption and violent appropriation. While the cogwheels clearly indicate industrial production, the decorative elements may depict flower garlands as well as electric cables. Binary distinctions such as natural and artificial, organic and technical, promise and decay lose their meaning.

In Tejal Shah's work, gendered embodiment and embodied agency and intimacy become means of queering the interconnections between economy, desire and justice. Based in India, Shah is interested in the asymmetry of the global North/South divide that is upheld by transnational economic exchange. Creating fantastic worlds mixing sci-fi and ancient myths, Shah unpacks how the effects of this asymmetry may be addressed – for instance, how waste exported from the global North to the global South is used for pleasure rather than for need, or how environmental damage may be healed through collective erotic practices. Shah is not referring to traditional female care relations or clean-up efforts. In the wider context of *Between the Waves*, the audience learns that the horned beast is a unicorn-like, bare-breasted figure in a magnificent harness, interested in sexual exchange that might or might not be called lesbian. Thus, Shah creates exactly those relationalities and interconnectivities between economy and its sexual subtexts and entanglements that, as this book tries to argue, open up new perspectives in economics and sexuality studies.

Queer politics, we suggest, is most compelling when artistic practices and intellectual debate, academic research and collective activism engage with one another. It could become socially transformative, while at the same time contributing to transdisciplinary fields such as gender, queer and postcolonial studies and the emerging field of cultural economy. Materializing in the context of an international conference that brought together many well-known and upcoming creative thinkers who were ready to face the conceptual challenge of transnational and transdisciplinary scholarship, the present volume addresses and incorporates critical work on the intersections of sexuality and economy. We hope that it opens a vibrant field of future inquiry and intervention.

Preface

> My sense is that our work is commonly motivated by a desire for a more radically restructured world, one which would have economic equality and political enfranchisement imagined in much more radical ways than they currently are. The question, though, that remains to be posed for us, I believe, is how we will make the translations between the philosophical commentary on the field of politics and the reimagining of political life. This is surely the kind of question which will render productive and dynamic the opposition between formalism and historicism, between the ostensibly a priori and the a posteriori. One might reply that any notion of economic equality will rely on a more generalized understanding of equality, and that that is part of what is interrogated by this kind of work. Or one might reply that any notion of a future of radically transformed economic relations will rely on a notion of futurity, and futurity is part of what is being attended to here. But such responses go only part of the distance in answering the question that is posed. For what happens to the notion of equality when it becomes economic equality? And what happens to the notion of the future when it becomes an economic future? We ought not simply to 'plug in' the economic as the particular field whose conditions of possibility can be thought out on an a priori level. It may also be that the very sphere of the economic needs to be rethought genealogically. Its separation from the cultural, for instance, by structuralist legacies within anthropology might need to be rethought against those who claim that the very separation of those spheres is a consequence of capital itself.
>
> Judith Butler (2000: 277–8)

Where does desire enter the economic? A common way of putting it is that our ability to obtain the goods and services we desire – whether things we need or things we want – is constrained by our economic circumstances. Conceptualizing the link between desire and economy as that of constraint acts as a 'common sense' starting point for much theorizing within and without the discipline of economics. While it finds its most obvious expression in the neoclassical economist's conception of the budget constraint, the concept of economy as constraint to desire is not limited to the narrowly utilitarian neoclassical tradition – Amartya Sen's capabilities approach and radical critiques of inequality that highlight conspicuous consumption by some and inability to consume by others also understand the economic in terms of constraint on our ability to attain desired outcomes. Framing the link between desire and economy through the lens of constraint leads us to a project and politics of relaxing the material constraints, whether expressed as a modernist project of growth and development or a social democratic project of wealth and income redistribution along with social safety nets.

But we can go much further than the redistributive politics of liberal social democracy when we move past understanding economy as constraint to desire, and instead approach economy as a set of social relations within which social subjects, and thus desire itself, get constituted: constraint on desire, nature/object/structure of desire, and desiring social subject all emerge out of the same set of processes, and co-constitute each other. Radically oriented scholarship and politics seeks to address this relation between desire and economy as an urgent one for a transformative politics beyond redistributive social democracy. Such scholarship both questions the origins and operation of desire (heteronormed desires, desires for objects of consumption, for equality under capitalism and recognition under modernity) and seeks out other desires (desires for just societies, for non-alienated forms of community, for other ways of engaging the world, for alternate futures). As a location from which both the potentials for containment and the possibilities for transformative agency can emerge, radical social theorists and political activists have sought to both analyse and break from the ways social structures and institutions, including those gathered under the sign of the 'economic', constitute desiring subjects and the objects of their desire.

Radical theorists and activists are not alone in seeking to account for and theorize desire. In neoclassical analyses of preferences and utility functions, bourgeois economics has marked desire as the core of its conception of individual decision-making and choice. Here, choice anchors neoclassical economics' conception of the social good, taking the place of ethical valuation. Even as it places desire at the ethical center of analysis through its commitment to the concept of individual choice, this approach tames desire, providing us with a lukewarm and vapid conception of what it means to hunger, to really *want* something. All that remains is a dry formulation of passionless orderings and rankings for various 'options' – usually, but not always, limited to options between various commodity bundles. All else is a transaction at arm's length experienced not as a passionate connection (or equally passionate disavowal) but as a movement between these varied choice sets. At best, one may add in other items such as needs for living wages through tweaks of the sets of options we may choose among and/or the ranking we provide them. Aspects of desires which cannot be adequately accommodated through such tweaking, such as desires for social justice or environmental sustainability, can enter as the need to address externalities, as infrastructural issues of law and health care and sewage due to 'market failure' – that is, as things that happen in some space outside the arm's length of exchange because they reflect desires whose fulfillment is not captured through individual transactions even if the desires themselves can be tweaked into the preference orderings. Even altruism, which occupies much attention in current efforts to model the bourgeois heteronorms of familial care, enters weakly as a tweak to preference orderings. Emotions such as grief, regret, or anger have little to no space in the analysis (regret or remorse are particularly difficult, since they entail disavowals of previously made choices – nobody looks back and laments past decisions in standard economics). Deep and powerful wells of 'base' desires such as Fanonian envy and fantasies of vengeance, of resentment at insult or murderous fury from collective memories of loss, do not have a place in the story. Desires for other ways of being in the world do not enter at all.

Other than greed redefined as self-interest (and even that greed palely rendered as rationality with little resemblance to the lusts for wealth and power that shape and define much of the actual working of economy), and despite desire-rendered-as-preference functioning as both analytic and ethical core for the concept of 'choice' in this approach, desire in bourgeois economics is a very weak and tame thing indeed. And, of course, this is not accidental. In its tame depiction of desire, bourgeois economics reflects the ideological self-imagination of bourgeois liberal modernity. If desire and passion enter the story in such vacuous ways, it is because bourgeois economics retains the evacuation of desire and passion resultant from the reason–emotion/rationality–passion divide instantiated by the subjective self-constitution of bourgeois liberal modernity. I will not repeat here the well-recounted histories of the origins of this episteme. As poststructuralist/postcolonial theorists in multiple fields have shown, this Self is constructed through opposition to a raced, classed, sexed, gendered, colonial Other.

It is, of course, quite easy to critique this formulation on purely realist grounds, and scholars within and beyond economics, liberal and radical, have provided substantial critiques. Economists allied under the umbrella rubric of heterodox economics, ranging across the political spectrum from conservative to liberal to radical, encompassing diverse schools of thought including Austrian, Post-Keynesian, Institutionalist, Marxist, and feminist economics, have devoted themselves to the task of providing a correct/alternate analysis of economic decision-making more aligned with 'reality'.[2] But the problem we face is not merely that

2 Lee and Jo (2013) define heterodox economics as 'economic theories and communities of economists that are in various ways an alternative to mainstream economics. It is a multi-level term that refers to a body of economic theories developed by economists who hold an irreverent position vis-à-vis mainstream economics and are typically rejected out of hand by the latter; to a community of heterodox economists [who] identify themselves as such and embrace a pluralistic attitude towards heterodox theories without rejecting contestability and incommensurability among heterodox theories; and to the development of a coherent economic theory that draws upon various theoretical contributions by heterodox approaches which stand in contrast to mainstream theory.' Heterodox economists come from a variety of schools of thought across the political spectrum, ranging from the pro-market anti-communist perspectives of the Austrian School to the radical perspective of Marxists. The boundaries between the differing traditions are not sharp since, as Lee and Jo note, scholars increasingly bring together concepts and approaches from differing heterodox traditions in developing their analyses. While heterodox economics includes scholars invested in challenging realist/

bourgeois economics gets it wrong. The problem with a modernist episteme such as this is that it is *constitutive*: what is left once we undertake such analysis is not merely description but prescription, a cause posing as an effect.

When we re-open this analysis to bring back desire and emotion, unless we grasp the ways in which this episteme functions as *generative* of subjectivity, our conclusions rehearse the modernist project. We begin by looking for the 'real' – which often becomes an accounting of the 'real' ways in which specific social subjects depart from this imagined-ideal. Since the imagined-ideal reflects a specific self-constitution, we would, not surprisingly, find that those who more closely align with the ideal seem to flourish better. From which follows the conclusion: if we can desire the right objects and attain the right and dutiful training into skill and citizenship, if we can just get the analysis right to identify where the blockage from the ideal vision lies for a specific group, we can then undertake appropriate policies that will lead us into class mobility, liberal democratic freedoms, development. Our radical projects devolve into 'fixing' efforts that instantiate the unfinished business of modernity, through, for example, gender training (to use Spivak's (2000) evocative phrase), or via integrative efforts at education-into-capitalist-labor. A crucial effect of this episteme, which the realist response can only rehearse, is a limiting of our imagination of radical alternatives to a combination of redistribution and safety nets, with all other 'change' imagined through a combination of recognition by and education into liberal capitalist citizenship.

Addressing the modernist evacuation of desires' multiple valences and locations from our understanding of the economic thus requires an effort that moves beyond simple social-scientific realist behaviourism, an *Other* way of narrating the relation between the two (Kaul 2004). This book takes on that project, bringing queer theory, postcolonial theory, race/ethnic studies, and poststructuralist/Althusserian Marxism to bear on a critical analysis of the relation between desire and economy. By centering justice rather than 'reality' as the term that organizes their conversation, the authors advance our understanding of the relationship between a politics of desire and a politics of economic transformation.

Such a project is necessarily fraught, as no text travels in a vacuum. A queer theoretic text taking up economy enters an intellectual terrain marked by legacies of earlier fights within the field of left scholarship and politics: fights about the implications of poststructuralist frameworks and the 'cultural turn' for Marxist thought, arguments about how the new social movements and the new interdisciplinary knowledge projects they gave rise to reflected an identity politics at the cost of economic radicalism and class politics. Rather than fruitlessly seeking to 'settle' questions such as whether the gay, lesbian, bisexual, trans, queer (GLBTQ) movements address or ignore issues of class, and whether queer

behaviorist approaches and highlighting the role of economic discourse itself in constituting social relations, a substantial portion of heterodox economics is committed to some form of realism in articulating critical alternatives to mainstream economics.

theoretic approaches take up or ignore questions of economy, the volume showcases multiple aspects of the limits and pitfalls, as well as the promise and potentialities, of GLBTQ communities and movements.

For example, Ferguson and Binnie highlight different aspects of GLBTQ communities/identities in England, with crucial differences in politics. Where Ferguson discusses black queer artistic and political practice in the 1980s and 1990s which responded to and critiqued Thatcher's neoliberal policies, Binnie describes a form of contemporary gay consumerism which reproduces highly classist representations of white working-class males. Read together, they show us that debates about whether 'the' GLBTQ movements accounted for class and economy ask the wrong question: clearly there are community formations where they have, and community formations in which they have not. Instead, the question becomes: how does a subjectivity organized around transgressive desire manage to foreground a radical practice and project? What are the constraints and limits that could curtail such a radical practice, and what strategies do we have for addressing these limits?

Three inter-related frames run through the volume's critical efforts to address the above questions:[3]

1 economy as context/capitalist neoliberalism;
2 economy as episteme/capitalist modernism; and
3 alternate economies/possibilities for communist futures.

In the first, economy as context or conjuncture, particular phases or stages of capitalist development provide the structural context within which we analyse queer political agendas. Given the contemporary focus of the contributions, neoliberalism/late capitalism takes center stage. For example, Weiss distinguishes transgressive from radical desire. Situating the activities of her objects of analysis

3 Each frame has two terms: a broad category followed by the particular form that category takes within a given context and conversation. In the first two frames, context and episteme, the formulation reminds us that the context of neoliberalism and the episteme of modernity are specific to a particular conjuncture of the capitalist mode of production, rather than standing in for context and episteme as such. This formulation ensures that we do not slip up and allow the specific term to stand in for the general term. When we slip and make the second stand in for the entirety of the first, we fall back into modernist teleology, which limits our ability to conceptualize alternatives to the current context. In the third, the general term is 'alternate economies', while the specific term is 'communist', allowing us to similarly clarify that there may be many visions of alternates, each reflecting a different type of politics. Without that, we stand in danger of imagining all actions as dissident merely because they reflect an alternate to the status quo (such as the slip which images anti-globalization as automatically pro-communist rather than, say, pro-nationalist or pro-nativist authenticity). The clarification in the final frame is the parallel for reimagining economics that the distinction between transgression and radical transformation provides for queer theory in assessing the politics of different types of non-normative desire.

(the queer BDSM community in San Francisco) within the context of neoliberal capitalism, she asks whether and how their transgressive activities are complicit in a fetish of the commodity (which, as Redecker's chapter discusses, is not, alas, a transgressive fetish under late capitalism). Gressgård highlights capitalist history (following Dipesh Chakrabarty's reworking of the original teleological Marxist formulation) as the register through which we may read the ways sexual rights have been trapped within a discourse of civilization. Sabsay anchors her critical discussion of the concept of choice and autonomy in a reflection on the discourses of trafficking and 'cleaning up' social spaces and their relation to spatial logics of gentrification in neoliberal/late capitalism.

But if capitalism/economy appears as conjuncture/social structural context across the volume, the authors share a critical understanding of the constructedness of the term itself – if modernism is the name we give the episteme that corresponds to the economic order we call capitalism, then we need to proceed with care. Since economy and capitalism constitute both a set of social relations and a set of frames for comprehending those relations, we can never take our frameworks as self-evident. It is not only the representations embedded in the desires of the gay consumers of Binnie's chapter, but equally those present in seemingly progressive desires and imaginations, including our own, that we need to take up for scrutiny. Thus, Weiss asks us to account not only for the complicity of the objects of our discussion (in her case, those who identify as and form part of the BDSM community in San Francisco) with neoliberal capitalism in our analyses, but equally for the ways in which we, as scholars, are complicit with these structures in our own scholarship.

One of the real strengths of this volume is the focused attention each author provides to this aspect of desire's relation to economy as episteme/capitalist modernism. Mascat's chapter examines the ongoing hold of modernist epistemes on our political imaginations, and asks us to consider which desires, and of what types, are even *legible* (let alone worthy of support) as reflective of autonomous/free desire. The difficulty in finding a frame within which subaltern desire can be legible cannot, of course, be 'solved' through mere addition/social science, since this is about the grid of intelligibility. Hence, the authors in this volume pursue genealogical and historical strategies which seek to situate and make sense of the frameworks we use to 'think' desire and economy.

Here, a dual move provides the basis for the rich analyses in this collection. For example, Ferguson shows how the radical politics of black queer artists get constituted through a move which breaks down sexuality, to constitute an identity which is always understood as dispersed and contingent. The acute self-consciousness that such a move creates for the category of sexuality in turn enables a far richer capacity to account for and take on the challenge of economic transformation, in contrast to the complicity that more naturalized and sedimented imaginations of sexual identity or sexual transgression (as in the examples from Binnie and Weiss) generate. Kapur, similarly, highlights the problems with imagining sexual non-normativity in terms of a singular heteronorm, dispersing the operations and meanings of sexual normativity around the terms of authentic, pre-colonial-cultural, Western, identity, practice, to anchor the far more ambivalent postcolonial landscape within which the rights-based struggles for decriminalization of sexual dissidence take place.

The counterpart to this move that self-consciously unpacks and breaks down sexuality is a move that breaks down the sedimented elements that constitute the seemingly coherent 'subjects' of economy. As noted above, Gressgård does not simply take 'capitalist economy' as the context for her discussion, but locates the operation of modernism precisely in the registers of History and history between and through which we make sense of economy's relation to modernity. Klapeer and Schönpflug examine the liberal notions of proprietary/property-owning selves that anchor the concepts of autonomy central to much radical imagination, including the radical imagination of freedom *from* control/regulation by society/others behind much feminist and queer thinking about reproductive and sexual freedom and choice. Sabsay similarly tackles the terms of 'choice' through which debates about sex work and sex trafficking are often articulated, providing a genealogy of how the concepts of 'autonomy' and 'self-possession' enact a racial logic – the trace of this logic resurfaces in the problem of subaltern desire addressed in Mascat's chapter.

The discussion of economy as episteme/capitalist modernism shows the importance of moving beyond simple realist analyses to changing the terms of our analysis. If our purposes are radical, then our accounting for desire's relation to economy cannot be limited to a social scientific realist recitation of the facts from within the parameters of the episteme. We must open up the possibilities both for alternate interpretations of 'reality' and for alternative imaginations beyond capitalism. The ability of queer desire to challenge economic relations is not automatic, but, as shown in the chapter by Kapur, such desire sits at multiple angles to various forms of normative desire and is thus available to potentially be mobilized *or* contained. Ossome's chapter reminds us that the economy–culture split is itself a product of the capitalist-modernist episteme, and to assume it as self-evident is to mistake both where economy is and how it relates to desire. Thus, Ossome picks up on Butler's insight about the link between heteronormativity and social reproduction of the mode of production to situate the radical potentials of the movements for GLBTQ rights in South Africa.

Apart from reimagining capitalism itself from outside the capitalist episteme, the chapters in this volume take up the question of alternate imaginations beyond capitalism. What would desire outside the capitalist-modernist frame look like? Redecker reworks the question of desire and commodity fetishism by way of an inter-articulation of Frankfurt School and queer-theoretic psychoanalysis, and develops the possibilities for communist sociality embedded in the figure of a lesbian desire not merely for another, but desire for the pleasure of – and, going further, taking pleasure in actions and practices (labor) that provide pleasure to – another. Klapeer and Schönpflug suggest that we rework our conceptions of sexual freedom through the lens of a 'queer commons' rather than through proprietary conceptions of self-ownership. And Heiliger combines the move of both reimagining 'economy' against the grain of the culture/economy split noted by Ossome and that of imagining desire beyond capitalism addressed by Redecker, Klapeer and Schönpflug, and other authors in this volume to theorize both desire and economy as simultaneously constituted. She suggests we navigate this co-constitution through a web of intentional interventions and tactical mobilizations for supporting the varied projects of dissident/queer subjects.

True to the spirit of radical politics which unsettles both the subjects and objects of desire that infuses its project, the volume cannot easily be pigeonholed into any single conversational community or (inter)disciplinary formation. While queer theory is no doubt a key anchor for the chapters, it acts more like an 'entry point' (in the sense developed by Resnick and Wolff 1987) than a boundary guarding the parameters of analysis and conversation. In their imaginations of alternatives to capitalism, the authors in this volume find points of contact with other dissident projects that seek to rework the question of desire, justice, and economy, such as the poststructuralist Althusserian Marxist tradition I identify with. For example, Redecker's discussion of the links between lesbian desire and communist imagination has parallels to Ceren Özselçuk and Yahya Madra's Lacanian retheorization of communism (Özselçuk and Madra 2005; Madra and Özselçuk 2010), and the work of J. K. Gibson-Graham (1996, 2006) in breaking down capitalcentrism is clearly at the center of analysis for Heiliger's tactical repositionings and maneuverings in the field of economic relations. This conversational openness can be seen in other locations as well, such as the link to conversations around commons in the chapter by Klapeer and Schönpflug, and to modernism and postcoloniality in the chapters by Mascat, Kapur, and others. As such, this is not a book that can or should be read primarily as an expansion of the parameters of a conversation within queer studies – though it is, no doubt, that as well. Rather, it forms one crucial node of a conversation about the possibility for another world.

S. Charusheela

References

Butler, J. (2000) 'Dynamic Conclusions', in J. Butler, E. Laclau, and S. Žižek, *Contingency, Hegemony, Universality: Contemporary Dialogues on the Left*, London: Verso, pp. 263–80.

Gibson-Graham, J. K. (1996) *The End of Capitalism (As We Knew It): A Feminist Critique of Political Economy*, Oxford: Blackwell Publishers.

—— (2006) *A Postcapitalist Politics*, Minneapolis: University of Minnesota Press.

Kaul, N. (2004) 'Writing Economic Theory AnOther Way', in E. Zein-Elabdin and S. Charusheela (eds) *Postcolonialism Meets Economics*, London: Routledge, pp. 183–200.

Lee, F. S. and Jo, T. -S. (2013) 'Chapter One: Introduction to Heterodox Economics', in *Heterodox Economics Directory* (5th edition). Available online at http://heterodoxnews.com/hed/intro (accessed 6 August 2014).

Madra, Y. M. and Özselçuk, C. (2010) '*Jouissance* and Antagonism in the Forms of the Commune: A Critique of Biopolitical Subjectivity', in C. Özselçuk and A. Curcio (eds) Special Issue on 'The Common and the Forms of the Commune', *Rethinking Marxism: A Journal of Economics, Culture and Society* 22(3): 481–97.

Özselçuk, C. and Madra, Y. M. (2005) 'Marxism and Psychoanalysis: From Capitalist-all to Communist Non-all', *Psychoanalysis, Culture and Society* 10(1): 79–97.

Resnick, S. A. and Wolff, R. D. (1987) *Knowledge and Class: A Marxian Critique of Political Economy*, Chicago, IL: University of Chicago Press.

Spivak. G. C. (2000) 'Other Things Are Never Equal: A Speech', *Rethinking Marxism: A Journal of Economics, Culture and Society* 12(4): 37–45.

Introduction

Nikita Dhawan, Antke Engel, Jule Jakob Govrin, Christoph F. E. Holzhey and Volker Woltersdorff

January 1st, 1912 marked the beginning of one of the most historic struggles of the American working class, when the textile workers of Lawrence, Massachusetts, staged a walkout. What was unique about the strike was that it brought together different immigrant communities under the leadership of the Industrial Workers of the World and was led to a large extent by women. As the legend goes, during a parade through Lawrence, a group of women workers carried banners demanding 'Bread and Roses'. The slogan is said to have been inspired by a speech delivered by Rose Schneiderman, wherein she proclaimed that 'The worker must have bread, but she must have roses, too' (cit. in Eisenstein 1983: 32). The slogan pairing bread and roses, appealing for both fair wages and dignified as well as pleasant work conditions, challenges the uncoupling of labour struggles for economic advances and struggles striving for recognition, dignity and quality of life. The 'Bread and Roses' logic that has inspired innumerable political movements goes against an economistic approach that reduces the question of justice to the fulfilment of bare needs. Challenging the happiness index that has become the global measure of sustainable well-being, it is instead driven by the desire for other, more just economies.

Unfortunately, this multifaceted approach to the question of justice is not always 'common sense'. In the past decades the ILO, UNESCO as well as the World Bank have advocated the 'basic needs' strategy, setting parameters for a minimum threshold below which no person should fall (Kapoor 2008: 22).[1] This entails setting up a minimum standard of living comprising food, shelter, clothing, sanitation, education and health. Although emphasis on 'basic needs'

1 The 'basic needs' strategy in the fight against 'absolute poverty' was introduced into international policy in 1976 by the International Labour Organization's World Employment Conference, and profoundly challenged by Amartya Sen in 1980 for its focus on consumption. Sen (1984), and subsequently Martha Nussbaum (2000) from a feminist perspective, instead proposed the 'capability approach', focusing on the conditions that enable socio-political participation. Nevertheless, 'roses' are not included in the capability approach, instead providing a different dimension of well-being and justice. This raises the crucial question of the complex intertwinement of material, socio-political and cultural dimensions of poverty and quality of life.

goes beyond the economic growth approach to poverty alleviation, Ilan Kapoor unpacks how the ideological construction of pure, universal, primary and natural 'basic needs' betrays a 'dubious cultural fiction' through erasure of socio-cultural contexts in which these are constituted (see Redecker, Chapter 1 in this volume). The dualisms constructed between needs and desires, or nature and culture, determine the legitimate demands for bare human necessities for survival by 'needy' beneficiaries. Kapoor contends that this constitutes a hierarchical distinction between 'primary' and 'secondary' needs, with the former being considered 'absolute socioeconomic prerequisites', while the latter are viewed as 'luxurious' indulgences (ibid.: 23). The upshot of this is an ahistorical narrative that flattens the multidimensionality of both needs and desires. Furthermore, this narrative divulges the desires of dominant groups who dictate what the needy 'really' need and deserve (ibid.: 24). Following Jean Baudrillard, Kapoor argues that 'basic needs' is a discursive construction that employs the figure of excess as its constitutive other. As such, the 'intimate links between luxury and survival, wealth and scarcity, inequality and poverty' are disavowed in economistic approaches (ibid.: 25). The logic of juxtaposing bread and roses rationalizes the capitalistic approach with clear categorization of individuals and groups that can make legitimate claims only to bread. In this framing, the demands by the poor and needy for 'roses' are deemed not only irrational and uneconomic but absurd, perverse and excessive (see Heiliger, Chapter 11 in this volume).

Historically, both Marxist and queer embrace of justice is marked by ambivalence. For Marx, justice was deeply entangled in ideology as there is no possibility of justice under capitalism and no need for justice after communism (Jakobsen 2011: 21). Furthermore, justice is traditionally associated with the idea of redistribution of goods and wealth, which leaves unaddressed the question of control of means of production (ibid). As sexual relations are also relations of production, this is also significant for queer politics. However, justice's opposing term, namely 'freedom', has also lost its attraction for contemporary Marxist and queer-feminist approaches. As outlined by queer theorists, the neoliberal interplay between politics of freedom and politics of sex reveals the inextricable link between sexual freedom/choice and capitalism (ibid.: 23).

Critical theorists are consequently drawing on the vocabulary of transnational in/justice to examine economic and political disenfranchisement in the era of neoliberal globalization. In addressing issues of economic justice and socio-political participation, feminist and queer scholars highlight the role of sexuality in addition to the gendered division of labour (Alexander 1997; Cornell 1998; Nussbaum 2000; Lorenz and Kuster 2007). They also draw connections between economic justice and sexual justice (Duggan 2003; Bedford and Jakobsen 2009), and reveal the heteronormative bias that fosters international gender and development policies (Bedford 2009; Lind 2010). In light of these discussions, this volume explores to what extent desire can provide an analytical tool in understanding sexual and economic justice. We are confronted with the following questions: How do justice, desire and economy intersect and conflict? How does their intertwinement form a complex dynamic of differential meanings, social effects and political affects? Taking these questions as the point of departure, the aim of this volume is to expound an understanding of economy as a key ingredient in the dynamic interplay between modes of subjectivity, governance and social life, and to explore how specific and different ways of doing economy may evolve from these dynamics. Employing feminist, queer and postcolonial perspectives, the volume focuses on questions of justice that emerge from economic processes. While these are questions of equality, distribution and recognition, we propose that they are also questions of desire and that analyzing justice through the lens of desire – as well as considering desire through the lens of justice – may prove useful to develop analytical tools for exploring economic processes. Since we understand analytical tools not merely as descriptive but also as unfolding performative potential, we suggest that the rethinking of justice/desire can foster transformative forces.

Despite the possible heteronormative connotations of romance, 'roses', as a metaphor of political protest, may signify a desire that is much more multifarious, a desire to subvert the distinction between natural needs and deviant desires, a desire that is sexual in polymorphous ways, perhaps also queer. Desire is considered both a motor of economy and a force to be generated and disciplined by economy. Challenging the presumption of economy as sexuality's other, we claim that desire is central to socio-economic processes, to the sphere of consumption, to working worlds, and to their modes of subjectivity; last but not least, it is embedded in economic exploitation, which often implies a lack of sexual autonomy and vulnerability to sexual violence (Castro Varela and Dhawan 2011b).

We focus on desire as a key term that facilitates exploring the entanglements of economy and sexuality. Like desire, sexuality is not separate from the ways in which we feed, clothe and house ourselves. Sex is always-already 'contaminated' by economic needs, wants and conditions, and ways of organizing sexual relations influence economic processes. Current global economic processes constitute specific sexual identities and practices that collaborate in relations of exploitation, domination and subjectivation, and they are often heteronormative (Kulpa and Mizielinska 2011; Castro Varela and Dhawan 2011b; Lind 2013). At the same time we also argue that heteronormativity is not the only modality for the regulation of desire, even as the salience of heteronormativity cannot be simply subverted by fostering non-normative sexualities and genders and the transgression of heteronorms.

Given the multiplicities of rationalities and technologies of power, we propose an approach that draws on queer theory, but does not reduce its scope to questions of gender and sexuality alone, instead understanding sex, gender, sexuality and desire as intricately intertwined and necessarily articulated through a whole set of complex, socio-historical differences. This view, which may be captured under the buzzword 'intersectionality' (Crenshaw 1989), has been extensively discussed within queer studies (Cohen 2005; Eng *et al.* 2005; Dietze *et al.* 2007; Hashemi *et al.* 2013). Accordingly, desire is understood to have constitutive effects not only on subjectivities and intimate social relations but also on normative symbolic orders and macro-political processes and institutions. Hierarchical gender arrangements, relations of exploitation and their colonial histories equally structure sexuality. We propose that queer theory and queer politics uphold the idea of a multiplicity of perspectives – the impossibility of foreclosing meaning or forms of social organizing – and accordingly fostering ongoing political struggles and non-dominant futures. The various chapters of this book explore how such forms of queer, feminist and postcolonial theory and politics, which are mutually productive, may contribute to more just and more desirable economies.

Herein, the term 'justice' is critically engaged with in order to explore both its enabling and disempowering functions in the context of debates about economy and desire. Instead of functioning as an ideal and universal norm, the term 'justice' is employed as a contestable term; it is open to debate *and* it offers possibilities for political practice. This means asking questions about the distribution of resources, forms of value and modes of recognition and representation. In order to articulate the demand for sexual justice as a crucial aspect of the struggles for economic justice, our understanding of justice must be reconfigured, so that struggles for economic justice do not marginalize sexual injustice and its economic consequences, even as struggles for sexual rights address economic issues (Bedford and Jakobsen 2009; Castro Varela and Dhawan 2011b). A postcolonial-queer-feminist critique of justice neither entails a rejection of the idea of justice for its Eurocentric origins nor claims to 'recover' pure, uncontaminated and authentic non-Western notions of justice (Randeria 2002; Dhawan 2011a, 2011b). Rather, justice may be understood as a 'travelling norm' whose *roots* must be distinguished from the *routes* of the idea (Gilroy 1995).

The three sections of the volume, 'Entanglements of desire and economy', 'Intersections of sexual and economic justice' and 'The political economy of queer embodiments', respectively address specific aspects of the key concepts outlined here. Furthermore, the variable interdependencies and unexpected interrelations of all three moments are peppered throughout the volume. Following such a complex, dynamic and open-ended approach enables the volume to draw attention to divergent, if not contradictory, geo-political formations in an unevenly globalized world, including countless internal differentiations that arise due to differing power relations and systems of knowledge. What difference does it make, for example, to employ the concept of neoliberalism, capitalism or cultural economy in order to understand sexualized class relations – in a Western rural region or a megacity in the global South? Why should one refer to love, desire or the erotic as a means of explaining property relations and the way they are – heteronormatively – reproduced? When is it politically more promising to draw on universal human rights than to highlight the unacknowledged legal pluralism in, for example, India or South Africa? What about queer desires that wish to participate in local power struggles of civil society rather than become cosmopolitan by adopting transnational discourses (cf. Gressgård, Chapter 5 in this volume)? Instead of answering such questions in a way that would subsume them under one overarching framework, this volume seeks to incite debate and a multiplicity of perspectives and politics.

Desire

We propose focusing on the notion of desire as an analytical tool to explore the *sexual* dimension of economy, the *economic* dimension of sexuality, and desire's potential for fostering justice. From this perspective, desire is most often grasped as sexual desire because sexuality is an important arena where desire and economy cooperate and conflict at the same time. Economy is not just run by desire; capitalism also produces desire to expand the manifold spheres of consumption. New consumer groups are being generated through sexualized wish production both in a wider sense and specifically in relation to sexual practices and socialities. Furthermore, the economization of sexual desire constitutes new neoliberal subject positions. It reorganizes the sexual field in terms of competition, consumption, personal optimization, financial capacity and body-normative beauty regimes. The neoliberal subject is interpellated to accumulate erotic capital in order to fulfil the socio-sexual standard of individual optimization, to be desirable and to design oneself as a sexual subject. Hence, the neoliberal diversification of sexuality integrates formations of desire in market logics, not only through consumption but also by creating more subtle forms of governmentality (Engel 2009). These forms of governing others and the self can be outlined in terms of sexual labour (Lorenz and Kuster 2007), sexual entrepreneurship (Harvey and Gill 2011) or governance through sexuality (Blasius 2013).

In light of these socio-political processes, desire is methodologically expedient not only to analyse the normative orders of sexual governance but also to unpack the potential of queering these orders. Of course, this entails reconceptualizing desire beyond its (hetero-)normative 'sexual structuring' (Lauretis 1994), which – at least historically – has functioned to legitimize and institutionalize class and gender differences, racializations and racist apartheid, human/animal distinctions, criminalizing and pathologizing exclusions, as well as hierarchizations of mental, bodily and moral health (Foucault 1980; Rubin 1992; McRuer 2006). Feminist and queer approaches to desire not only challenge the heterosexual norm and the premise of binary gender difference, they also criticize the complementary and hierarchical divide of the 'subject' and 'object' of desire as a structural moment that effects and legitimizes relations of desire as domination, submission and appropriation (Rubin 1975; Butler 1993; Grosz 1995; Weiss, Chapter 4; Klapper and Schönpflug, Chapter 9; and Sabsay, Chapter 10 in this volume).[2] In light of these queer-theoretical approaches, critiques of

2 Elizabeth Grosz (1995) provides a historical overview of theories of desire from Plato to Freud, showing how the position of a desiring subject is secured by expecting someone to embody the object of desire: to function as the recipient of the subject's activity, or even to be appropriated as a possession. As early as 1975 Gayle Rubin argues in her essay 'Traffic in

psychoanalytic conceptions of desire continue to be important in order to elaborate desire in other ways, for instance as ***productivity*** (Probyn 1996; Shildrick 2009; MacCormack 2009). Elspeth Probyn's (1996) notion of 'desire travelling in images' is inspired by Gilles Deleuze and Félix Guattari (2004) in presenting desire as drawing connections on the surface of the social and forming assemblages of objects, signs and bodies. It subverts any kind of naturalized desire caught in the depth of a subject. At the same time, Probyn points out that power analysis is necessary and may unfold whether concrete connections repeat well-known patterns of identity, difference and their stratified power relations, or whether desire is travelling in images that confuse and disrupt established normalities and invoke surprising assemblages.

While it would be implausible to argue that desire is transformative in itself or that, ontologically, desire is inherently queer, its manifold articulations suggest that desire contains a paradox, which allows for queer re-articulations. This paradox – provided that it is played out as a productive tension – holds the promise of linking Foucault's insights into desire as a product of historical power/knowledge with a Deleuzo-Guattarian understanding of desire as movement and becoming. The former sees desire as a regulatory force, disciplining bodies, regulating populations and constituting normative sexual identities (Foucault 1980, 1990), whereas the latter underlines the potential of desire to break up established power relations (Deleuze 1997).[3] While Foucault, in order to think sex otherwise,

Women: Notes on the "Political Economy" of Sex' that the hierarchical 'sex/gender system' is built upon a heterosexual order of males exchanging females as 'gifts'. In her 1974 book *Speculum de l'autre femme* (Engl. translation 1985), Luce Irigaray discloses this as a phallocentric order built upon a certain form of 'hommosexualité', which secures an understanding of sexual difference that excludes women from the subject position and declares feminine desire an impossibility. Audre Lorde (1984), in her 1978 essay 'Uses of the Erotic', therefore suggests that women should reclaim and share with each other the power of the erotic in order to get away from patriarchal notions of desire. Judith Butler not only denaturalizes the binary distinction of the sexes, which she discovers as functioning as the precondition of normative or compulsory heterosexuality (1990), but also offers a feminist interpretation of Hegel's 'Begierde' as a desire for recognition that constitutes an 'ek-static self' (2004). Taking up Jessica Benjamin's *Bonds of Love* (1988), she translates the Lacanian notion of the 'desire of the Other' (Lacan 1977) into the 'desire of the Other of the Other' (Butler 2004), thus asking us to embrace the uncontrollable affectedness by irreducible otherness as a psychic as much as a social experience. Other queer/feminist re-readings of psychoanalytic theories have been brought forward, for instance by Teresa de Lauretis (1994), who suggests understanding desire as taking place in 'shared fantasy scenarios' where positions of subject and object are no longer distinguishable, or by Leo Bersani (2010, originally 1987), who foregrounds that Freud, while on the one hand enforcing a normative heterosexual, phallocentric development, on the other hand promotes the shattering of the subject of mastery in practices of sexuality as 'the precondition for the very establishment of a relation to the other' (24).

3 Michel Foucault (1980) criticized the psychoanalytic understanding of desire as a discursive regime, which constitutes bodies, subjectivities and populations in such a way that they actively make themselves adapt to normative gender identities, heteronormative family structures and capitalist ways of production and consumption.

proposed shifting attention to economies of pleasures, Gilles Deleuze and Felix Guattari (2004) focused their critique on psychoanalysis's preoccupation with a supposedly constitutive lack that incites desire. According to these authors, this psychoanalytical perspective fails to understand the productivity of desire, which is not only, as Foucault suggests, constituted by and constitutive of the dominant social order but also a vital force of its own – a force that may inspire unexpected connections and transformations (cf. Ferguson, Chapter 3 and Heiliger, Chapter 11 in this volume).

While advocating a more versatile understanding of desire as an itinerant category, oscillating between lack and productivity, it is also important not to overlook dimensions of need, self-interest and power. There certainly can be no question of naively believing in desire as remedy for political and economic injustices. Instead, we suggest that in seeking to bring together economic and sexual justice through queer reconceptualizations of desire it is helpful to maintain tensions between desire, need and interest, as well as between desire as a 'conservative' and desire as a 'transformative' force (Gibson-Graham 2006). Furthermore, it seems necessary to capture a complex intertwinement of bodily pleasures, fantasies, effects, relationalities and institutions of desire – all of which might carry rational as well as irrational dimensions.

In the face of the problematic heteronormative sexual structuring of desire and the various critiques of desire, we nonetheless do not abandon desire nor subtract the sexual from desire, as some current queer-theoretical thinking does (Halley and Parker 2011). Rather, we insist on desire as sexual. In the context of queer theory, sexuality is understood not solely as a dimension of embodied subjectivity but also as a discourse that works in tandem with material forms, institutions and regimes of social relationships (Foucault 1980; Rubin 1992; Butler 1990; Weeks *et al.* 2003; Blasius 2013; Lind 2013; Mesquita *et al.* 2012; Hashemi *et al.* 2013). A queer-theoretical perspective not only analyses how institutions regulate sexuality but also explores: 'How do assumptions about sexuality inform and constitute social institutions and our notions of the "social world"?' (Richardson and Seidman 2002: 7). Thus, the queer-theoretical term 'heteronormativity' describes how normative or compulsory heterosexuality as a social institution is based on rigid binary sexual difference and reproduces it (Warner 1993; Hartmann *et al.* 2007). Enforcing the norm of coherence of sex, gender and desire (Butler 1990), heteronormativity 'sets the conditions of possibility and impossibility for gender intelligibility' (Carver and Chambers 2008: 144). Gayatri Spivak (2012) proposes the term 'reproductive heteronormativity (RHN)' in order to examine how a 'complicated semiotic system of organizing the sexual/gendered differential', which is intricately intertwined with passion, 'extends to reproduction, with all its psychic uses' (124). This system, she argues, may be challenged through a 'rearrangement of desire' (ibid.: 125). Spivak's terminology asks us to draw explicit connections to global sexual justice – including controversial debates about natalism, biopolitics in the name of 'population control', homophobia, adoption rights, artificial insemination, abortion and sexual self-determination – that concern communities usually not in alliance: heterosexual as well as lesbian, gay and transgender ways of existence; ethnicized and racialized constituencies; and people with debilities or disabilities. For these reasons and others, it becomes clear that the critique of heteronormativity must include the critique of identity categories and processes of exclusion and normalization, including economic ones (Butler 1990; Warner 1993; Castro Varela and Dhawan 2011a).

A queer-theoretical understanding of desire as sexual stands in contrast to approaches in political philosophy that conceptualize desire as beyond the sexual, for example as the desire for recognition (Hegel 1970), the will to power (Nietzsche 1999) or the desire to secure one's existence (Spinoza 1996). In *The Politics of Friendship*, Jacques Derrida (2005) unfolds the role of male homosocial bonding for the understanding of politics over the centuries, and critically points out that these notions and practices of friendship are built upon the foreclosure of the feminine (as the sexualized other), heterosexual friendship and desire in politics. To some extent, insisting on the political role of sexuality recalls Freudo-Marxist or Frankfurt School thinking from the early and mid-twentieth century (Marcuse 1955; Reich 1972; Fromm 1995). However, this former theorizing mostly considered sexuality in terms of instincts, drives, needs, desires or libido, and tended to take normative heterosexuality for granted, while naturalizing or even idealizing binary gender complementarity (see Redecker, Chapter 1 in this volume, for a more complex reading of Marcuse).

The genealogy of desire in the history of philosophy and psychoanalysis should be borne in mind when deploying the epistemological links between desire and economy. It reveals how desire and economy intertwine by oscillating between lack and productivity. Hegelian but also psychoanalytic concepts of desire share the idea that desire operates as a mode of intersubjectivity. Desire here is grasped as a 'longing for recognition' (Hegel 1970; Butler 1987, 2004) and an unconscious wish for complementarity and wholeness, and hence motivated by a constitutive lack (Freud 1982; Lacan 1985). Within an understanding of desire as grounded in a fundamental lack and incited by a longing for recognition, the quest for capital, property and consumption appears as an attempt to be reassured of one's value and as an ultimately futile effort to cover up lack. This raises questions such as the following: To what extent do existing and imagined alternative economies challenge this false promise? How far do they replicate scarcity in a symbolic register and use symbolic recognition as a cheap, exploitative substitute for financial compensation? The conception of desire as lack conjures up not only desire's regulation according to binary sex/gender differences and heterosexual coupling, but also the economic register of scarcity.[4] However, are we always speaking of the same lack? Not only does lack function differently – for example,

4 Furthermore, this conception links up with the fetish as a defence against lack, which provides another bridge to the economic field through the notion of commodity fetishism (Lauretis 1994; Hennessy 2000; Weiss, Chapter 4 in this volume).

in economic scarcity or austerity and in the sexual fetish – but lack can also be taken to imply the impossibility of the closure of signification, of achieving stable meaning or of constituting a coherent identity. Only a small shift of perspective is therefore necessary to arrive at a notion of desire as excess and productivity. While this opens up further connections with economic processes, the view of desire as productivity is not necessarily closer to queering desire than desire as lack is, and in our view either perspective may be productively confronted with questions of need.

How, then, may the manifold entanglements of sexuality and economy be conceptualized? It seems essential to ask critically how specific economies deploy desire, and which concepts of desire allow for what kind of economic thinking. If we assume that desire sustains current economies, but also carries the potential for orchestrating new forms of understanding and doing economy, are we then referring to different or even contradictory forms of desire or to an inherent paradox in desire? For example, if we try to understand the desire of the broker to speculate on the stock market, is this bound to the pleasure of gambling, the excitement of risk, the affective investment in hegemonic masculinity, the belief in destiny, the interest in profit-making, or all of this at once? Although desire should not be conflated with interest, the question arises if the interest in profit-making is driven by economy or desire, and how the interest to subvert the hegemonic order can be understood in terms of desire. What, then, could 'queering' economy mean? Could we, for example, imagine a form of speculation that draws pleasure from risking the exit from the normative orders of capitalism and heteronormativity? A broker who desires to undermine forms of profit-making built upon exploitation and personal enrichment? Could we imagine a stock market exchange that explicates the sexual pleasure underlying its transactions? Or which queers these transactions not by fostering homonormative alliances but by creating axes of solidarity and redistribution with disenfranchised and underprivileged communities? And, if we cannot (which might be quite likely), where can we then imagine a ground for these differing economies of desire to come into being?

The challenge consists in recognizing the dangers of neoliberal co-optation of queer desire (Hennessy 2000; Cruz-Malavé and Manalansan 2002; Duggan 2003), while simultaneously exploring whether queering identity and new forms of queer sociality may subvert neoliberalism's logics of individualized interests and profits (Gibson-Graham 2006; Engel 2009; Woltersdorff 2011). Focus on different social, cultural and geopolitical contexts raises the question of where or when the term 'queer' might be inappropriate or even objectionable. For example, the term 'queer' might not adequately capture the emerging solidarities between union workers, self-sustaining peasant farmers (of all genders), sex workers (of all genders), a sexual health movement equally concerned with HIV/AIDS politics and reproductive rights, and people with disabilities struggling for self-determination. While a queer movement aiming to fight all forms of domination, exploitation, injustice and violence might be happy to claim the label, other political groups might well be sceptical about whether the term appropriately reflects their specific interests, even as the concerned parties might fear to lose political ground by being subsumed under this category, or forfeit hard-earned gains. By problematizing both universalist and cultural relativist approaches in different socio-discursive fields – such as consumerism and sex work, hate crime legislation and queer-of-colour film production, exoticizing erotic literature and globalized market economies – this volume emphasizes the very particular socio-historical conjunctures of various relations between sexualities and economies.

Economies

In light of recurrent economic crises, critical scholarship has focused on the multiple forms of crises and the ongoing crisis of capitalism that is endemic to its functioning. These insights and interpretations have also been discussed in relation to historical transformations of sex and gender systems (Demirović and Maihofer 2013; Grabel 2013; Dück 2014), to queer studies (Rosenberg and Villarejo 2012) and to the limited role of feminist economics (Fukuda-Parr *et al.* 2013). The recent financial and economic crisis has made even privileged Eurocentric thinkers aware of the importance of varieties of capitalism and the global operations of political economy, and urged them to consider the field of economy in new ways, drawing insights from thinkers and activists from the global South, to whom the relevance of global economic processes has long been self-evident. This volume therefore not only critically analyses current global capitalism(s), but also envisions and explores possibilities of new forms of economies that challenge the present economic regimes. The presumption here is that global capitalism is not a monolith; rather, diverse capitalisms and diverse economies exist. For instance, ethnic economies in diasporic communities, subcultural economies, gift-and-barter economies and cooperative economies do not all conform to the capitalist logic (Gibson-Graham 1996; Joseph 2002). Going beyond the disciplinary framework of economics, contributions from diverse socio-cultural and geo-political backgrounds inquire into how (queer) reconceptualizations of desire may emerge as a destabilizing and transformative force for economic relations. They thereby fashion spaces for imagining 'other' economies or imagining economy 'otherwise', as well as for the deployment of the concept of desire in ways that allow for a reworking of social relationships and economic practices (Gibson-Graham 1996, 2006; Schönpflug 2008; Engel 2010; Madra and Özcelçuk 2010).

One focus in this volume is on investigating further the relation between heteronormativity and neoliberal capitalism. There is a long-standing controversy over whether capitalism relies on heteronormative orders or not (Los Angeles Research Group 1975; Rubin 1975; D'Emilio 1983; Hennessy 2000; Jakobsen 2011). While the orthodox Marxist tradition tends to reduce all modes of domination to the principal contradiction of capital and labour, other strands of political thinking have observed the (relative) autonomy of gendered and sexualized modes of domination. John D'Emilio (1983) delineated in capitalism a paradoxical simultaneity of doing and undoing heteronormative arrangements.

In this vein, Rosemary Hennessy (2000) pinpoints the co-optation of lesbian and gay communities and argues that capitalism does not need heteronormativity to function. Rather, she affirms, neoliberal capitalism mobilizes desire in order to obtain compliance from individuals. At the same time, the neoliberal precarization of workforce undermines traditional gender identities (Völker 2011) as much as precarization builds upon the feminization of labour and the continuity of coloniality, for example in domestic care work (cf. Gutiérrez Rodríguez 2011). Acknowledging the danger of co-optation, yet turning it into a case for an anti-capitalist queer politics, Lisa Duggan (2003) demands that a queer politics of rights and cultural representations be thoroughly intertwined with a politics of economic justice, in order to halt the politics of upward redistribution enforced by neoliberal politicians. Thus, the increasing socio-cultural integration of diversified genders and sexualities cannot simply be celebrated, but has to be analysed in its double-edged role (Engel 2013). Nonetheless, neoliberal policies can equally rely on the neo-traditionalization of heteronormative and patriarchal family structures, on nationalist and racist identity constructions, and on an intensification of the exploitative global division of labour. Accordingly, other authors address the contradictory effects of capitalism as simultaneously liberatory and exploitative of precarious bodies and subjects, arguing that resistance and anti-capitalist politics have to be developed from within neoliberal subjectivation (Cruz-Malavé and Manalansan 2002; Pühl 2003; Engel 2009; Kolářová 2011; Woltersdorff 2011).

Yet, how does this translate into the field of economic globalization and what does it mean for engaging critically with the transnational mechanisms of sexual and economic exclusion, exploitation and superexploitation? Penny Griffin (2007) and Kate Bedford (2009) highlight the role of the World Bank in reproducing heteronormative gender arrangements through neoliberal policies and securing neoliberal policies by relying on heteronormative notions of sex, gender and sexuality. Some of the contradictory aspects that need to be considered here are the powers of producing within a market economy, powers connected to the control of wages and of conditions of work, and powers to renegotiate roles in the family and the everyday pleasures one enjoys in these roles as a part of the production process and in the market (Dhawan 2011b). More often than not, feminist and queer political struggles in the global North inadvertently reinforce injustice in the South. For instance, neoliberal capitalism has invited bourgeois women of the West into the labour market and thus increased their financial autonomy, but at the same time reinforced gendered international division of labour. A queer perspective on sexual and economic justice cannot refrain from building intersectional and transnational alliances that contest occidentalist dominance (Dietze 2010) and use Northern privilege for dehierarchizing purposes (Alexander 2001; Binnie 2004; Wilson 2004; Bedford 2005; Luibheid and Cantu 2005; Drucker 2009; Menon 2010). Otherwise there is the danger that stereotypical images of economic exploitation in the global South are instrumentalized to enable the self-constitution of the West as a space where capitalism and democracy converge harmoniously, thereby consolidating its global hegemonic position (Spivak 1999; Mohanty 2003; Kapur 2005; Puar 2008; El-Tayeb 2011).

In the examination of capitalism's existing contradictions and alternatives, a perspective on labour has shown to be a productive focal point where questions of economy, desire and justice intersect very clearly. It has inspired investigations in 'immaterial' or 'affective' labour (Hardt and Negri 2004; Lazzarato 1996), but, unfortunately, this research is not informed by queer, feminist and postcolonial critical knowledge. It ignores, for instance, the feminist concept of emotional labour developed by Arlie Hochschild (1983), which extends the analysis of work and exploitation to gendered and sexualized forms of subjectivation and service. This feminist concept of emotional labour was subsequently adopted and refined with a special emphasis on the heteronormativity of work relations as 'sexual labour' (Lorenz and Kuster 2007) and 'gender labour' (Ward 2010). It has equally inspired feminist and queer research on care work and affective labour (Folbre 2012; Jochimsen 2003; Gutiérrez-Rodríguez 2011). This volume follows this strand of thinking when it scrutinizes how exploitative work relations produce desiring subjects and how desire is mobilized for the acceptance or contestation of such work relations (cf. Klapeer and Schönpflug, Chapter 9 in this volume).

Within the broad field of exploring other economies and their potential to unsettle global capitalisms, the widely discussed approach by J. K. Gibson-Graham (2006), which opts for a 'postcapitalist politics of economic difference', provides an important background for some authors in the volume. Gibson-Graham propose a combination of anticipatory thinking, self-cultivation and 'the collaborative pursuit of economic experimentation' (xxiii) in order to enable a heterogeneity of economic practices that do not take the logics of capital and profit maximization for granted. Furthermore, Gibson-Graham propose the term 'queering economy'. This suggestive, though not systematically elaborated concept is particularly interesting for the discussions of *Global Justice and Desire: Queering Economy* since it enables a double perspective on desire: on the one hand desire is seen as a promising driving force of 'imagining otherwise' as well as of 'economic experimentation', while on the other hand it appears as a conservative force that reproduces 'normalities' and upholds the status quo. Apart from suggesting the term 'queering economy', Gibson-Graham promote the development of 'communal economies', thereby contributing to the vibrant debate on the concept of the commons that has inspired recent political thinking and activism. Like Gibson-Graham, many authors in this volume explore the role of desire for developing perspectives of doing economy otherwise.[5]

5 Postcolonial, queer, feminist scholarship has been struggling with these questions for the past decades: Gayle Rubin's early essay 'The Traffic in Women' (1975), Jacqui Alexander's postcolonial analysis 'Erotic Autonomy as a Politics of Decolonization' (1997) and monographs such as Rosemary Hennessy's *Profit and Pleasure* (2000), John D'Emilio's *Sexual Politics,*

Justice

There has been a resurrection of juxtaposing materialist and non-materialist struggles in recent scholarship on justice. One of the most widely discussed examples of the 'bread versus roses' logic is Nancy Fraser's critique of the politics of recognition, including queer politics and anti-racist politics, which in her view emerged in a post-socialist zeitgeist with a resurgence of neoliberal globalization (Fraser 2008).[6] Shifts to a politics of recognition, according to her, have displaced the focus from anti-capitalism to cultural questions. Fraser diagnoses a dovetailing

Sexual Communities (1983) and David Evans's *Sexual Citizenship* (1993) provided groundbreaking work on economic analyses of sexual relations that also question heteronormative premises. They also initiated explorations on the economic costs and benefits of gay, lesbian and transgender life, which were subsequently elaborated in publications such as Amy Gluckman and Betsy Reed's *Homo Economics* (1997), Lee Badgett's *Money, Myths, and Change* (2001), Lisa Duggan's *The Twilight of Equality* (2003) and Arnaldo Cruz-Malavé and Martin F. Manalansan's *Queer Globalizations* (2002). Feminist economics has for decades reflected on the relationship of gender, sexuality and economy (Kuiper and Sap 1995; Nelson 1996; Hewitson 1999; Barker and Kuiper 2003; Gutiérrez 2003; Zein-Elabdin and Charusheela 2004; Schönpflug 2008). Moreover, it further develops the rethinking of relations of desire, economy and justice that was addressed in the various issues of the journal *Rethinking Marxism*. It participates in debates on community economy (Gibson-Graham 1996, 2006; Joseph 2002) and on the commercialization of sexual diversity emanating from the global North (Gluckman and Reed 1997; Altman 2002; Sender 2005). Furthermore, it connects both these fields directly to questions of justice rather than to legal regulations, for example of intimacy (Zelizer 2005). The present volume supplements these analyses and reflects on methodological considerations of poststructural political economy (de Goede 2006), especially regarding how to analyse heteronormativity in economics (Cornwall 1997; Badgett 2001; Charusheela 2008). It is highly affirmative of and enriched by complex and well-argued debates on intersectionality (Grabham *et al.* 2008; Taylor *et al.* 2011), while taking inspiration from insights provided by queer approaches to economics (Jacobsen and Zeller 2008). However, several of these texts often focus specifically on the critical role and the critique of neoliberalism, while neglecting a postcolonial critique. As a corrective to this, there have been a number of recent publications that intertwine queer and postcolonial perspectives – for example, *Queer Diasporas* (2000), edited by Benigno Sánchez-Eppler and Cindy Patton; *Queer Migrations* (2005), edited by Eithne Luibheid and Lionel Cantu; Roderick Ferguson's *Aberrations in Black* (2004); Gayatri Gopinath's *Impossible Desires* (2005); Ratna Kapur's *Erotic Justice* (2005); and Jasbir Puar's *Terrorist Assemblages* (2008).

6 The controversial exchange between Nancy Fraser, Iris Marion Young and Judith Butler that took place in 1997/98 in *New Left Review* and was republished and extended in a later publication (Fraser 2008) has greatly enriched discussions about the appropriate parameters of struggles for justice. Calling Fraser's approach 'Dual Systems Theory', Young criticizes it for creating artificial borders between struggles over distribution of wealth and struggles against discrimination, which Young terms as 'marginalization' and 'cultural imperialism'. Judith Butler's reply to Fraser with the title 'Merely Cultural' equally critiques a politics of division within the Left, yet also makes a strong point of foregrounding how lack of recognition goes along with material exclusion and economic hardship, and resonates with the socialist feminist argument that capitalist re-/production is built upon heterosexual division of labour. For a queer-theoretical evaluation of the debate, see Engel (2002: 206–11).

of the politics of recognition and neoliberalism. She warns against the dangers of the current decoupling of identity politics from class politics, or of the cultural left from the social left (ibid.).

However, Fraser's critique depends on drawing a rigid border between politics of distribution and politics of recognition. In her account, cultural politics is the same as identity politics, which fight for the recognition of essentialized differences. She does not allow for cultural politics as a means rather than a topic of struggle, and thus cannot acknowledge politics that fight through cultural means against economic and symbolic constructions of difference (Engel 2002, 2007).[7] While partly agreeing on the dangers of marginalizing class politics in critical discourses, we propose not to ignore anti-capitalist positions within queer theory and politics (Duggan 2003; Sears 2005; Floyd 2009; Woltersdorff 2011; Rosenberg and Villarejo 2012). For example, the New York-based project Queers for Economic Justice (QEJ), which was initiated in 2002, but had to close down due to lack of funding in 2013, focused on poverty in lesbian, gay, bisexual, trans(gender/sexual), intersexual and queer (LGBTQI) communities, seeing 'queer realities shaped by race, class, and desire'.[8] Furthermore, the arguments made by Fraser and similar voices ignore the failure of socialist struggles to adopt an intersectional perspective that would address the co-constitutive nature of race, class, gender, sexuality, religion, able-bodiedness, etc. (Dhawan 2011a, 2011b). For instance, trade unions remain male-dominated and particularly in the global South they are being increasingly superseded by NGOs because of their failure to address issues such as child care, health care and sexual health, which are still gendered and heteronormative in nature. Accordingly, many of the authors in Sokari Ekine and Hakima Abbas's *Queer African Reader* (2013) emphasize that LGBTQI politics depends on and should build solidarity and strong alliances with different social groups in order to address the 'multiple and intersecting causes of political oppression and persecution' (Ossome 2013: 43). They are sceptical about aid conditionalities stipulated by donors from the global North that support struggles against homophobia and transphobia in African countries because they endanger the solidarity in common struggles over issues of poverty, health and food security, and socio-economic and environmental justice.

7 Among others, the colloquia 'Toward a Vision of Sexual and Economic Justice' (2009) and 'Gender, Justice, and Neoliberal Transformation' (2013), organized by the Barnard Center for Research on Women in New York, aim at overcoming this distinction. See: http://sfonline.barnard.edu/sexecon/issue.htm and http://sfonline.barnard.edu/gender-justice-and-neoliberal-transformations (accessed 23 June 2014).

8 See: http://archive.today/q4ej.org (accessed 9 December 2014). Apart from initiating debates, Queers for Economic Justice had organized a homeless shelter for LGBTQI adults and fostered, under the headline 'Queer Survival Economies', policy development and 'cross-community alliances [...] with labor, economic policy think tanks, immigrants' rights organizers, and the Excluded Workers Congress'. On critical attitudes towards QEJ, see Weiss, Chapter 4 in this volume.

We would propose that an intersectional approach to social and cultural struggles is imperative, one that is as critical of identity politics that marginalize class politics as it is of the failures of class politics to build alliances.

We acknowledge that contemporary queer civil rights politics has favoured the legal and social recognition of same-sex marriages, the growth of the pink economy through the integration of LGBTQI people into global consumerism, and the increased corporatization of queer collectivization through pride marches, for instance, and that it has been instrumentalized and become complicit with legitimizing militarization and imperialism. Some queers have thereby been transformed from figures of death associated with AIDS to reproductive citizens associated with increased purchasing power, gay marriage and family values, integrated into the biopolitical optimization of life (Duggan 2003; Puar 2008; Haritaworn *et al.* 2014). Yet we do not agree with a distinction between politics of recognition as 'affirmative' versus politics of redistribution as 'transformative', as it has frequently been made in the controversy between materialist and non-materialist political thinkers. Such a distinction ignores that queer politics can be both affirmative and transformative at the same time. For instance, in the context of the AIDS crisis, the ongoing fight *against* pharmaceutical companies that control the research, price and distribution of antiretroviral drugs should be seen as transformative politics. At the same time, limiting recognition of citizenship and subjects of legal rights to the small group of gay men who are designated as consumers of their products *by* the pharmaceutical industry is a form of affirmative politics. Similarly, transgender politics might be called affirmative insofar as 'transgender' or 'third gender' are recognized as social or even legal categories in several countries worldwide; however, this does not end the transformative struggles against group pressure, social and familial sanctions, normative, psychic and physical violence, nor the hardships of exclusion from or discrimination in education or on the job market. Nicolas Beger (2004) understands the 'desire for rights' as a decisive moment of queer/LGBTQI struggles for justice, yet points out the queer dilemma at work here: while queer theory questions the normative and exclusionary effects of categorizations, queer politics finds categories still necessary in order to make claims for rights. In combining affirmative and transformative dimensions, the controversial term 'sexual justice' embodies this dilemma.

Like Hennessy (2000) and Duggan (2003), Fraser (1997, 2008) rightly unfolds how the vocabulary of difference and diversity along with that of justice and rights has been appropriated in the service of capital and compromised in its critical potential. However, while this produces new forms of discrimination, exclusion and differentiation through integration, shifting the gaze away from the global North further complicates the picture. The (re-)criminalization of homosexuality in Uganda, Nigeria and India (Kapur, Chapter 6 in this volume), with homophobic sentiments whipped up by foreign Evangelical groups, the introduction of American-style defence of marriage acts in countries such as Romania, and the 2004 declaration of the Doha International Family Institute, which brings together Christian and Muslim civil society groups that reinforce normative ideas of family and marriage, necessitate a more complex, multi-directional politics of critique. While recognition of same-sex marriages in postcolonial countries such as South Africa and Brazil has ushered in civil rights for postcolonial queers, the prevalence of 'corrective rapes' of lesbians (Ossome, Chapter 7 in this volume) or the routine experiences of discrimination on the labour market is an everyday reality. It is not just religion that is a site of marginalization but also the free market as well as the examples mentioned above of trade unions and leftist social movements that contribute to the precarity of non-normative sexualities (Dhawan 2013).

Furthermore, sexuality is increasingly becoming a foreign policy issue (Weiss and Bosia 2013), even as the norm of 'sexual justice' is mobilized by Evangelical groups to call for protection of traditional families and heterosexual relations. This confronts us with the challenges of pursuing gender and sexual justice in this over-determined discursive terrain, fashioning spaces for re-imagining the relation between desires, pleasures and 'other economies', and thereby reworking social relationships and economic practices globally. In order to tackle these challenges, it is necessary to engage critically with the global mechanisms of sexual and economic exclusion and superexploitation as well as emancipation and empowerment. Although postcolonial queer-feminist organizing is increasingly transnational, both theorization and activism in the field of economic and sexual justice is often plagued by 'methodological nationalism'. At the same time, universal blueprints for implementing justice have been challenged for eroding the legitimacy and efficacy of 'local' mechanisms and practices through 'top-down' models of transnational justice that ignore the singularity of the context in which it is supposed to be implemented.

One of the key questions for critical social theory in general, and postcolonial, queer, feminist in particular, is the challenging question of why subjects desire their own subjugation. In one of the most interesting analyses of the complex discontinuity between desire and interest, Gayatri Spivak in 'Can the Subaltern Speak?' (1988) critiques Deleuze and Foucault's claim that the oppressed know about the conditions of their exploitation and are able to speak for themselves. In Spivak's view, their position risks conflating desire and interest, thus constructing an undivided political subject. They thereby fail to address contemporary forms of economic exploitation, especially the superexploitation of women in the global South, by ignoring the gendered ideological subject constitution on both sides of the colonial divide. By focusing on the incoherence between desire and interest, Spivak emphasizes the importance of critique of ideology even as she contests any simplistic understanding of politics as the rational and economic pursuit of justice and rights (Castro Varela and Dhawan 2014; also cf. Weiss, Chapter 4 in this volume). According to her, economic and political transformation is incomplete without the accompanying intervention in the subject production of the hegemon and subaltern in both the global North and South.

While desire for economic justice is often coded in terms of reducing all value to its pecuniary equivalent, desiring *other* economies can take the form of envisaging alternate modes of recognizing value other than financial compensation (Gibson-Graham 2006). In contrast to discussions on sexual and economic justice that primarily attend to demands for redistribution and recognition, often presenting them as oppositional or adversarial (Hennessy 2000; Fraser and Honneth 2003), we suggest a shift of focus. Supplementing debates about redistribution and recognition, we propose that issues of representation are equally essential (Gibson-Graham 1996; Butler 1998; Spivak 1999; Engel 2002; Kapur 2005; Gressgård, Chapter 5; Binnie, Chapter 8; and Kapur, Chapter 6 in this volume). Accordingly, it is imperative to assess whether the subjects who are affected by unjust structures have a say in the apparatuses of value-coding (Spivak 2012: 59). Thus, a politics of sexual and socio-economic justice raises the question of how people are involved in the decision-making processes of intervening in and transforming these arrangements of value-coding. Drawing on Marx, Spivak argues that 'the logic of capitalism weaves the socius like the textile of a particular set of relationships. Power and validation within this socius are secured by denying that web and transforming/ displacing it into "natural" readability' (Spivak 2012: 59). From a queer perspective, naturalized heterosexuality is part of weaving the socius – like kinship, ethnic and transnational relations – into the structures of neoliberal political economy, while at the same time rendering these mechanisms invisible. Problematizing any straightforward relations between justice and capitalism, this book highlights how postcolonial-queer-feminist struggles for economic and sexual justice are not just about organizing material goods for the suffering classes or mobilizing (sexual) rights for disenfranchised communities – where the deprived are reduced to their needs, which are coded as transparent to our reading practices. Rather, they are about engaging with the imagination and desires of both dispensers as well as receivers of justice.

About the contributions

The contributions to this volume offer various approaches for capturing different historical and geo-political forms, narrations and normative regulations of the complex and dynamic interplay of justice and desire in socio-economic processes. Not only do they avoid an economistic view of global economic processes, they also acknowledge a simultaneity and complexity of forces and relations of power, domination and violence that are sometimes coherent and sometimes contradictory. Intertwining the key terms 'desire', 'economy' and 'justice' in different ways, this volume is organized into three sections: 'Entanglements of desire and economy', 'Intersections of sexual and economic justice' and 'The political economy of queer embodiments'. The four chapters in the first section highlight in different ways that transgressive desires and radical sexualities need not be transformative, but can feed into fantasies that reproduce inequalities – be they (neo-)colonial, orientalist, racist, classist or elitist. At the same time, they insist that such sexualities and desires are not fully determined by neoliberal capitalism, which has a remarkable capacity for inciting and absorbing them, but also allow for alternative configurations.

Eva von Redecker's chapter 'Marx's concept of radical needs in the guise of queer desire' (Chapter 1) argues that for a theorization of 'revolutionary desire' we need an account of 'how a certain type of desire turns efficacious – that is, an account of desire-becoming-need'. Rather than merely combining Marxist and queer-poststructuralist approaches with their supposed focus on economy and sexuality, respectively, she proposes 'folding the two bodies of critical theory back onto each other'. After working through converging internal contradictions and loose ends in Karl Marx, Herbert Marcuse and Michel Foucault, Redecker turns to Teresa de Lauretis' notions of 'perverse desire' and 'habit changes' based on socially shared fantasies that undermine the distinction 'between the labour for someone else's satisfaction and one's own pleasure' as a path towards queer anti-capitalist practices.

Jamila Mascat's 'Can the subaltern desire? The erotic as a power and disempowerment of the erotic' (Chapter 2) explores the commodification and consumption of the sexual and racial Other. It does this while unpacking the sexual politics surrounding three contemporary Arab women writers whose narratives of postcolonial erotic desires are caught between being censored in the Arab world and feeding into a neo-orientalist imagery as the condition for getting symbolic and economic recognition in the West, where media have celebrated them as the authentic 'sexual intifada'. Invoking Audre Lorde's 'Uses of the Erotic', Mascat concludes by suggesting that if there is, on the one hand, a desire exceeding the erotic in the texts considered – namely a desire to gain recognition by conforming to the Western interpellation into a 'subject supposed to desire' – the erotic can, on the other hand, also constitute 'a tool for self-assertion that works in the opposite direction from the subaltern "desire to be desired"'. This requires the postcolonial narrator to renounce the 'authority of the authentic author' as theorized by Foucault, switching to other interlocutors and 'displacing desires [...] by imagining, sharing and experimenting with alternative scenarios of interlocution'.

Roderick Ferguson also invokes Lorde's definition of the erotic in Chapter 3, 'The associations of black queer life: reading and seeing the nineteen-eighties'. He links it to a particular activation of sexuality in the visual and literary works of black queer artists in the UK and the US during the neoliberal emergencies of the 1980s – an activation that he theorizes, alluding to the functioning of Deleuze and Guattari's desiring machines, as being 'born out of the breaking down and the reassembling of sexuality into a mode of difference that could attach itself to other histories, cultures, and struggles'. Taking a cue from Isaac Julien's statement that he wanted his 1989 film *Looking for Langston* to be about black gay identity without being straightforwardly about sexuality, the chapter concludes by envisioning a history of sexuality that complicates Foucault's insofar as it is 'not only an account of hegemonic power but an examination of sexuality's visions for justice, visions that were – in the context of black queer formations in the nineteen-eighties – part of sexuality's erotics'.

In Chapter 4, 'Queer economic justice: desire, critique and the practice of knowledge', Margot D. Weiss questions the scholarly desire – hers included – for queer and transgressive sexuality to be a site of radical resistance to economic inequality and confronts it with the extraordinary commercialization of its actual practice. Ironically, she suggests, 'our desires for queer transformation [...] might in the end obscure the conditions of their production' and create 'a situation where we continuously attempt to re-politicize both our objects and ourselves, while simultaneously, necessarily, turning away from the social and political conditions of our analysis'. Insisting on the necessity of critique, Weiss takes issue with the ways in which dichotomies between cultural criticism and activism have been established both by those who object to the necessarily compromised work of activist research and by those who subscribe to the presumption of masterful distance to critique. Invoking the work of Queers for Economic Justice, she insists instead that 'they are already doing activism as cultural critique', even if it is necessarily compromised. Against 'scholars' desires to find emancipatory politics *in our objects, rather than in the contradictions of the historical conditions we share*' (our italics) and against the false opposition of critique and desire, the chapter concludes by suggesting that 'we see critique as a form of desire' – as 'the desire for collective transformation'.

The chapters of the second part, 'Intersections of sexual and economic justice', explore the interplay and transformative potential of political struggles for sexual and for economic justice within contemporary neoliberal capitalisms. The section tests the hypothesis of whether the notion of justice can help as a guiding norm for the critique and transformation of neoliberalism. The contributions in this section combine perspectives from the global South and North with reflections on political agency and exploitation, thus focusing on the co-constitution of sexual and economic dimensions of justice from a transnational perspective.

In 'Unruly desires, gay governance and the makeover of sexuality in postcolonial India' (Chapter 6), Ratna Kapur explores the openings and closures of spaces of desiring just economies by investigating whether the market offers more liberatory possibilities in postcolonial India than national law was able to offer – or whether it is simply recoding the sexual subaltern as the consumer citizen. Randi Gressgård's chapter 'The instrumentalization of sexual diversity in a civilizational frame of cosmopolitanism and tolerance' (Chapter 5) scrutinizes the relationship of queer desire and neoliberal city space, focusing particularly on urban planning and its fantasy of the tolerant cosmopolitan metropolis. Discussing Richard Florida's (2002) influential conflation of high-tech economy and a tolerance toward sexual diversity, Gressgård problematizes the concomitance of economic and sexual justice in the global North and the global South. She unmasks the ideology of cosmopolitanism and sexual diversity by pointing at their material exclusions and strategic instrumentalization, as, for example, in the practice of pink-washing. Following this critique, Chapter 7 challenges very similar projections of queer political thinking and activism. In 'Intergrating sexual and economic justice: challenges for queer feminist activism against sexual violence in

South Africa', Lyn Ossome focuses on the political, social and economic contexts of activism in which queer groups seek to intervene in processes of economic and sexual injustice in the South African context. Ossome demonstrates how issues of class and economic justice get disarticulated in the struggle against anti-lesbian violence. Against this background, the author challenges the current use of hate crime legislation and its usage of the infamous terms 'curative' or 'corrective' rape. The next and final chapter of this section similarly insists on the relevance of class privileges in queer communities and academic research in a British context. In Chapter 8, 'Classing desire: erotics, politics, value', Jon Binnie critically examines the 'economic turn' within queer studies by unpacking the class biases within queer formations of the economized erotic sphere. In particular, he scrutinizes gay desire for working-class masculinity for its problematic assumptions about class and heterosexuality that both fetishize and depreciate working-class masculinity, while associating it with steadfast heterosexuality. He also draws on the critical use value of the concept of homonormativity.

The third section of the book, entitled 'The political economy of queer embodiments', explores the limiting factors, potentials and future perspectives of economic transformations, driven by the desire to create space for envisioning new forms of doing economy. Concepts of property and ownership, extended to the liberal idea of self-ownership of one's body, are problematized, as is the economist modelling of the presumably autonomous subject. In contrast to an understanding of freedom as 'freedom of choice' and justice as 'redistribution of property', the authors explore non-commercial forms of relationality, the commons and embodiments that acknowledge interdependencies. They conjoin freedom, survival and collective practices; they value utopian thinking, activist wisdom, queer desires, which 'inspire complex weavings of market, alternative market, and non-market economic activities' (Heiliger, Chapter 11 in this volume).

Christine Klapeer's and Karin Schönpflug's contribution 'Queer needs commons! Transgressing the fiction of self-ownership, challenging Westocentric proprietism' (Chapter 9) focuses on the liberal notion of self-ownership and its problematic role for developing queer subjectivities. How does the fictional idea of self-ownership influence queer claims for self-determined/self-defined identities, genders and sexualities? And how far does this contribute to the reproduction of Westocentric proprietism also in current struggles for (subversive) queer subjectivities? Klapeer and Schönpflug critically discuss commodification processes of labour, based on recent debates on the compatibility of capitalist logics and non-heteronormative identities, as well as current notions of 'a common' and 'the commons' and their potentials for developing new understandings of property. With the aim of going beyond liberal concepts of (self-)ownership, they suggest a radical epistemological and political reconceptualization of the relationship between 'having' and 'being', which they see realized, for example, in some ecofeminist or ecosexual practices. Finally, they come up with a proposal for what they call a 'queer commons' based on the idea of 'a general interrelatedness and connectedness, a one-ness or a world's "commons"'.

Also for Leticia Sabsay's 'The ruse of sexual freedom: neoliberalism, self-ownership and commercial sex' (Chapter 10), the notion of self-ownership is central, when she intervenes into current debates on sex work, which paradoxically legitimize new forms of criminalizing sex work through fostering a delimited idea of choice. One of the central questions that have established the terms of these vexed debates is whether those who make a living from commercial sex were *really* free to choose to do so. Departing from this question, Sabsay argues that the imaginary of individual freedom has not only been central to the deployment of liberal and later neoliberal governmentality but is also modelled by the paradigm of private property convenient for the capital form, understood in Marxist terms as a social relation, and the colonial enterprise that shaped it. Building on the Foucaultian notion of governmentality, where the liberal subject is governed through freedom and owns its body as a property, alternative notions of justice and freedom that are not based on the idea of self-ownership are explored. Sabsay brings forward the challenges that both the postcolonial condition and relational approaches to subject formations pose to possessive individualism.

In 'Queer economies: possibilities of queer desires and economic bodies (because "the economy" is not enough)' (Chapter 11), Evangeline Heiliger argues that re-theorizing economies as 'desiring bodies' is not merely a metaphorical undertaking but a way to value forms of embodied economic activity not generally visible within conventional, or even alternative, capitalisms. With her chapter, Heiliger engages in the project of queering economy, which for her is by no means an abstract or utopian affair. Rather, she provides the reader with five very concrete examples of 'doing economy otherwise' – examples that explicitly address challenges of class politics and poverty from a queer-theoretical perspective. In particular, Heiliger suggests that porous, mutually interacting queer economic bodies have a powerful potential for desire and economy outside the (re-) productive. Against the powerful ideology of 'the economy' as a closed, monolithic system, the final contribution in this section proposes a more complex picture of economic processes based on the interaction, attraction and recognition/invisibility of 'economic bodies'.

All three sections outline how questions of economic transformation on a global level may very well start from local practices. Yet it also becomes clear that 'queering economy' does not limit justice to sexual or economic dimensions. As a 'reading for difference rather than dominance' (Gibson-Graham 2006: xxxi), it instead addresses the various forms and unprecedented connections that dominance takes on. We hope that the chapters of this volume provide new insights into the tensions and interactions between bread and roses. Thus the struggles for fair wages and decent work are also about reconfiguring the sexualized division of labour and gender and the capitalist mode of production in the era of neoliberal globalization. As two famous political slogans of the 1970s radical left proclaim: 'We don't just want a bigger slice of the cake, we want to change the recipe' and 'We don't want just one cake, we want the whole fucking bakery'. And, we would add, the poppy field for fucking, too.

References

Alexander, M. J. (1997) 'Erotic Autonomy as a Politics of Decolonization: An Anatomy of Feminist and State Practice in the Bahamas Tourist Economy', in M. J. Alexander and C. T. Mohanty (eds) *Feminist Genealogies, Colonial Legacies, Democratic Futures*, London/New York: Routledge, pp. 63–100.

—— (2001) 'Imperial Desire/Sexual Utopias: White Gay Capital and Transnational Tourism', in E. Shohat (ed.) *Talking Visions: Multicultural Feminism in a Transnational Age*, Cambridge, MA: MIT Press, pp. 281–305.

Altman, D. (2002) 'Globalization and the International Gay/Lesbian Movement', in D. Richardson and S. Seidman (eds) *Handbook of Lesbian and Gay Studies*, London/Thousand Oaks, CA/New Delhi: Sage, pp. 415–25.

Badgett, L. (2001) *Money, Myths, and Change: The Economic Lives of Lesbians and Gay Men*, Chicago, IL: University of Chicago Press.

Barker, D. K. and Kuiper, E. (eds) (2003) *Towards a Feminist Philosophy of Economics*, London/New York: Routledge.

Bedford, K. (2005) 'Loving to Straighten Out Development: Sexuality and "Ethnodevelopment" in the World Bank's Ecuadorian Lending', *Feminist Legal Studies* 13(3): 295–322.

—— (2009) *Developing Partnerships: Gender, Sexuality, and the Reformed World Bank*, Minneapolis: University of Minnesota Press.

Bedford, K. and Jakobsen, J. (2009) *Towards A Vision of Sexual and Economic Justice*, Report for the Ford Foundation.

Benjamin, J. (1988) *The Bonds of Love: Psychoanalysis, Feminism, and the Problem of Domination*, New York: Pantheon.

Binnie, J. (2004) *The Globalization of Sexuality*, London/Thousand Oaks, CA/New Delhi: Sage.

Beger, N. J. (2004) *Tensions in the Struggle for Sexual Minority Rights in Europe: Que(e)rying Political Practices*, Manchester: Manchester University Press.

Bersani, L. (2010) 'Is the Rectum a Grave?', in L. Bersani *Is the Rectum a Grave? And Other Essays*, Chicago, IL: University of Chicago Press, pp. 3–30.

Blasius, M. (2013) 'Theorizing the Politics of (Homo)Sexualities across Cultures', in M. L. Weiss and M.J. Bosia (eds) *Global Homophobia: States, Movements, and the Politics of Oppression*, Urbana/Chicago/Springfields, IL: University of Illinois Press, pp. 218–45.

Butler, J. (1987) *Subjects of Desire: Hegelian Reflections in 20th-Century France*, New York: Columbia University Press.

—— (1990) *Gender Trouble: Feminism and the Subversion of Identity*, New York: Routledge.

—— (1993) *Bodies that Matter: On the Discursive Limits of 'Sex'*, New York: Routledge.

—— (1998) 'Merely Cultural', *New Left Review* 227(1): 33–44.

—— (2004) *Undoing Gender*, London/New York: Routledge.

Carver, T. and Chambers, S. (2008) *Judith Butler and Political Theory: Troubling Politics*, London/New York: Routledge.

Castro Varela, M. and Dhawan, N. (2011a) 'Normative Dilemmas and the Hegemony of Counter-Hegemony', in M. Castro Varela, N. Dhawan and A. Engel (eds) *Hegemony and Heteronormativity: Revisiting 'the Political' in Queer Politics*, Hampshire: Ashgate, pp. 91–119.

—— (2011b) 'Sexual and Economic Justice: Sex, Work and the Politics of Representation', in Tadej Pogacar (ed.) *Code: Red*, Ljubliana: PARASITE Institute, pp. 11–16, 45–7.

—— (2014) *Postkoloniale Theorie: Eine kritische Einführung*, Bielefeld: transcript.

Charusheela, S. (2008) 'Gender and the Stability of Consumption: A Feminist Contribution to Post Keynesian Economics', *Cambridge Journal of Economics* 34(6): 1145–56.

Cohen, C. J. (2005) 'Punks, Bulldaggers, and Welfare Queens: The Radical Potential of Queer Politics?', in P. E. Johnson and M. G. Henderson (eds) *Black Queer Studies: A Critical Anthology*, Durham, NC/London: Duke University Press, pp. 21–51.

Cornell, D. (1998) *At the Heart of Freedom: Feminism, Sex, and Equality*, Princeton, NJ: Princeton University Press.

Cornwall, R. (1997) 'Deconstructing Silence: The Queer Political Economy of the Social Articulation of Desire', *Review of Radical Political Economics* 29(1): 1–130.

Crenshaw, K. (1989) 'Mapping the Margins: Intersectionality, Identity Politics, and Violence Against Women of Color', in M. A. Fineman and R. Mykitiuk (eds) *The Public Nature of Private Violence*, New York/London: Routledge, pp. 93–118.

Cruz-Malavé, A. and Manalansan IV, M. F. (eds) (2002) *Queer Globalizations: Citizenship and the Afterlife of Colonialism*, New York/London: New York University Press.

Deleuze, G. (1997) *Desire and Pleasure*, trans. M. McMahon, *globe* 5; 'Désir et plaisir', *Magazine littéraire* 325, October 1994: 59–65.

Deleuze, G. and Guattari, F. (1980/1987) *A Thousand Plateaus: Capitalism and Schizophrenia 2*, Minneapolis: University of Minnesota Press.

—— (1994/2004) *Anti-Oedipus: Capitalism and Schizophrenia*, London: Continuum.

D'Emilio, J. (1983) 'Capitalism and Gay Identity', in A. Snitow, C. Stansell and S. Thompson (eds) *Desire: The Politics of Sexuality*, New York/London: Virago, pp. 10–113.

Demirović, A. and Maihofer, A. (2013) 'Vielfachkrise und die Krise der Geschlechterverhältnisse', in H. M. Nickel and A. Heilmann (eds) *Krise, Kritik, Allianzen. Arbeits- und geschlechtersoziologische Perspektiven*, Weinheim/Basel: Beltz, pp. 30–48.

Derrida, J. (2005) *The Politics of Friendship* [1994], trans. G. Collins, London: Verso.

Dhawan, N. (2011a) 'Transitions to Justice', in S. Buckley-Zistel and R. Stanley (eds) *Gender in Transitional Justice*, Basingstoke: Palgrave Macmillan, pp. 264-83.

—— (2011b) 'Transnationale Gerechtigkeit in einer Postkolonialen Welt', in M. Castro Varela and N. Dhawan (eds) *Soziale (Un)Gerechtigkeit: Kritische Perspektive auf Diversität, Intersektionalität und Anti-Diskriminierung*, Münster: LIT, pp. 12–35.

—— (2013) 'The Empire Prays Back: Religion, Secularity and Queer Critique', *Boundary 2* 40(1): 191–222.

Dietze, G. (2010) 'The Critique of Occidentalism', in H. Brunkhorst and G. Grözinger (eds) *The Study of Europe*, Baden-Baden: Nomos, pp. 87–116.

Dietze, G., Haschemi Yekani, E. and Michaelis, B. (2007) 'Checks and Balances. Zum Verhältnis von Intersektionalität und Queer Theory', in K. Walgenbach, Dietze, G., Hornscheidt, L. and Palm, K. (eds) *Gender als interdependente Kategorie: Neue Perspektiven auf Intersektionalität, Diversität und Heterogenität*, Opladen: Budrich, pp. 107–39.

Drucker, P. (2009) 'Changing Families and Communities: An LGBT Contribution to an Alternative Development Path', *Development in Practice* 19(7): 825–36.

Dück, J. (2014) 'Krise und Geschlecht. Überlegungen zu einem feministisch-materialistischen Krisenverständnis', *PROKLA* 174, 44(1): 53–70.

Duggan, L. (2003) *The Twilight of Equality: Neoliberalism, Cultural Politics, and the Attack on Democracy*, Boston, MA: Beacon Press.

Eisenstein, S. (1983) *Give Us Bread but Give Us Roses: Working Women's Consciousness in the United States, 1890 to the First World War*, London: Routledge.

Ekine, S. and Abbas, H. (2013) *Queer African Reader*, Dakar/Nairobi/Oxford: Pambazuka Press.

El-Tayeb, F. (2011) *European Others: Queering Ethnicity in Postnational Europe*, Minneapolis: University of Minnesota Press.

Eng, D. L., Halberstam, J. and Muñoz, J. E. (eds) (2005) *What's Queer about Queer Studies Now?*, *Social Text* 84/85, Durham, NC: Duke University Press.

Engel, A. (2002) *Wider die Eindeutigkeit: Sexualität und Geschlecht im Fokus queerer Politik der Repräsentation*, Frankfurt am Main: Campus.

—— (2009) *Sexualität und Ökonomie: Queere kulturelle Politiken im Neoliberalismus*, Bielefeld: transcript.

—— (2010) 'Desire for/within Economic Transformation', *e-flux journal* 17(6). Available online at www.e-flux.com/journal/view/156 (accessed 20 November 2014).

—— (2013) 'The Surplus of Paradoxes: Queer/ing Images of Sexuality and Economy', in C. Pascale (ed.) *Social Inequalities and the Politics of Representation: A Global Landscape*, London/New Delhi/Thousand Oaks, CA: Sage, pp. 176–88.

Evans, D. T. (1993) *Sexual Citizenship: The Material Construction of Sexualities*, New York/London: Routledge.

Ferguson, R. A. (2004) *Aberrations In Black: Toward A Queer Of Color Critique*, Minneapolis: University of Minnesota Press.

Florida, R. (2002) *The Rise of the Creative Class. And How It's Transforming Work, Leisure, Community and Everyday Life*, New York: Basic Books.

Floyd, K. (2009) *The Reification of Desire: Toward a Queer Marxism*, Minneapolis: University of Minnesota Press.

Folbre, N. (2012) *For Love and Money: Care Provision in the United States*, New York: Russell Sage Foundation.

Foucault, M. (1980) *The History of Sexuality* Vol. 1. [1976], trans. R. Hurley, New York: Vintage/Random House.

—— (1990) 'Sexual Discourse and Power', in J. Alexander and S. Seidmann (eds) *Culture and Society: Contemporary Debates*, Cambridge/New York: Cambridge University Press, pp. 199–204.

Fraser, N. (1997) *Justice Interruptus: Critical Reflections on the 'Postsocialist' Condition*, London/New York: Routledge.

—— (2008) *Adding Insult to Injury: Nancy Fraser Debates her Critics: Debating Redistribution, Recognition and Representation*, London/New York: Verso.

Fraser, N. and Honneth, A. (2003) *Redistribution or Recognition? A Political-Philosophical Exchange*, London/New York: Verso.

Freud, S. (1982) *Die Traumdeutung* [1900], in Studienausgabe Bd. II, Frankfurt am Main: Fischer.

Freud, S. (1982) "Traumdeutung": The Interpretation of Dreams. New York: Avon, 1980.

Fromm, E. (1995) *The Art of Loving* [1956], New York: HarperCollins.

Gibson-Graham, J. K. (1996) *The End of Capitalism (As We Knew It)*, Cambridge, MA: Blackwell.
—— (2006) *A Postcapitalist Politics*, Minneapolis: University of Minnesota Press.
Gilroy, P. (1995) 'Roots and Routes: Black Identity as an Outernational Project', in W. H. Herbert, C.B. Howard and E.H. Griffith (eds) *Racial and Ethnic Identity: Psychological Development and Creative Expression*, London: Routledge, pp. 15–30.
Gluckman, A. and Reed, B. (eds) (1997) *Homo Economics: Capitalism, Community, and Lesbian and Gay Life*, London: Routledge.
de Goede, M. (ed.) (2006) *International Political Economy and Poststructural Politics*, London: Palgrave.
Gopinath, G. (2005) *Impossible Desires: Queer Diaspora and South Asian Public Culture*, Durham, NC/London: Duke University Press.
Grabel, I. (2013) 'Global Financial Governance and Development Finance in the Wake of the 2008 Financial Crisis', *Feminist Economics* 19(3): 32–54.
Grabham, E., Cooper, D., Krishnadas, J. and Herman, D. (eds) (2008) *Intersectionality and Beyond: Law, Power and the Politics of Location*, London/New York: Routledge-Cavendish.
Griffin, P. (2007) 'Sexing the Economy in a Neo-liberal World Order: Neo-liberal Discourse and the (Re)production of Heteronormative Heterosexuality', *British Journal of Politics and International Relations* 9: 220–38.
Grosz, E. (1995) *Space, Time, and Perversion: Essays on the Politics of Bodies*, New York: Routledge.
Gutiérrez, M. (ed.) (2003) *Macro-Economics: Making Gender Matter: Concepts, Policies, Changes in Developing Countries*, New York: Zed Books.
Gutiérrez Rodríguez, E. (2011) 'Politics of Affect. Transversal Conviviality'. Available online at http://eipcp.net/transversal/0811/gutierrezrodriguez/en (accessed 21 November 2014).
Fukuda-Parr, S., Heintz, J. and Seguino, S. (eds) (2013) *Special Issue on Critical and Feminist Perspectives on Financial and Economic Crises*, in *Feminist Economics* 19(3).
Halley, J. and Parker, A. (2011) *After Sex? On Writing since Queer Theory*, Durham, NC/London: Duke University Press.
Hardt, M. and Negri, A. (2004) *Multitude: War and Democracy in the Age of Empire*, New York: Penguin Books.
Haritaworn, J., Kuntsman, A. and Posocco, S. (eds) (2014) *Queer Necropolitics*, London/New York: Routledge.
Hartmann, J., Klesse, C., Wagenknecht, P., Fritzsche, B. and Hackmann, K. (eds) (2007) *Heteronormativität. Empirische Studien zu Heterosexualität als gesellschaftlichem Machtverhältnis*, Wiesbaden: VS Verlag für Sozialwissenschaften.
Harvey, L. and Gill, R. (2011) 'Spicing It Up: Sexual Entrepreneurs and The Sex Inspectors', in R. Gill and C. Scharff (eds) *New Femininities: Postfeminism, Neoliberalism and Subjectivity*, New York: Palgrave Macmillan, pp. 52–68.
Hashemi Yekani, E., Kilian, E. and Michaelis, B. (eds) (2013) *Queer Futures: Reconsidering Ethics, Activism, and the Political*, Surrey: Ashgate.
Hegel, G. W. F. (1970) *The Phenomenology of Spirit* [1807], trans. A. V. Miller, Oxford: Oxford University Press.
Hennessy, R. (2000) *Profit and Pleasure: Sexual Identities in Late Capitalism*, New York: Routledge.

Hewitson, G. (1999) *Feminist Economics: Interrogating the Masculinity of Rational Economic Man*, Cheltenham: Edward Elgar.
Hochschild, A. R. (1983) *The Managed Heart: Commercialization of Human Feeling*, Berkeley: University of California Press.
Irigaray, L. (1985) *Speculum of the Other Woman* [1974], trans. G. C. Gill, Ithaca, NY: Cornell University Press.
Jakobsen, J. R. (2011) 'Perverse Justice', *GLQ: A Journal of Lesbian and Gay Studies* 18(1): 19–45.
Jacobsen, J. and Zeller, A. (eds) (2008) *Queer Economics: A Reader*, London/New York: Routledge.
Jochimsen, M. A. (2003) *Careful Economics: Integrating Caring Activities and Economic Science*, Boston, MA/London: Kluwer Academic.
Joseph, M. (2002) *Against the Romance of Community*, Minneapolis: University of Minnesota Press.
Kapoor, I. (2008) *The Postcolonial Politics of Development*, London/New York: Routledge.
Kapur, R. (2005) *Erotic Justice: Law and the New Politics of Postcolonialism*, London: Glasshouse Press.
Kolářová, K. (2011) 'How Sam Became a Father, Became a Citizen: Scripts of Neoliberal Inclusion of Disability', in M. Castro Varela, N. Dhawan and A. Engel (eds) *Hegemony and Heteronormativity: Revisiting 'the Political' in Queer Politics*, Hampshire: Ashgate, pp. 121–42.
Kuiper, E. and Sap, J. (eds) (1995) *Out of the Margin: Feminist Perspectives on Economics*, London: Routledge.
Kulpa, R. and Mizielińska, J. (eds) (2011) *De-Centring Western Sexualities: Central and Eastern European Perspectives*, Surrey: Ashgate.
Lacan, J. (1977) 'The Mirror Stage as Formative of the Function of the "I" as Revealed in Psychoanalytic Experience' [1949], in *Écrits: A Selection*, trans. A. Sheridan, New York: Norton, pp. 1–7.
—— (1985) 'The Meaning of the Phallus' [1958], in J. Mitchell and J. Rose (eds) *Feminine Sexuality: Jacques Lacan and the École Freudienne*, New York/London: Norton, pp. 74–85.
de Lauretis, T. (1994) *The Practice of Love: Lesbian Sexuality and Perverse Desire*, Bloomington: Indiana University Press.
Lazzarato, M. (1996) 'Immaterial Labour', in P. Virno and M. Hardt (eds) *Radical Thought in Italy: A Potential Politics*, Minneapolis: University of Minnesota Press, pp. 132–46.
Lind, A. (ed.) (2010) *Development, Sexual Rights, and Global Governance*, London: Routledge.
—— (2013) 'Heteronormativity and Sexuality', in G. Waylen, K. Celis, J. Kantola and L. S. Weldon (eds) *The Oxford Handbook of Gender and Politics*, Oxford: Oxford University Press, pp. 189–213.
Lorde, A. (1984) 'Uses of the Erotic: The Erotic as Power', in *Sister Outsider: Essays and Speeches*, Freedom, CA: Crossing Press, pp. 53–9.
Lorenz, R. and Kuster, B. (2007) *sexuell arbeiten: eine queere perspektive auf arbeit und prekäres leben*, Berlin: b-ooks.
Los Angeles Research Group (1975) *Toward a Scientific Analysis of the Gay Question*, Cudahy, CA: The Group.

Luibheid, E. and Cantu, L. Jr. (eds) (2005) *Queer Migrations: Sexuality, U.S. Citizenship, and Border Crossings*, Minneapolis: University of Minnesota Press.
MacCormack, P. (2009) 'Unnatural Alliances', in C. Nigianni and M. Storr (eds) *Deleuze and Queer Theory*, Edinburgh: Edinburgh University Press, pp. 134–49.
Madra, Y. M. and Özcelçuk, C. (2010) '*Jouissance* and Antagonism in the Forms of the Commune: A Critique of Biopolitical Subjectivity', *Rethinking Marxism* 22(3): 481–97.
Marcuse, H. (1955) *Eros and Civilization*, Boston, MA: Beacon Press.
McRuer, R. (2006) *Crip Theory: Cultural Signs of Queerness and Disability*, New York: New York University Press.
Menon, G. A. (2010) 'Recoveries of Space and Subjectivity in the Shadow of Violence: The Clandestine Politics of Pavement Dwellers in Mumbai', in P. McMichael (ed.) *Contesting Development*, New York: Routledge, pp. 151–64.
Mesquita, S., Wiedlack, M. K. and Lasthofer, K. (eds) (2012) *Import-Export-Transport: Queer Theory, Queer Critique and Activism in Motion*, Wien: Zaglossus.
Mohanty, C. T. (2003) *Feminism Without Borders: Decolonizing Theory, Practicing Solidarity*, Durham, NC: Duke University Press.
Nelson, J. A. (1996) *Feminism, Objectivity, and Economics*, London/New York: Routledge.
Nietzche, F. (1967) *The Will to Power* [1888], trans. W. Kaufmann, New York: Random House.
Nussbaum, M. (2000) *Sex and Social Justice*, Oxford/New York: Oxford University Press.
Ossome, L. (2013) 'Postcolonial Discourses of Queer Activism and Class in Africa', in S. Ekine and H. Abbas (eds) *Queer African Reader*, Dakar/Nairobi/Oxford: Pambazuka Press, pp. 32–47.
Probyn, E. (1996) *Outside Belongings*, London/New York: Routledge.
Puar, J. (2008) *Terrorist Assemblages: Homonationalism in Queer Times*, Durham, NC/London: Duke University Press.
Pühl, K. (2003) 'Der Bericht der Hartz-Kommission und die "Unternehmerin ihrer Selbst": Geschlechterverhältnisse, Gouvernementalität und Neoliberalismus', in E. Gutiérrez Rodríguez and M. Pieper (eds) *Gouvernementalität: Eine sozialwissenschaftliche Debatte im Anschluss an Foucault*, Frankfurt am Main: Campus, pp. 111–35.
Randeria, S. (2002) 'Entangled Histories: Civil Society, Caste Solidarities and Legal Pluralism in Post-Colonial India', in J. Keane (ed.) *Civil Society: Berlin Perspectives*, New York: Berghahn, pp. 213–42.
Reich, W. (1972) *Sex-Pol: Essays 1929–1934*, ed. L. Baxandall, New York: Vintage Books.
Richardson, D. and Seidman, S. (eds) (2002) *Handbook of Lesbian and Gay Studies*, London: Routledge.
Rosenberg, J. and Villarejo, A. (eds) (2012) 'Queer Studies and the Crises of Capitalism', *GLQ: A Journal of Lesbian and Gay Studies* 18(1): 127–47.
Rubin, G. (1975) 'The Traffic in Women: Notes on the "Political Economy of Sex"', in R. Reiter (ed.) *Toward an Anthropology of Women*, New York: Monthly Review Press, pp. 157–210.
—— (1992) 'Thinking Sex: Notes for a Radical Theory of the Politics of Sexuality', in C. Vance (ed.) *Pleasure and Danger: Exploring Female Sexuality* [1984], London: Pandora, pp. 267–319.

Sánchez-Eppler, B. and Patton, C. (eds) (2000) *Queer Diasporas*, Durham, NC/London: Duke University Press.

Schönpflug, K. (2008) *Feminism, Economics and Utopia: Time Travelling through Paradigms*, London/New York: Routledge.

Shildrick, M. (2009) 'Prosthetic Performativity: Deleuzian Connections and Queer Corporealities', in C. Nigianni and M. Storr (eds) *Deleuze and Queer Theory*, Edinburgh: Edinburgh University Press, pp. 115–33.

Sears, A. (2005) 'Queer Anti-Capitalism: What's Left of Lesbian and Gay Liberation?', *Science and Society* 69(1): 92–112.

Sen, A. (1984) *Resources, Values, and Development*, Cambridge, MA: Harvard University Press, reprinted 1997.

Sender, K. (2005) *Business, Not Politics: The Making of the Gay Market*, New York: Columbia University Press.

Spinoza, Baruch de (1996) *Ethics*, London: Penguin Books.

Spivak, G. C. (1988) 'Can the Subaltern Speak?', in C. Nelson and L. Grossberg (eds) *Marxism and the Interpretation of Culture*, Urbana/Chicago: University of Illinois Press, pp. 271–313.

—— (1999) *A Critique of Postcolonial Reason: Towards a History of the Vanishing Present*, Cambridge, MA/London: Harvard University Press.

—— (2012) *An Aesthetic Education in the Era of Globalization*, Cambridge, MA: Harvard University Press.

Taylor, Y., Hines, S. and Casey, M. (eds) (2011) *Theorizing Intersectionality and Sexuality*, New York: Palgrave Macmillan.

Völker, S. (2011) 'Praktiken sozialer Reproduktion von prekär beschäftigten Männern (Practices of Social Reproduction by Men in Precarious Employment)', *WSI-Mitteilungen* 8: 423–9.

Ward, J. (2010) 'Gender Labor: Transmen, Femmes, and Collective Work of Transgression', *Sexualities* 13(2): 236–54.

Warner, M. (ed.) (1993) *Fear of a Queer Planet: Queer Politics and Social Theory*, Minneapolis: University of Minnesota Press.

Weeks, J., Holland, J. and Waites, M. (eds) (2003) *Sexualities and Society: A Reader*, Cambridge: Polity Bridge.

Weiss, M. L. and Bosia, M. J. (2013) 'Political Homophobia in Comparative Perspective', in M. L. Weiss and M. J. Bosia (eds) *Global Homophobia: States, Movements, and the Politics of Oppression*, Urbana/Chicago/Springfield: University of Illinois Press, pp. 1–29.

Wilson, A. (2004) *The Intimate Economies of Bangkok: Tomboys, Tycoons, and Avon Ladies in the World City*, Berkeley: University of California Press.

Woltersdorff, V. (2011) 'The Paradoxes of Precarious Sexualities: Sexuality in Neoliberalism', *Cultural Studies* 25(2) (Special Issue 'Queer Adventures in Cultural Studies', ed. Angela McRobbie): 164–82.

Zein-Elabdin, E. O. (2004) 'Articulating the Postcolonial (with Economics in Mind)', in E. Zein-Elabdin and S. Charusheela (eds) (2004) *Postcolonialism Meets Economics*, London/New York: Routledge, pp. 21–39.

Zelizer, V. (2005) *The Purchase of Intimacy*, Princeton, NJ: Princeton University Press.

Part I

Entanglements of desire and economy

Chapter 1

Marx's concept of radical needs in the guise of queer desire

Eva von Redecker

> We believe that life really is too short to settle for second best and that simple, honest pleasures are often the most rewarding.
>
> Whether it's breakfast in bed made by someone you love, or a lazy afternoon spent looking through old photos, we think it's important to make the most of the little things that really put a spring in your step.
>
> (Dorset Cereals packet; sell-by date August 2012)

> Pleasure is everything
> Give in to happiness
> Reject propriety; embrace variety
> Prudence is sooo 1658
> Life is fleeting; clasp it hard with both hands
> Seek delight
> Trust your impulses
> Ordinary is pointless
> Break free
> All hail the Gü decadents
> Smooth passion fruit cheesecake with a crumbly
> biscuit base and fragrant passion fruit and mango curd.
>
> (Gü Afternoon Cheesecakes packet; sell-by date 17.03.12)

The two mottos opening this chapter caution, from the start, against a simple opposition between transgressive desire and capitalism. We might analyse the muesli advert as wedding consumerism to heteronormative idyll. But teatime has us face that a more excessively phrased, decadent discourse of desire serves just as well to advance capitalist exchange. Why not rebel against propriety by spending on impudently overpriced industrial confectionery?

Capitalism's cunning potential for reintegrating mere transgressions into its untransformed logics has for some time now posed a challenge to queer theories – a problematic which Margot Weiss renders particularly acute in

Chapter 4, exploring what politics queer theorists habitually project onto their objects of study without linking them to broader projects of structural change.[1] One way of filling the gap would be to try to add a Marxist or materialist analysis to queer theory's theoretical toolkit, as Rob Cover suggested in his influential paper 'Material/Queer Theory' (Cover 2004). Yet what worries me in such attempts is the simplifying assumption that we are dealing with two bodies of theory displaying different strengths, as if the Marxist and the queer/poststructuralist traditions of critique weren't in themselves full of contradictions, impasses and loose ends – full, especially, of potentiality to be transposed onto other domains than their alleged proper objects (sexuality and economy, respectively).[2]

So what I want to put forward in this chapter is not so much a set of singular, free-standing claims, as a particular (dis)integrating perspective on part of our received theoretical landscape. My chapter attempts to pick up the Marxist debates around the subjective factor in revolution by translating their key term, 'new' or 'radical needs', back and forth into poststructuralist and queer terminology of 'desire'.

Anti-capitalist thought is thereby pushed to broaden its focus beyond forever desiring 'just' (only) economies. It might encompass the desire for different relationalities, different genders and not least the desire for different, revolutionary desire. Queer theory, solving a particular dead end of Freudo-Marxism, for its part then addresses more than 'just' economies of *desire*. Its themes re-emerge within the economies of needs, goods and practice.

My actual discussion is limited to few, exemplary texts by the early Marx, by Herbert Marcuse, Michel Foucault and Teresa de Lauretis. Both Marcuse in his Frankfurt School context and the queer theorist de Lauretis draw from the work of Sigmund Freud. My account of desire therefore moves within the confines of a psychoanalytical understanding of desire as lack, a paradigm that is not without critics and alternatives in queer theory. Elisabeth Grosz, for example, in her 'Refiguring Lesbian Desire', compellingly advocates abandoning the motive of desire as lack and negativity which runs from Plato through Hegel to Freud in favour of a Spinozist/Deleuzian framework of positivity and productivity:

> Now this notion of desire as an absence, lack, or hole, an abyss seeking to be engulfed, stuffed to satisfaction, is not only uniquely useful in capitalist

1 Such co-optation is of course not a capacity of capitalism alone. Jamila Mascat shows in Chapter 2 how allegedly transgressive depictions of Muslim female sexuality end up reinscribing a deeply orientalist logic.

2 My concern is not so much to follow the well-meaning admonishments that queer or feminist theory should become more self-consciously anti-capitalist or to counter the denunciations that it cannot (Toiland 2011), but to show that concepts and considerations from within queer theory can be productively transposed to other emancipatory debates and their particular impasses. My 'Feministische Strategie und Revolution' is a similar exercise, trying to replenish the missing 'objective' scenarios of transition in common theories of revolution with notions of transformation as formulated in second-wave feminism (Redecker 2012).

> models of acquisition, propriety, and ownership (seeing the object of desire on the model of the consumable commodity), but it also inherently sexualizes desire, coding it in terms of the prevailing characteristics to the masculine/feminine opposition, presence and absence.
>
> (Grosz 1994: 71)

Grosz suspects that the force of desire lends itself particularly well to capitalist and heterosexist articulations if we conceive of it as endowed by an absence. I would like to bear this warning in mind, yet try to address it from within a psychoanalytic understanding of desire. The task emphasized by Grosz's rejection of desire-as-lack would then be to conceptually surmount a gendered, consumerist logic of subject and object of desire – in other words, theorize 'revolutionary' desire.

My key concepts, as stated, are the notion of need – 'radical needs' for Marx, 'new needs' for Marcuse – on the one hand and the queer-theoretical notion of desire, specified as 'perverse desire' by de Lauretis, on the other. It is comparatively easy, with the hindsight of the academically later-educated, to point out the problems the Marxist theory of emancipatory needs runs into. As I hope to explicate, the totalizing analyses of society proposed by Marx and Marcuse render the emergence of the 'new needs' required by their theory of revolution thoroughly paradoxical. Marcuse's solution – to present the erotic energy bound by repressed sexuality as a revolutionary force – falters in the light of Foucault's *History of Sexuality Vol. 1* (1998[1976]) which refutes any attempts to situate sexuality outside social power dynamics. However, if on the side of critical theory it is the emergence of new needs that remains implausible, then at the poststructuralist end the efficacy of readily present heterogeneous desires threatens to drop out of sight. I want to present de Lauretis' work on perverse desire and habit change as a resource to fill this desideratum, since it provides a model for the validation of deviant desire so as to structure practice and subjectivity.

Yet countering this somewhat triumphalist ascent of queer theory to repair the ruins of Marxism runs another trend, backwards as it were. Certain shifts of perspective, which Foucault seems to prop up against Marcuse, at a second glance serve rather as an opening to kindred elements in both oeuvres. Whoever else might have maintained the repressive hypothesis slashed by Foucault, Marcuse did not think of sexuality and instincts as located outside of the history of power. And despite his own terminology of social totality (if not totalitarianism; cf. Marcuse 1955: 93), he does at times weave complicated discontinuities in his account of the social, thus rendering his concept of 'new needs' more tentative and more plausible than it initially seemed. Finally, de Lauretis' consolidation of perverse desire into a structuring fantasy, rather than as an alternative to the Marxist take on revolution's 'subjective factor', could be read as a variant of it. Outlining how desire turns efficacious, we could read her as presenting us with a theory of the emergence of new needs.

Folding the two bodies of critical theory back onto each other in this way might call for a much more extensive and detailed investigation which would no doubt be productive of manifold further and more nuanced tensions. Nevertheless, my conclusion merely resumes the motif of co-implication in a more condensed and sketchy way. I present the content of the most complex of Marx's radical needs, the form of non-alienated labour in communism, as congruent with a hyperbolic lesbianism taking its cues from de Lauretis. Both the former and the latter overcome the distinction between subject and object not only of desire but of work and pleasure, too.

Totality and need

As understood by Marx, the concept of need does not just cover anthropological or biological must-haves. As the satisfaction of needs is always socially and culturally mediated, even the basic needs assume particular shapes relative to a given life form and mode of production. It is not just need for nutrition but for food processed in a particular way – 'Hunger is hunger, but the hunger gratified by cooked meat eaten with a knife and fork is a different hunger from that which bolts down raw meat with the aid of hand, nail and tooth' (Marx 1986[1857]: 20); it is need not just for what it takes to survive but for all the goods that we consider part of the good life. The perpetual creation and satisfaction of needs is a basic feature of human societies according to Marx; their progress consists in the ever greater power to satisfy ever richer needs.

In line with Hegel, Marx conceives societies as organized wholes. Not simply the coincidence of sharing a space–time slot but a distinctive mechanism of integration individuates societies. Whereas Hegel distinguishes societies or life-forms according to their respective stage in the self-realization of freedom, Marx locates the basic organizing principle in the particular modes of production that are predominant in the society in question. Interestingly, needs play a double role in this picture. They feature in the argument for why, in the first place, the mode of production should organize the 'totality' of society and they provide a focal point for the revolutionary transition to a new society. The first argument, which Marx presents in the *Grundrisse*, establishes that different spheres of society, some of which bourgeois economists have studied in isolation, are inherently linked (Marx 1986[1857]: 26f.). The production, distribution, circulation and consumption of goods always reflect each other, because they are played out – much like language, Marx suggests – socially. Production might seem to precede consumption, but in fact it itself consumes material, while also shaping the skills of the producing subjects. Consumption, in turn, not only uses up certain goods but instils new needs in the consumers, needs that will again guide the production that instigated them. The mode of production, for Marx, therefore functions like a coloured filter; it is not that everything is exactly the same colour in capitalism (or feudalism or communism), but everything is tinted in a particular tone:

> In all forms of society there is one specific kind of production which predominates over the rest, whose relations thus assign rank and influence to

> the others. It is a general illumination which bathes all the other colours and modifies their particularity.
>
> (Marx 1986[1857]: 46)

But how does the scene change? Since Marx assumed that communism would be more productive than capitalism, the mere increase of needs points in the historically progressive direction – according to his philosophy of history, a given mode of social organization is overcome in revolution when it has turned into 'fetters' for the productive forces (Marx 1987[1859]: 164). Yet besides this quantitative role of needs in Marx's account of historical development – which is largely discredited both for its teleology and its productivism – he also offers a qualitative account of a particularly revolutionary class of needs in his early writings. 'Radical needs' are construed as those needs that necessarily arise in the capitalist mode of production, yet require the latter's overthrow in order to be fulfilled.[3] They range from the wish for drastically reduced labour time and the desire to overcome the limitations set on personal development by a rigid, involuntary model of the division of labour to more complexly utopian notions of how unalienated labour would come to be a manifestation of freedom (Heller 1976: 26f.). This, according to the early Marx, amounts to an entire transformation of our relation to need or our 'way of needing' (Chitty 1993: 26). In capitalism, needs bind together humans in an instrumental, thing-like fashion (cf. Marx 1975[1843]: 219). I need something (new red shoes), so I need to work (teach classes) in order to earn the money it takes to pay the shoemaker, who herself only makes red shoes in order to be able to buy pink crémant for her girlfriend's birthday. I see my teaching simply as an instrument to get boots which were produced as an instrument to get bubbly. In communism as the early Marx envisions it, contrarily, there would be no shortage of shoes, crémant and philosophy classes for anybody. Shoemaking would be done for the pleasure of shoemaking and, importantly, the pleasure of pleasing those in need of shoes. Being able to see one's work for what it is – satisfaction of fellow humans' needs – would make production so enjoyable that it itself would take on the character of a need. I would feel the need to exercise my teaching powers just as much as my shoe-wearing powers. 'My work', as Marx puts it, 'would be a *free manifestation of life*, hence an *enjoyment of life*' (Marx 1975[1843]: 227).[4]

The hope that the experience of the alienated activity – teaching as instrumental activity, at hours I don't choose, while involuntarily being turned into 'a teacher'[5] – would give rise to radical needs, however, seems not to find much

3 'Radical needs' are not used as consistent terminology by Marx himself. The term was suggested by Agnes Heller in her most encompassing study of Marx's concept of needs; see Heller 1976: 88f. for the textual evidence guiding her choice.

4 My reconstruction leaves aside the details of the thematic of alienation and the relation of need and labour to Marx's concept of species-being. An excellent account can be found in Kübler 2013.

5 For a much more detailed exegetic account of this point, see Furner 2011.

historical support. This is at least how the first generation of theorists from the Frankfurt School assessed the situation after nearly another hundred years without revolution in the West. Their theories of ideology can be seen as the 'negative' of Marx's account of subjective emancipatory needs – false consciousness is what prevents the workers from entering open class struggle.

The uniformity of social totality, adopted from Marx, is thus reinforced by being traced back not solely to economic organization but to human consciousness as well. Like a thick unicoloured coat, ideology now seals the social. The following quotation is from Marcuse's *Eros and Civilization*, which actually still proposes a more nuanced diagnosis of social conformity than the later *One-Dimensional Man* (Marcuse 1964):

> People dwell in apartment concentrations – and have private automobiles with which they can no longer escape into a different world. They have huge refrigerators filled with frozen foods. They have dozens of newspapers and magazines that espouse the same ideals. They have innumerable choices, innumerable gadgets which are all of the same sort and keep them occupied and divert their attention from the real issue – which is awareness that they could both work less and determine their own needs and satisfactions.
>
> (Marcuse 1955: 100)

Given Marcuse's analysis of society as lacking in imagination and creativity and trapped in the capitalist everyday life governed by the performance principle,[6] he seems hard-pressed to account for the resources of possible resistance. His theoretical framework mirrors Marx's in that he, too, considers needs the crucial vehicle for human action and binds the possibility of revolution to the emergence of 'new needs', which diametrically oppose the existing order. Yet where in a flawlessly one-dimensional order should those new needs originate? Marcuse's solution is to move beyond the reigning social system and present the erotic forces bound by repressed sexuality as revolutionary potential.

This sets him two major challenges. The first is to refute Freud's own pessimism about the compatibility of instinctual liberation and civilization; the second is to account for the actual accumulation of this potential into new needs entertained by a decisive part of the population.

In Freud's metapsychology, as laid out in *Civilization and its Discontents* (Freud 2002[1930]), civilization rests in several ways on the constraint of instincts ('Triebverzicht'). The pleasure principle or life instinct which aims at immediate gratification needs to be held off, because a world of scarce resources requires humans to work and organize themselves. Maturity both of societies and in individuals comes with the acknowledgment of the reality principle, the insight into the fact that the

6 'Performance principle' is Marcuse's translation of the well-established German term 'Leistungsprinzip', which means being governed above all else by the standards of achievement and efficiency.

world is not what the pleasure principle's wishes would have it to be. Moreover, the death instinct which Freud introduces later in the text constantly works against the achievements of social cooperation and development, as it is striving for a relief of tension beyond the grasp of complex life forms, found only in inanimate matter or, indeed, death. Thanatos, as Freud also calls the death drive, thus needs to be constantly held at bay if it is not to unravel and destroy civilized life. Marcuse makes several decisive moves to rework this picture. The first and most fundamental is to bring the Marxist regard for historicity to bear on the theory of the drives. Even the libidinal 'first' human nature can be seen as a sedimentation of humanity's historical interaction with nature. Thus, despite the fact that Marcuse, in line with the *General Edition* of Freud's works in English, uses 'instinct' to refer to the German 'Trieb', he makes a de-naturalizing move that Laplanche later put forward by the preference of 'drive' over 'instinct' as the correct translation of 'Trieb'.[7] It is in a specific course of history that the drives and their vicissitude must be located, namely the history of domination. Marcuse introduces the term 'surplus repression' to distinguish the restraint necessitated by scarce resources from that imposed by the differential distribution of resources – that is, domination. Many of the aggression-inducing and guilt-producing effects which Freud attributes to the struggle between life and death drives are better accounted for as results of surplus repression, Marcuse argues. In the current era, when – according to Marcuse's progressivist view – technology would allow scarcity to be overcome, ideological repression of the life instincts has become so pressing precisely because surplus repression has never been as irrational (Marcuse 1955: 93). In wrongly universalizing a specific reality principle, namely the capitalist 'performance principle', as representing reality *tout court*, Freudianism, according to Marcuse, actually contributed to this ideology. As reread by him, however, the exposure of the performance principle as an outlived definition of 'reality', a particular 'promethean' reality principle, opens the space for reconsidering the possible libidinal dynamics under another reality principle (Marcuse 1955: 138f.). Its shape, Marcuse claims, can already be made out in an array of manifestations which escape the reach of the current reality principle, namely fantasy, utopia, perversions and aesthetic representations. From all of them, Marcuse reads off a new definition of work and existence, which he defines as 'Orphic-Narcissistic'.[8]

> They have not become the culture-heroes of the Western world: theirs is the image of joy and fulfillment; the voice which does not command but sings;

7 In line with Marcuse, I use 'drive' and 'instincts' interchangeably in the following. For further clarification on the translation of 'Trieb', see Lauretis 2010: 20f.

8 In a certain way, however, Marcuse remains sadly trapped in the 'promethic' model. His notion of work seems completely blind towards care work or reproductive labour. An interesting alternative is suggested by the psychoanalyst Elisabeth Young-Bruehl, drawing on another cast of mythological characters, namely Philemon and Baucis (see Young-Bruehl 2003: 13). A summary of the feminist critique of Marx's own negligence regarding reproductive labour can be found in Himmelweit 1991.

> the gesture which offers and receives; the deed which is peace and ends the labor of conquest; the liberation from time which unites man with god, man with nature. Literature has preserved their image.
>
> (Marcuse 1955: 162)

In another formulation, Marcuse's alternative is captured in the terms of 'play and display', pointing towards the reorganization of human activity, work included, into pleasure (Marcuse 1955: 195). This does not mean that work would end, but that its form would change. We might be doing some of the same things, but they would now be experienced not as the suspension but as the realization of pleasure. 'For example, if work were accompanied by a reactivation of pregenital polymorphous eroticism, it would tend to become gratifying in itself without losing its *work* content' (Marcuse 1955: 215).

However, so far all manifestations of this order are of marginal, even 'unreal' status. The Orphic-Narcissistic principle 'has retained its freedom from the reality principle at the price of being ineffective in the reality' (Marcuse 1955: 172). It would have to move out of, as Marcuse puts it, 'the unreal atmosphere of the museum and Bohemia' (Marcuse 1955: 176) in order to restructure society effectively. So while Marcuse convincingly stipulates the possibility of a non-tragic libidinal dynamics, thus meeting Freud's challenge, he seems to fall short of his own Marxist aspiration, namely to sketch a plausible theory of social transformation. Marcuse's position could be summarized as 'libidinal materialism', leaning on Marx's own historical materialism. He suggests that a particular 'ripeness' of libidinal dispositions needs to be reached to create the preconditions for revolution. This, however, amounts to the temporality of historicism so trenchantly criticized by postcolonial thinkers. Dipesh Chakrabarty, for instance, argues that any such idea of steady historical progress can be used both to construe the advance and superiority of the theorists' own society over other, typically non-Western societies and to assign them to the 'waiting rooms of history' (Chakrabarty 2007: 10). Even the development Marcuse projects for Western capitalist societies seems paradoxical. They do not only require the technological means to overcome scarcity and intensive labour in order for revolution to be possible, but they also need to have reached a stage in the development of their instincts which allows a transition from the tragic opposition of pleasure principle and performance principle to the reconciliation between liberated instincts and aesthetic reality (cf. Marcuse 1955: 214; 1969: 4). Yet the refigured instincts alone would not automatically be stronger than the repression they face. Moreover, unlike the means of production, they seem to depend on freedom from repression to fully form themselves (Marcuse 1955: 222). To be effective for revolution, they would need to accumulate into what Marcuse calls 'the Great Refusal' (Marcuse 1955: 170; 1969: *passim*) antecedently, a refusal with a positive core, which aims 'not only against the reality principle, at non-being, but also beyond the reality principle – at another mode of being' (Marcuse 1955: 109). But is it possible to imagine a revolutionary subject of new needs, situated in a present firmly in the grip of the past, being animated entirely by the future? Marcuse himself acknowledges this dilemma as a vicious circle (Marcuse 1969: 18f.).

Disparity and desire

In his *History of Sexuality. Vol. 1* (1998[1976]) Foucault takes issue with Marxist historical explanations only very vaguely and from a fair distance, polemically discarding them in occasional side comments. Yet the counter-evidence he assembles methodologically undermines both the main stakes of Marcuse's Freudo-Marxism, the notion of social totality and the conception of repressed sexual forces underwriting revolutionary needs.

At the core of Foucault's argument is an analysis which shifts the understanding of power from a juridical one to one that conceives of it as productive. It is not, Foucault stresses, that power never occurred in the guise of the law, as a negative and prohibiting force, but this form would have to be explained in the course of an analysis, not assumed at its outset. The more so since, as Foucault – putting forward his own piece of ideology critique – points out, such narrow conception of power as law serves as its legitimating guise, obscuring power's omnipresence in its manifold other manifestations.

To prove his point, Foucault deliberately resorts to its most counterintuitive domain, namely sexuality, as his paradigm case (Foucault 1998: 90). More than Marcuse's actual text, he thereby diametrically opposes the atmosphère of which *Eros and Civilization* was an early manifestation. Pontificating about the necessity to free sexuality from its alleged repression, in Foucault's provocative re-periodization, simply prolongs a peculiar Western discourse of sexuality, dominant since the eighteenth century. This 'regime of power-knowledge-pleasure that sustains the discourse on human sexuality in our part of the world' is singled out by the fact that 'sex was constituted as a problem of truth' (Foucault 1998: 56), not in a pedagogical model as in ancient Greece, but in a pastoral one: 'For us, it is in the confession that truth and sex are joined, through the obligatory and exhaustive expression of an individual secret' (Foucault 1998: 61). The perversions, which Marcuse singled out not only as symptoms of present contradictions but also as anticipated articulations of a liberated future, are, for Foucault, a focal point of the standard operation of productive power and pastoral discourse (cf. Foucault 1998: 45f.). They are not, as Marcuse envisions it, discontinuous with the powers that be (a discontinuity curiously highlighted in Marcuse's text by the fact that almost all the material he quotes to convey his idea of the Orphic-Narcissistic is printed in a different language from the main text – modernist French poetry or writings from the German romanticist tradition). What is more, the perversions as accounted for by Foucault do not point to a development heading towards the replacement of the current by a future order. This position is, however, not to be mistaken with a strict structuralism. Being in continuity with the present regime of power does not reduce desire to be its mere expression.

Therefore a possible Lacanian critique of the repressive hypothesis according to which 'the law is what constitutes both desire and the lack on which it is predicated' (Foucault 1998: 81) is, according to Foucault, itself still in the grasp of a juridical model of power, this time attributing to power the unilateral force to shape reality (Foucault 1998: 85). His own view, contrarily, makes power productive but not deterministic; it depends on the tension between relatively opposing poles. The question of whether or not power positively establishes something thus seems less defining of Foucault's 'productive power' than its mode of operation: power proceeds not by commanding obedience but by instigating, aligning, dispersing reactions.

Nevertheless, this is not entirely at odds with Marcuse's view of a complex, mutually reinforcing formation of a particular regime of allocation, oppression and sexuality. He precisely does not think that one-dimensional society represses polymorphous sexuality, but that a particular (why not say discursive?) regime of the 'performance principle' goes along with a particular organization of sexuality in tension with civilization. *Eros and Civilization* sets out to show that this performance principle is historically specific – just as *Will to Knowledge* proves the peculiar particularity of sexuality-cum-truth-in-confession. Yet the more we concede to Marcuse that he presents the Orphic-Narcissistic not as an actual erotic potential repressed by present society but merely as a future possibility, presupposing a different mode of social or power relations, the more a materialist, dialectical solution to the problem of transition moves out of sight.

In his totalizing account of society, Marcuse seems to have only two choices about moments of resistance: either they belong to the future or they are violently repressed. The present is only allowed to refer negatively to a better future. The car, the fridge, the frozen food symbolize nothing but one-dimensionality. In a Foucauldian perspective, each node of power, contrarily, is endowed with ambivalence. His notion of power presupposes the combination of continuity – nothing social 'beyond' or 'outside' power – and heterogeneity – no relation of power in the first place if it wasn't for the inflected element's relative and ongoing unpredictability. Against the unicoloured, Marxist picture of society, Foucault utilizes the metaphor of the mosaic (Foucault 1998: 53, 64). The metaphor is spatial and suggests the discursive simultaneity of asynchronous moments. Yet Foucault's view does not amount to the disintegration of any and all patterns – obviously he discerned a particular pattern for the Western discourse of sexuality, but it is a pattern compatible with disparity. The model of the mosaic allows the social theorist to highlight certain moments as resistant or heterogeneous – Foucault speaks of 'heterotopias' (Foucault 1984); it even allows the political subject to embrace some as interesting, promising, desirable. Teresa de Lauretis, following Foucault's shift to spatial metaphors, summarizes aptly how this proceeds without severing those moments from their location in the present:

> For that 'elsewhere' is not some mythic past or some utopian future history: it is the elsewhere of discourse here and now, the blind spots, or the

> space-off, of its representations. I think of it as spaces in the margins of hegemonic discourses, social spaces carved in the interstices of institutions and in the chinks and cracks of the power-knowledge apparati [...].
>
> (de Lauretis 1987: 24)

Why not, then, redefine Marcuse's repertoire of the Orphic-Narcissistic, his surrealist poems and his allusions to non-reproductive and homo-sexuality as simply such 'elsewheres', precariously and contingently realized in the interstices of the present? This would mitigate the dilemma of new needs' emergence. The mosaic of sociality allows them to be prefigured: we can regard them as coming from somewhere more reliable than *the* future; they would reside in the unruly desires of the present.[9]

However, the theoretical problem thereby turns out to be merely postponed one step. As soon as we favour a particular trajectory of social change, as soon as we single out a particular set of desires as revolutionary, what we are lacking is any account of their efficacy. The conceptual implication of a need was that once a subject has it, it will follow through with fulfilling it. Needs are unequivocal. Either you need something or you do not. Only in rare cases do desires lend themselves to such unambiguousness. Desires can be contradictory and do not necessarily direct action, and even when they do, they do not directly aim at satisfaction – as de Lauretis emphasizes, the sexual drive aims for a lost object's '*promise* of a perfect state of bliss' (de Lauretis 2010: 29; my italics), not for satisfaction unmediated. What makes desire so stubborn, its resilience in the face of non-fulfilment, thus simultaneously makes it a frail and far from sufficient revolutionary force. Maybe the owners of that fridge Marcuse laments about did constantly entertain fancies about more meaningful choices and more profound escapes, but held those desires as nothing more than a background noise to their 'real' daily lives, disjoint from any serious attempts of implementation, pursued in the approximations Marcuse mentions – a ride in the car through the countryside – but not fulfilled by them. Just as the grocery boxes allude to economies of pleasure outside the exchange of work and money without bringing their consumer any nearer to those. What is lacking, then, is an account of how a certain type of desire turns efficacious – that is, an account of desire-becoming-need.

If Marcuse seems to have a case in point when emphasizing the alleged 'unreality' of fantasy and perversion, his judgement nevertheless betrays a hegemonial perspective. As a potential model for future polymorphous pleasures, perversions might be as 'unreal' as he supposes (cf. Marcuse 1955: 176) – seen from within established

9 José Esteban Muñoz has most beautifully pursued such readings of the utopian in the present. Especially his discussion of O'Hara's and Warhol's 'praise' of the Coke bottle would lend itself as a direct contrast to Marcuse's bleak view of the fridge quoted above (Muñoz 2009: 5f.). However, the question of how such utopian moments found in the present could attain transformative power remains bracketed in his work, too.

interstitial practices of perversity, however, the question about their own reality rings cynical. From the interstitial angle, the question is not how perversion could be made real, because it already is, but how more of reality could be made perverse.

Teresa de Lauretis' book *The Practice of Love: Lesbian Sexuality and Perverse Desire* (1994) can be seen as a theoretical treatment of exactly this question. In a similar vein to Marcuse's, de Lauretis rereads Freud against the more naturalizing and deterministic strands in his work. Where Marcuse qualified the tragic dynamics of the drives as dependent on a specific history of domination, de Lauretis emphasizes the dependency of the drives' direction on mediating fantasies. Freud himself supposed the content of fantasy to be structured by certain primal fantasies – intra-uterine existence, parental intercourse, castration, seduction (cf. Laplanche and Pontalis 1973: 331f.). Yet while Freud traced the content of those 'Urphantasien' back to supposedly phylogenetic origins, de Lauretis, following Laplanche and Pontalis, insists on the cultural content of whatever comes to stand as a structuring fantasy (de Lauretis 1994: 284; Laplanche and Pontalis 1968: 16f.). Finally, what she tries to develop under the name of 'habit change' is an account of how lesbianism, against a mainstream of heterosexual cultural representations, can assume the status of a structuring fantasy.

The first and decisive manoeuvre in *The Practice of Love* is to redescribe *all* sexuality as 'perverse'. Drawn from a close reading of Freud, de Lauretis reveals a nexus between fantasy scenario and fetish as underlying any sexual orientation, notably also that of heterosexuality. De Lauretis summarizes her journey from Freud as follows:

> I began this study in chapter 1 from Freud's assertion in the *Three Essays* that the sexual instinct is *in the first instance* independent of its objects. Now, in light of the various texts through which I have developed the notion of perverse desire, I think it is possible to conclude that *in the last instance* the sexual instinct *as* perverse desire is dependent on a fantasy scenario which the object evokes and helps to restage; conversely, it is in that scenario, in that restaging, that the object acquires its fantasmatic value as object.
>
> (de Lauretis 1994: 309)

But what, then, makes for a habit change, for the transition to a new structuring fantasy? De Lauretis locates the habit-changing mediation from social to psychic world on three levels. The first concerns the actual content of a fantasy, the second its representational setting, and the third its collective dynamics.

The content of a fantasy determines the subsequent object of desire, the fetish, as its defence and reminder. The fantasy that comes to stand as a primal fantasy for lesbian desire, according to de Lauretis, is not the familiar version of castration but a traumatic loss of the henceforth sought-after feminine body image, maternally or narcissistically invested but prohibited or denigrated within a patriarchal order. It is against this loss that the lesbian fetish, the (wounded) female body image, gains shape (de Lauretis 1994: 262).

Yet to account for the efficacy of such changes in fantasy-content, de Lauretis directs the attention also to the form or structure of representations. Only particular spectatorial settings, according to de Lauretis, can account for the restructuring effect of certain representations. Like primal fantasies, particular films or performances implicate the fantasizing subject from all angles: she is part of the scene and simultaneously the onlooker who can identify with multiple positions in it (though, crucially, not a priori with any and all of them); 'that is to say, the film would address the spectator as subject of its fantasy in its different levels and forms, would provide at once the fantasy and the means of access to it' (de Lauretis 1994: 98). By seeing herself in the scene, the subject is not only the passive recipient of a scene and the object in it but also self-reflective subject. Not bound to either object or subject position, to either desire for or identification with the figures in the scene, the spectator can thus, in a certain respect, be rendered as a lesbian subject irrespective of her actual self-definition and practices (de Lauretis 1994: 89; Engel 2002: 159). Shifting focus from the content level to the formal structure of perception, de Lauretis thus introduces a hyperbolic definition of 'lesbianism' (clearly highlighting the *homo*sexuality of lesbian sexual practice over, for instance, a particular butch-femme dynamic) as the cipher for a relation which frees its protagonists from the fixation to either the subject or the object position.

De Lauretis' account of habit change combines the restructuring of fantasy with the catalysing effect of what she calls, with a term borrowed from Helene Deutsch, 'consent to activity'. Effective encouragement, as isolated in the psychoanalytic scene, comes from concrete others with whom a particular fantasy is shared as well as from public representations. With such discursive tailwind, different and new scenes can fall in the place of 'primary fantasy', thus turning constantly into the source informing desire. In her analysis of Sheila McLaughlin's film *She Must Be Seeing Things*, de Lauretis sees this process represented as well:

> This is a film about two women who share a common fantasy, a lesbian fantasy of origins; and if 'the origin of the subject [her]self' is located 'in the field of fantasy', as Laplanche and Pontalis say, then this very fantasy, which they share, is part of what constitutes them as a lesbian subject. Not the least implication of which is that it takes two women, not one, to make a lesbian.
>
> (de Lauretis 1994: 92)

This passage is also the first mention of the line that forms a sort of refrain throughout de Lauretis' book – 'that it takes [at least] two women to make a lesbian' (de Lauretis 1994: 96, 99, 123, 235, 251, 283, 296).

When de Lauretis sees desire anchored in the stage set by fantasy scenarios, she defies a neat opposition between fantasy on the one hand and reality on the other (thereby again following Laplanche and Pontalis 1968). Marcuse has done much work to criticize Freud's particular account of reality as the only reality. Yet he himself seems to assume that what escapes the 'reality' defined by the performance principle is, as fantasy, without any anchors in actual practice. In a way, he seems to have a one-dimensional account of fantasy, only sourcing it for its content and preparing the metapsychological ground for its future possibility.

De Lauretis brings in the practical and collective dimensions which render fantasies structuring. Her three-dimensional account of habit change might be demanding, but is not dependent on a whole new social totality. It might, however, implant the desire for one.

Needs in the guise of desire

But how should we, in turn, discern the fantasy scenarios productive of anti-capitalist desire? And what entitles us to carry de Lauretis' 'passionate fiction' (de Lauretis 1994: xiv) over to the scene of political economy? Interestingly, she does prompt this herself in a sweeping reference on the very last pages of *The Practice of Love* to a theorist notably absent from her preceding discussion – Karl Marx:

> Finally, my understanding of sexual structuring [...] also finds a welcome coincidence in Foucault's statement that 'every technique of production requires modification of individual conduct – not only skills but also attitudes'. But that his reference to a nowadays unpopular text, Marx's *Capital*, intersects with references to Peirce and Freud [...] in these closing pages of a study of perverse desire is perhaps not a coincidence, after all.
>
> (de Lauretis 1994: 312)

To exemplify what this ending of *The Practice of Love* might open up to, and sketch a somewhat more palpable proposal, I want to return to Marx's formula for radical needs introduced earlier. Could we not strip them from their historical necessity, yet reintroduce their content in the guise of queer revolutionary desire? In communism, Marx had claimed, the structure of need will profoundly have surpassed the logic of an individual requiring means to achieve its ends – that is, working in order to gain what it costs to exchange one's products for what it takes to satisfy one's needs. In an economy geared at fulfilling needs rather than making profit, production would directly aim at satisfaction. The punchline was that this satisfaction would not be restricted to the consumption side of things, but satisfaction would already derive from the unalienated need-oriented production. In communism, labour will itself have become a need, so that the distinction between having a need satisfied and working for the satisfaction of a need is overcome. For Marx, this process is seen as the realization of full human potentiality for freedom, of what he calls the 'species-essence' – 'Our products would be so many mirrors in which we saw reflected our essential nature' (Marx 1975[1843]: 228). But for present purposes I would like to suggest that we can also recognize in this communist conception of need a basic tenet of hyperbolic lesbianism as encountered before in de Lauretis' ideal of the indeterminacy between subject and object position. The idea of not distinguishing between the labour for someone else's satisfaction and one's own pleasure rings familiar for anyone versed in the myths of butch* relationality.[10] As Sally Munt puts it in her aptly titled book *Heroic Desire*, 'the *butch* embodies a potent fusion of female *desire*; as de Lauretis has said, she is both desiring subject and desiring object' (Munt 1998: 82). And more than that, the definitions of give and take conventionally associated with object and subject positions are overcome in various formulations of lesbian lore. Thus the British glossy lesbian magazine *Diva* displayed on one of their covers a quote from DJ Mz Fontaine: 'My pleasure is pleasing women'. Or, to move from the mainstream to the hardcore of lesbian erotic self-understanding, we can follow Patrick Califia's protagonist from 'A Dash of Vanilla': 'I get worn down to my stubborn core, the tough silent part of me that does not question the decision to perform a difficult task [...]. Perversely [...], I get very turned on by the idea of servicing you, of having you use my mouth for hours' (Califia 2009[1988]: 368).[11]

In whichever way we fantasize the exact translation of that particular scenario of desire onto other areas of exchange, a society which learned to perform this for hunger as well as for love would consume truly communist cookies.

References

Califia, P. (2009) *Macho Sluts* [1988], Vancouver: Arsenal Pulp Press.

Chakrabarty, D. (2007) *Provincializing Europe* [2000], Princeton, NJ: Princeton University Press.

Chitty, A. (1993) 'The Early Marx on Needs', *Radical Philosophy* 64: 23–32.

Cover, R. (2004) 'Material/Queer Theory: Performativity, Subjectivity, and Affinity-Based Struggles in the Culture of Late Capitalism', *Rethinking Marxism* 16: 293–310.

DIVA Magazine 112 (September 2005).

Engel, A. (2002) *Wider die Eindeutigkeit: Sexualität und Geschlecht im Fokus queerer Politik der Repräsentation*, Frankfurt am Main: Campus.

Foucault, M. (1998) *The History of Sexuality Vol. 1: The Will to Knowledge* [1976], London: Penguin.

—— (1984) 'Of Other Spaces', *Architecture, Mouvement, Continuité* 5: 46–9.

Freud, S. (2002) *Civilization and Its Discontents* [1930], London: Penguin.

10 I use the '*' here to emphasize the openness of the idealized subject positions of lesbian, butch and femme to all sexes. Obviously, I am not providing an empirically accurate analysis of lesbian practices here – entirely different research would be required to that end. I employ the *hyperbolic* figure of lesbian sexuality to highlight a certain anti-capitalist economy of exchange as well as to queer the usual terms in which we account for left utopias.

11 This quotation, taken from a collection of sadomasochism stories, in particular invites the suggestion that the dynamics of Marx's radical needs are much better described as masochistic than as hyperbolically lesbian (perhaps following Bersani in claiming that all sexuality was at its core masochistic, striving for the abandonment of the self). I decided not to pursue this tempting reading here, since it might obfuscate the radical edge of Marx's idea of labour in communism, namely that work completely loses the character of being service, toil, instrumental. The idea seems less to be to make the pain of working pleasurable but rather to move beyond a distinction between working for somebody and being worked for, between giving and receiving.

Furner, J. (2011) 'Marx's Sketch of Communist Society in *The German Ideology* and the Problems of Occupational Confinement and Occupational Identity', *Philosophy and Social Criticism* 37(2): 189–215.

Grosz, E. (1994) 'Refiguring Lesbian Desire', in L. Doan (ed.) *The Lesbian Postmodern*, New York: Columbia University Press, pp. 67–84.

Heller, A. (1976) *The Theory of Need in Marx*, London: Allison and Busby.

Himmelweit, S. (1991) 'Reproduction and the Materialist Conception of History: A Feminist Critique', in T. Carver (ed.) *The Cambridge Companion to Marx*, Cambridge: Cambridge University Press, pp. 196–221.

Kübler, L. (2013) 'Marx's Theorie der Entfremdung', in R. Jaeggi and D. Loick (eds) *Karl Marx: Perspektiven der Gesellschaftskritik*, Berlin: Akademieverlag, pp. 47–66.

Laplanche, J. and Pontalis, J. -B. (1968) 'Fantasy and the Origins of Sexuality' [1964], *International Journal of Psycho-Analysis* 49(1): 1–18.

—— (1973) *The Language of Psycho-Analysis*, London: Hogarth Press and the Institute of Psycho-Analysis.

de Lauretis, T. (1987) *Technologies of Gender: Essays on Film, Theory, and Fiction*, Bloomington: Indiana University Press.

—— (1994) *The Practice of Love: Lesbian Sexuality and Perverse Desire*, Bloomington: Indiana University Press.

—— (2010) *Freud's Drive: Psychoanalysis, Literature, and Film*, London: Palgrave Macmillan.

Marcuse, H. (1955) *Eros and Civilization*, Boston, MA: Beacon Press.

—— (1964) *One-Dimensional Man*, Boston, MA: Beacon Press.

—— (1969) *Essay on Liberation*, London: Penguin Press.

Marx, K. (1975) 'Comments on James Mill', in *Marx/Engels Collected Works Vol. 3* [1843], London: Lawrence & Wishart, pp. 211–28.

—— (1986) 'Grundrisse', in *Marx/Engels Collected Works Vol.28* [1857], London: Lawrence & Wishart, pp. 17–540.

—— (1987) 'A Contribution to the Critique of Political Economy', in *Marx/Engels Collected Works Vol.29* [1859], London: Lawrence & Wishart, pp. 257–420.

Muñoz, J. E. (2009) *Cruising Utopia: The Then and There of Queer Futurity*, New York: New York University Press.

Munt, S. (1998) *Heroic Desire: Lesbian Identity and Cultural Space*, New York: New York University Press.

von Redecker, E. (2012) 'Feministische Strategie und Revolution', in C. Kley, C. Newark and S. Miller (eds) *Peripherie und Zentrum: Geschlechterforschung und die Potenziale der Philosophie*, Bielefeld: Transcript, pp. 17–36.

Toiland, T. (2011) 'Queer, flexibel, erfolgreich', *Analyse und Kritik* 558. Available online at www.akweb.de/ak_s/ak558/27.htm (accessed 18 January 2014).

Young-Bruehl, E. (2003) *Where Do We Fall When We Fall in Love?* New York: The Other Press.

Chapter 2

Can the subaltern desire?

The erotic as a power and disempowerment of the erotic

Jamila M. H. Mascat

Don't wanna be your exotic
your lovin of my beauty ain't more than
funky fornication plain pink perversion
in fact nasty necrophilia
cause my beauty is dead to you
I am dead to you
not your
harem girl geisha doll banana picker
pom pom girl pum pum shorts coffee maker
town whore belly dancer private dancer
la malinche venus hottentot laundry girl
your immaculate vessel emasculating princess
don't wanna be
your erotic
not your exotic

Suheir Hammad (2010)

'For Arabs, desire was all-powerful' (Al Neimi 2009: 79): so states the nameless protagonist of Salwa Al Neimi's *The Proof of the Honey*, a novel that revisits the most intimate secrets and memories of a Syrian librarian who lives in Paris and has become a clandestine expert in ancient Arabic erotica. Al Neimi's book is emblematic of a *nouvelle vague* of feminine erotic literature written by Arab women writers that has been warmly welcomed by European critics as the emergence of a 'sexual intifada' (*Der Spiegel*) and as the start of an 'unstoppable revolution' in the Arab world (*The Guardian*). By focusing on some selected works of three authors – *The Proof of the Honey* by Salwa al Neimi from Syria, *The Almond* by Nedjma from Morocco and *I Killed Scheherazade* by Joumana Haddad from Lebanon,[1] this chapter intends to show how and to what extent

1 The list of the authors who participate in this publishing trend of Arab literature written by women, where intimacy plays a crucial narrative role, might well be lengthened to include Algerian Ahlam Mosteghanemi (*Chaos of the Senses*, 2004); Lebanese Alawyia Sobh (*Maryam*

gendered stereotypes of nineteenth-century Orientalism (Lewis 2004; Mernissi 2001; Valassopoulos 2007; Yegenoglu 1998) have been reactivated in contemporary women's postcolonial narrative (first and second sections). At the same time, by analysing the enthusiastic reception that these works have encountered in the West, it aims to reflect on the cultural and political implications of this relatively new literary phenomenon against the backdrop of the transnational debate on gender justice and women rights (third section).

Al Neimi's *Borhàn al 'Asal* (*The Proof of the Honey*) was first published in Beirut in 2007, by Riad El Rayyes, and it was banned almost everywhere in the Arab world, the few exceptions being Tunisia, Morocco, Algeria and the Arab Emirates. Censorship and sensational advertising – such as 'Al Neimi announces the end of a taboo in the Arab world: that of sex!' (Reuters 2009) – helped the novel become a bestseller in the West. *The Almond*, billed on the original back cover as an 'exceptional testimony' in which 'for the first time a Muslim woman freely gives account of her intimate life', is an erotic memoir published in France in 2004 by Nedjma – the pen-name of a writer who has never revealed her real identity. The book quickly sold tens of thousands of copies, so many as to persuade the author to rack up another success with *La traversée des sens: conte intime* (2009), a second *Bildungsroman* that describes the sentimental and sexual education of an Algerian girl guided by a more experienced woman who was 'born with an inclination towards pleasure' (Nedjma 2009: 23). *I Killed Scheherazade*, published in English in 2010, collects the 'confessions of an angry Arab woman' – the Lebanese poet Joumana Haddad – in a violent invective against repressive bigotry of Arab societies, and pleads in prose and verse the cause of feminine pleasure in the name of emancipation. The three writings considered here share the same themes (sex, women, religions and traditions in the Arab world), the same demands (liberty and libertinism) and a similar promise to challenge traditional taboos and prohibitions in order to reveal, through an intimate and private storytelling, the true erotic vitality of ancient and contemporary Arab culture. They also received a similar publishing treatment: labelled under the banner 'exotic and erotic' in the Western book market, they have all been praised in the reviews that appeared in most of European leading newspapers and sold a conspicuous number of copies.[2]

ou le passé décomposé, 2007) and Iman Humaydan Younes (*Wild Mulberries*, 2008); Saudi Seba Al Herz (*The Others*, 2009) and Rajaa Al Sanea (*Girls of Riyadh*, 2007); and French writer Lounja Charif (*La Maghrébine: Du voile à la guépière*, 2010; *Désirs voilés*, 2012), whose country of origin remains unknown.

2 *The Proof of the Honey* has been translated into 19 languages. *I Killed Scheherazade* has been published in 12 editions. *The Almond* has sold rights in 17 countries. Moreover, while only few authors from the Arab world succeed in selling more than 10,000 copies of their translations in Europe, the three books considered here have largely crossed the line. As an example, the Italian edition of *The Proof of the Honey* has been reprinted six times and sold tens of thousands of copies in the first weeks after publication, while in France Nedjma's novel has sold 50,000 copies in a few months and has spent weeks on *Der Spiegel*'s bestseller list in Germany.

Reflecting on the material and discursive conditions that enabled the success of the 'postcolonial erotic' genre through the books of Al Neimi, Nedjma and Haddad, this chapter aims to show how, despite adopting a gender perspective, the process of re-appropriating abused *topoi* of 'oriental' sexuality – a process whose stated intent is to rescue Arab culture from the mistaken and stereotyped portrait circulating in the West of a sexophobic Arab-Muslim world – ends up re-establishing a fabricated view of the 'Orient' and turning classical Western fantasies of the erotic East into a *canon*. In the current context, such erotic canon, when it is assigned to women, may seem to be new if we compare it with the one of the 'monolithic woman as a victim' (Spivak 2000: 305) created in the name of the gender-and-development ideology by international feminist elites as 'culturally incapable of democracy and feminism' (Spivak 2000: 332) – but it is actually just an old one that has been resurrected from the colonial repertory.

A second element of analysis concerns the postulates of this canonization, which is grounded on a very controversial notion of *authenticity*: the idea of an *authentic*/traditional Eastern world (a world devoted to the pleasures and delights of sex) and the assumption of an *authentic*/reliable spokesperson (the 'oriental' woman herself as an *author*) whose epistemic location and political positioning remain ostensibly unquestioned.

In the lecture 'What is an author?' held in 1969 at the Collège de France in Paris, Foucault quoted Samuel Beckett – '"What does it matter who is speaking", someone said, "what does it matter who is speaking"' – as a starting point to raise the issue of the disappearance of the author in contemporary literature (Foucault 1980: 141). In lieu of the author's *persona*, which in the last analysis represents only 'the surface *effect* of more firmly grounded unities' (Foucault 2002: 29), Foucault introduces the device of the *author function* to shed light on the regimes of appropriation of discourse. In this regard, according to Foucault, what needs to be accounted for is *how* the right to speak is defined, which desires, interests and power relations are at play, what makes a discourse possible and who can be invested with the authoriality of producing it. The shift from the author's persona to the author function enables the philosopher to wonder about the set of material and formal conditions that allow specific discursive practices to emerge. In this way, he writes, 'we would no longer hear the questions that have been heard for so long: Who really spoke? Is it he and not someone else? With what authority and originality and what part of his deepest self did he express in his discourse?' At this point, following Foucault, new questions would arise, such as: 'What are the modes of existence of this discourse? Where has it been used, how can it circulate, and who can appropriate it for himself? What are the places in it where there is room for possible subjects? Who can assume these various subject functions?' (Foucault 1980: 160).

Investigating the author function contingently performed by the three writers here discussed implies taking account of the question of *authority* – authority to speak, to write and to represent – in the context of postcolonial neo-orientalist narrative. What gives authority to the act of speaking and what gives legitimacy to storytelling? Or, as Hamid Dabashi puts it, 'who gets to represent whom and by what authority?' (Dabashi 2009: xi).

Through narrative, the voices of privileged postcolonial writing subjects measure themselves against the reception by metropolitan readers and critics and simultaneously affirm their presence at the expense of the subaltern voices that are exiled from the spectrum of the discourse. Moreover, both authors and audiences are entangled in the structural constraints of cultural imperialism that promotes the circulation and consumption of exotic literary commodities (Huggan 2001). The textuality of erotic desire within which the novels by Haddad, Nedjma and Al Neimi are located will therefore be explored by taking into consideration the discursive setting that defines the conditions for the emergence of the genre. After mapping and reconstructing how postcolonial erotic literature gains access to the Western book market and enters the field of the neo-orientalist debate, a further question will still remain to be addressed. It concerns the extent to which erotic desire can contribute to the invention and the transmission of new forms of resistant agency (see Weiss, Chapter 4 in this volume). In other words, paraphrasing Spivak, is 'strategic eroticism' possible? And, to borrow Audre Lorde's formulation, how can the *erotic as a power* (Lorde 1984) play a role in disrupting the neo-colonial and patriarchal symbolic capital that pertains to the hegemonic discourse (fourth section)?

A secret named desire

In each of the three books analysed here, desire is the narrative device that weaves the storylines. Desire for carnal pleasure and knowledge is what drives the anonymous protagonist of *The Proof of the Honey* through the series of her amorous encounters: 'All that matters is my own desire, my rare desire', she proclaims (Al Neimi 2009: 14). The narrator begins to put into practice the theories that she has learned in many years of clandestine reading of Arabic erotica and ancient Islamic texts in which sexual desire is viewed as a foretaste of the delights of paradise. The tale of her passionate experiences – starting from her meeting a man, 'the Thinker', who helps her explore a previously unknown world of pleasure – is sprinkled with erudite quotes from the patrimony of classic erotic writings where the protagonist seeks redemption of the sensuality that the Arab world once glorified but now disregards. 'Three things I need in life. I cannot exist without them', she confesses. 'I have physical need for water, semen, and words' (Al Neimi 2009: 49). Indeed, words matter in Al Neimi's novel, since the flux of the erotic endlessly circulates through texts and bodies. The texts are commentaries on the joys and techniques of sex written by classical Arab writers such as Al Junayd (830–910), Ahmad Al Tifashi (1184–1253), Muhammad Al Nafzawy (fifteenth century), Jalaladdin Al Suyuti (1445–1505) and Ahmad Al Tijani (1735–1815). Their works demonstrate that sex was never a sin in the Islamic world, and that, on the contrary, Muslims are the only people for whom *eros* is a 'blessing' for which one should be grateful to God (Al Neimi 2009: 43). These texts prove, according to the narrator, that 'Arabic [...] is the language of sex' (Al Neimi 2009: 21). Therefore it should be time to return this language to its original sexual matrix, by recuperating banned and forgotten words, by inventing new ones and by transgressing (as the protagonist does) the restrictions imposed by a 'castrated' computer that behaves like a 'shrinking violet' and whose spell-check corrector systematically underlines in red the verb 'to fuck' (Al Neimi 2009: 110).

If Al Neimi's novel argues for the recovery of Arab eroticism and its language, Joumana Haddad shares the same determination to rebel against the 'spineless fear of Arabic words' (Haddad 2010: 65). Like Al Neimi, she wishes to give back to the Arabic language its original imaginative and expressive potential, which has vanished over the centuries, by referring to that classic literary heritage 'loaded with works that would make even the most liberated Western writer blush' (Haddad 2010: 80f.). In *I Killed Scheherazade*, which blends the registers of the pamphlet and of the memoir, Haddad offers to a hypothetical Western interlocutor (the 'dear Westerner' whom she addresses from page one on) 'a meditation on what being *an Arab woman* does and *could* mean today' (Haddad 2010: 20). She accomplishes the task by retracing her biography as an 'insatiable, insubordinate and aware' woman (Haddad 2010: 36): from her childhood passions – 'only two things were worth doing whenever I had the chance of being alone: reading and masturbating (Haddad 2010: 33–4) – and her early discovery of Sade's works in her father's bookshelves, to her choosing to write erotic poetry – 'a woman writing erotic/explicit literature in the Arab world is claiming freedom as a vital necessity' (Haddad 2010: 74) – and finally her controversial 2008 decision to found the quarterly cultural magazine *Jasad*, a journal in Arabic specialized in the arts, sciences and literatures of the body. The erotic desire that pervades Haddad's work embodies a longing for recourse and rebellion that operates as a tool for denouncing the hypocrisy of Arab societies. It is a cry against patriarchy and religions, and against the complicit condescension of Arab women who, according to the author, prefer to settle for 'compromises', just as Scheherazade, the storyteller in the *Arabian Nights*, did. Hence the choice to commit murder:

> Yes, I killed Scheherazade. I killed her in me. And I am quite determined to kill everything and everyone that even remotely looks or behaves like her [...]. So her sisters, daughters and grand-daughters and all her descendants had better close down the concessions' business, or stay away, far away from me.
> (Haddad 2010: 146–7)

Yet the murder still needs to be proved.

The protagonist in *The Almond* (subtitled *The Sexual Awakening of a Muslim Woman* in the English translation published in 2005) is Badra, a young Moroccan Berber woman, who flees from her native village to escape the husband she was forced to marry against her will, and seeks refuge in the home of her aunt who lives in Tangiers. There, Badra begins an affair with a wealthy and sophisticated doctor named Driss, who introduces her to the pleasures of the flesh. With him she explores passion, down to its most obsessive and turbid facets. The novel is written in the form of a retrospective autobiographical account that the narrator, now nearly 50 years old, has decided to write 'freely, informally, with a clear head and a quivering sex' (Nedjma 2005: 10). 'Through these lines, in which *sperm* and *prayer* are joined', she explains in the prologue, 'I have attempted to break down the walls that now separate the celestial from the terrestrial, body from soul, the mystical from the erotic.' For Nedjma, as for Haddad, 'literature alone has the efficacy of a "lethal weapon"' and the author uses it:

> to *give back* to the *women* of my blood the power of speech *confiscated* by *their fathers*, brothers, and husbands. In tribute to the ancient Arab civilization in which desire came in many forms [...] where love was liberated from being sinful, in which both having and giving pleasure was one of the duties of the believer.
>
> (Nedjma 2005: 1)

In all three books, erotic desire, anchored to the experience of bodies and conveyed through writing, seemingly functions as a means for subverting both the Western cliché that interprets Arab culture as an enemy of sex and the mainstream Arab world's self-representation, which does not do justice to its past heritage. However, despite the constant claim for a female sexual revolution yet to come, in the novels there is no trace of feminist stances; rather we are confronted with occasional assertions of gender equality grounded, though, on unchallenged normative gender orders.[3] Moreover, it is worth noting that the erotic fantasies narrated here describe some undoubtedly conventional pictures, where sexuality is always portrayed as heterosexuality, traditional gendered roles are emphasized through the teacher–learner relationship scheme, masculinity mainly coincides with logos and mastery, while femininity matches with corporeality and carnality that deserve to be awakened by the male's gaze.

On the other hand, the plea for a return to a somewhat mythical erotic Golden Age in Arab-Muslim history and the attempt to revive in literature the atmosphere of a world lost and corrupted over the centuries by barbarity and obscurantism have the tenor of a statement of *cultural authenticity*. A second implicit claim for authenticity is evinced through the choice of a first-person narrator. Autobiography, whether real or fictional, is meant as a testimony of an indisputable point of view from the inside delivered to Western readers (Huggan 2001:

3 In the chapter entitled 'An Arab Woman Redefining Her Womanhood', Haddad states: 'I definitely am what you would call a woman "with balls". [...] I am a highly paid *career woman*, but I hate having to pay the *restaurant* bill when a *man* takes me out on a date. [...] I am not superficial, but a woman's oily hair, messy clothes and hairy armpits are on my scale as much a "no-no" as silicon lips/cheeks/tits, and wherever else they inject that substance nowadays. [...] I am an initiative-taking woman, but I lose my "erection" in front of a spineless, gutless man. [...] In short, I am what you would call a fanatic of femininity' (Haddad 2010: 95f.).

155–7). It is proof, as reported in Haddad's novel, that an '"other" Arab woman exists' (Haddad 2010: 32). This presumed *other* Arab woman should counter the discredit imposed by Western trivial depiction of all Arab women as victims and oppressed as well as the trivial mystifications orchestrated by Arab societies to the detriment of women's freedom. Like the protagonist of Al Neimi's novel, this *other* Arab woman aims at distinguishing herself from those who decide to accept the laws of 'Arab dissimulation' (Al Neimi 2009: 99) and sets herself, as Badra does in *The Almond*, against the 'the imbeciles who wear the veil because they refuse to live in their time and are angling for paradise at half price' (Nedjma 2005: 5). The *other* Arab woman is precisely the one who, with her courage and her daring, will be able to redeem them all.

The autobiographical form therefore does not dissemble the universalist vocation that permeates each story despite the first-person account, so that the register of intimate confession reveals an unacknowledged will to echo the voices of those who supposedly have no voice, in order to express their forbidden and unrevealed desires.

At this point, some of Foucault's questions on the author function become relevant again and call attention to the matter of authority, specifically to the locational privilege from which authority derives. Haddad, Al Neimi and Nedjma certainly don't belong to the realm of subalternity, 'cut off from the lines of social mobility' (Spivak 2000: 328). They lead mobile lives, cross borders, are familiar with multiple languages and cultures, and exercise their freedom of speech: they speak, write and represent. On the narrative plane, the erotic desire that circulates in their novels driving the experiences of the protagonists is meant to mark a rigid divide between the heaven of women's liberty and the hell of women's oppression, thereby imposing a reductionist understanding of Arab women's lives, practices and choices, and thus setting off a sort of ungrounded normative view of *what they are* and *should desire* (interestingly enough, no social demand is evoked, as if sexual freedom were all Arab women strive for). Such a textual performance engenders on a metanarrative plane the foreclosure of the incommensurable and heterogeneous constellation of subaltern desires that do not fit that canon: at worst they are dismissed as 'desperate' remnants that 'would be capable of taming even the fiercest erection' (Al Neimi 2009: 129), while at best they just remain unexpressed and unrepresented. In this sense the *author*'s speech becomes parasitical on subaltern silence, since her *authority*, as an *authentic* subject who is allowed and willing 'to speak for', emerges at the expense of the desubjectivation of subaltern desires that the neo-orientalist hegemonic discourse makes it impossible to articulate, hence to properly 'desire'.

Neo-orientalist imagery and postcolonial desire

Eroticism and subalternity are traditionally interwoven in the unconscious libidinal economy of classical Orientalism, within which the desire to possess the subaltern Other has always played a constitutive function. In fact, as Said argued,

Orientalism as a field of study has always circumscribed 'a male province' (Said 2003: 207) in which the 'Orient' has often been metaphorized in a feminine register through the icons of fabled 'oriental' women – the odalisque, the slave, the belly-dancer frequently portrayed in European orientalist paintings – that Western fantasy projected onto the exotic East (Said 1985). The 'Orient' – imagined and falsified, colonized and subalternized – has been at the same time eroticized 'in its feminine penetrability' and turned into the object *par excellence* of Westerners' voracious desire to possess and dominate. Thus the exotic became erotic (Said 2003: 206).

Beyond metaphors, in his *Constantinople* (1853) French writer Théophile Gautier recalls that the first question addressed to every traveller returning from the East was: 'Well, and the women?' (Gautier 1991: 235). This question seems still to be the one that appeals and drives the West's *will to knowledge* about that legendary and enchanted entity that used to be the 'East', and that since 9/11 has taken on the features of the 'Arab-Muslim world'.

In the last fifteen years, indeed, together with an escalation of the West's economic and military investments in the East, the orientalist apparatus has been going through a new phase of revitalization. The last decade, in a context of increasing ideologization of the relationship between East and West, has set powerfully in motion again the practice of producing knowledge about the Islamic 'Orient' and it is precisely within this framework that the novels considered here need to be interpreted. In this regard it seems more appropriate to use the term Neo-Orientalism – rather than 'Post-Orientalism' (Dabashi 2009) or 'After Orientalism' (Boer 2003) – to characterize what Said had once described as 'the corporate institution for dealing with the Orient by making statements about it, authorizing views of it, describing it, teaching it, settling it, ruling over it' (Said 2003: 3).

The neo-orientalist discourse has inherited the old Orientalism's main devices: it shows the rehabilitation of traditional orientalist approaches (culturalism and essentialism) and of classical dichotomies (modern West vs. anti-modern East, civilization vs. barbarity, democracy vs. oppression, secularism vs. theocracy, evolution vs. immobility, progress vs. backwardness). Speaking of Neo-Orientalism thus requires analysing the current state of affairs in light of the ensemble of political and cultural implications that derive from the continuity of the present with the history of the past (Turner 1994). At the same time, it requires rethinking and reflecting upon times and spaces of contemporary Orientalism within the New World Order and in relation to the socio-political dynamics that characterize it. Indeed, the 'othering machine' – the classical orientalist apparatus of ideological domination – has progressively integrated a new wide range of practical and discursive forms which, profiting from advanced technological supports, has reached a field of resonance that is infinitely wider and more powerful than in the past. Lastly, Neo-Orientalism shows a 'politics of value' that is worthy of analysis for its capacity to establish global strategies of commodification and consumption of the postcolonial Other in the cultural world market (Appadurai 1986; Huggan 2001). If, as hooks points out, 'it is by eating the Other that one asserts power and privilege', we should then recognize that today's 'gastronomical' setting and techniques seem much more sophisticated than the ones available to old-school Orientalism (hooks 1992).

It is therefore necessary to pinpoint some significant changes that mark the original physiognomy of the neo-orientalist discourse (Samiei 2010). The first concerns *borders*. In the nineteenth century, when travelling headed mainly in one direction from West to East (Said 2003: 204), the Orient had more measurable geographic frontiers. The neo-orientalist geography, by contrast, is hybrid, incommensurable and boundless, since the East, due to the change of migratory routes that occurred in the last decades, has attained a stable demographic presence in the West.

A second element concerns the *stance* of the discourse. Because of the current geopolitical conflicts and harsh ideological battles, the new discourse about the Orient appears more fiercely denigrating than ever before by polarizing Western ethos and Eastern barbarism. In the nineteenth century a large number of Westerners who travelled to the East – Flaubert, Gautier, Rimbaud, Lamartine, Burton, Byron, just to mention some among the most famous writers of the time – were fascinated by the exotic Orient. This fascination mainly consisted in 'praise without knowledge', and their superficially benevolent attitude played an important role in setting the register of the orientalist style (Todorov 1994: 265). In recent times the lure of the East has instead been replaced by a more disparaging attitude fostered by a political climate of paranoid and alarming islamophobia (Caldwell 2009; Lewis 2002; Fallaci 2001, 2004; Sarrazin 2010; Levy 2010).

A third aspect deals with the *spread of information*. The evolution of communication technology has accelerated and widened the circulation of data, contents and images. While classical Orientalism was a terrain of erudition, a field of knowledge for experts only, Neo-Orientalism seems to be accessible to anyone who is willing to engage in the process of producing information about the East: think tanks and news media as much as ordinary people. As a result, the neo-orientalist inventory has accumulated a mainstream patrimony of representations shared at all levels of society and has become a sort of background music in everyday lives. However, the multiplication of the channels for generating information has improved the volume of contents in inverse proportion to the increase in their variety. As Said sharply foresaw in his *Covering Islam* (1981), the media's ever more intense fabrication of a *newsworthy* Islamic world has proceeded at the same pace as restrictions on the repertory of the news reports, and as the production of 'unacceptable generalizations of the most irresponsible sort' (Said 1997: xvi). The stories multiply, yet they seem to converge toward a very limited range of restrictive plots and pictures of the Arab-Muslim world which the revolutions of 2011 managed to erode only in part, while demonstrating the existence of enduring mindsets. *Covering* displays then its ambiguous nature as a process of obscuring-through-revealing whose only purpose is to 'determine how we see the rest of the world' (Said 1997).

The last element to be highlighted concerns a significant change that has occurred in the neo-orientalist *storytelling* since the subjects of enunciation are not necessarily Westerners, but may be Easterners, or Easterners living in the West. The aspect that is most worthy of interest in the new wave of erotic Arabic literature is the fact that the authors are not the orientalists of two centuries ago, all of whom were white Western men. They do not resemble Flaubert (2002), who in *Cinq lettres d'Egypte* (1849–1850) described the licentious habit of Kuchuk Hanem as a typically dissolute oriental woman. In this case we are confronted with the words of flesh-and-blood Arab women who write about sexuality and provide intense confessions about their intimate fantasies. What happens then when *the oriental* speaks about *the Orient*? And what happens when *the oriental woman* speaks about *oriental women*? When the *author* becomes '*authentic*'?

The new scenario reveals several entanglements. On the one hand it shows the ambivalent ways in which postcolonial subjects negotiate their identity between old patterns and new inventions, on the edge of the epistemic violence that they suffer within the context of the dominant culture, and at the same time indirectly perpetrate against the subalterns. On the other hand it raises further questions about how postcolonial literary production gains access to mass consumption while postcolonial writers attain the privileged status of '*authentic*' *authors*. The focus then shifts to the discursive procedure that allows *only* some acts of speech to emerge and become audible.

Imperial narrative and strategic eroticism

Narrative can be considered as a site of interpellation, insofar as both writing and reading are accountable for the process of subject formation, for subjectivation as well as for desubjectivation. Writing interpellates the textual addressee to whom the complementary act of reading pertains, whereas reading interpellates the writer and her authority. The *writer as an author* is thus constituted within and by means of the discourse, through a set of forms and rules according to which her act of writing takes shape (Butler 1993: 226–8).

'The writer is a speaker', Sartre maintained in 'What's Literature?'; 'he designates, demonstrates, orders, refuses, interpolates, begs, insults, persuades, insinuates' (Sartre 1988: 34). In the same way, we may argue, the writer *is* designated, ordered, refused, persuaded, and accordingly created as a subject of enunciation. Therefore in literature, as a political terrain of contention, agency and subjection are enacted as critical and contingent variables under the power-knowledge dispositif. Postcolonial erotic literature exemplarily reveals such complex intersection of expressive registers and regimes of authority that underlies narrative, always fluctuating between creation and reproduction, mirroring and subversion. To focus on the issue only as it concerns the milieu discussed here, it is essential to look at the matrix of desire embodied in the novels written by Al Neimi, Nedjma and Haddad. In none of these books does the erotic saturate the dimension of desire. There is indeed a desiring dimension that goes beyond the field of eroticism. In *The Proof of the Honey*, erotic desire is intellectualized as a source of inspiration for writing: 'The Thinker [who initiated her into the joys of sex] was a writer's device, a ruse', states the protagonist at the end of Al Neimi's novel (Al Neimi 2009: 139). In Nedjma's novel, Badra's erotic desire exceeds the boundaries of the body to express a desire of intimate storytelling. Badra begins to write when she 'is no longer hungry'. She writes 'to untangle the web', to relive her life 'and enjoy it a second time around instead of fantasizing about a new one'. 'I blushed about what I had written', the narrator admits, 'then found it to be very right. What is to stop me from continuing? [...] The world is turning. So am I. What should I be ashamed of?' (Nedjma 2005: 6–8). Lastly, Haddad uses erotic desire as a truth-teaching device. 'I will attempt [...] to disenchant you', she writes, addressing her hypothetical Western interlocutor, 'and to deprive you of your chimeras and ready-to-wear opinions' (Haddad 2010: 17). The act of narrating thus manifests a desire for recognition that transcends the sphere of erotic pleasure. But how does this desire meet the Western audience's *will to knowledge*?

'Shocking', 'audacious', 'revolutionary', 'unsubdued': these were some of the epithets that appeared in the culture pages of the major Western newspapers and magazine to describe the impact of the new publishing trend of which the books by Al Neimi, Haddad and Nedjma are among the most successful examples. Yet Salwa Al Neimi's 'impertinent confessions' – so states the blurb of the Italian edition – aroused much clamour but no astonishment. There was no bewilderment at the appearance of Nedjma's 'erotic masterpiece', which the French synopsis described as 'a shock'. No fear induced by the prose of Joumana Haddad, regardless of the 'anger' recalled in the subtitle of her book. In fact, the three erotic novels seem to fit perfectly into the neo-orientalist canon. In the last instance, despite the supposedly insubordinate import and the claim to violate taboos and stereotypes, none of these daring narrative revolutions succeed in challenging well-established Western exoticism. Instead, in the context where 'women and their role became a stick with which the West can beat the East' (Malti-Douglas 1991: 35), erotic literature written by Arab women writers wins a privileged position in a way that is only seemingly unexpected. In fact, beyond the authors' intention, their pleas for desire as an antidote to the repressive habits of the Islamic societies can be easily mobilized in the name of the 'occidentalist gender pact' that has declared war against religious and patriarchal oppression in the Arab-Muslim world – and precisely through this pact, as it has been remarked, 'by stigmatizing "oriental woman" as oppressed, suddenly women's liberation [...] becomes sexy again and acknowledged as necessary' (Dietze 2010: 99).

With regard to the erotic novels analysed here, the 'authentic' location implicitly claimed by the authors and explicitly granted to them – their being 'oriental women' speaking about the 'Orient' – provides *authority* to their words. As a consequence, the *authenticity* of their apparently subversive tales, besides illustrating a quite predictable representation of heterosexual desire, also contributes to reconsolidating the mainstream cartography that marks a deep cultural divide between 'freedom in the West' and 'segregation in the East', so as to lend indirectly *authentic* legitimacy to imperialist crusades undertaken for the sake of gender justice and gender liberation.

In this case, the narrative of postcolonial erotic desire runs the risk only to match the hegemonic desire to hear *authentic* tales of the Other, tales that offer reassuring confirmations of the conventional portraits in which the Other is always imagined, depicted, disseminated and consumed in the West (Huggan 2001: 159). Such narrative may end up responding to an old colonial conditioning: the traditionally Western drive to reveal-and-violate by forcing the doors of the harem and ripping off the women's veils, the sole difference being the fact that in the recent *nouvelle vague* of erotic Arabic literature 'oriental' women take the initiative in opening wide the harem doors and choose to narrate their life behind the veils.

As Huggan notes, this proves the existence of 'significant continuities between older forms of imperial exoticist representation and some of their more recent, allegedly postcolonial, counterparts' (Huggan 2001: 16). These continuities are rooted in the permanence of a common discursive register – both the old colonial subjects and the postcolonial ones adopt the same language, share the same metaphors and icons, and inhabit the same imagery – that still needs to be decolonized.

The 'postcolonial exotic' thus reveals its constitutive ambivalent function as a (re)producer of otherness that is in one way eccentric and in another already tamed. For eroticism to be 'strategic' and to resist the neo-orientalist symbolic capital, it needs to be *recoded* against the prescriptions of comfortable exoticism. By contrast, the exotic-erotic desire that is set on stage in the novels of Al Neimi, Haddad and Nedjma does not seem to emancipate itself from its status of subordination to the neo-orientalist 'desiring machine'. The entanglement lies in the dialectic of interlocution to which such desire remains imprisoned. It can't produce any significant epistemological break because its 'permission to narrate' (Said 1984) derives precisely from its epistemic continuity with the structures and practices of the dominant discourse. In fact, the neo-orientalist register resignifies postcolonial desire by imposing upon it a purely reflexive form of existence: the form of *a desire to be desired* – and thus recognized and legitimized – according to the wishes of the imperial master narrative. In such a way the 'erotic match' can only occur through reaffirming the persistent primacy of the hegemonic Western desire at the expense of its desirable counterparts. Whenever this happens, the 'postcolonial erotic' loses all potential to destabilize the symbolic and material relationships of domination.

Rearranging desires, decolonizing the erotic

To come full circle: can the subaltern then desire? The question recalls the issue that Foucault pointed out in his preface to Gilles Deleuze and Félix Guattari's *Anti-Oedipus* (2004): 'How does one introduce desire into thought, discourse and action? And how can and must desire deploy its forces in the sphere of politics and intensify itself in the process of overturning the established order?' (Foucault

2004: xiv). With regard to the matter discussed here, a more specific query takes shape concerning whether and how the erotic can challenge the ambivalent textuality of postcolonial desire so as to dismantle the discursive dichotomies within which it takes shape.

The erotic desire that operates in Haddad's, Al Neimi's and Nedjma's novels, insofar as it is essentialized and fetishized as the *authentic* expression of an oriental femininity to be revealed, remains caught in the grammar of the neo-orientalist discourse. In this context, erotic narrative, far from being able to alter the status quo of representations, has mainly the effect of alienating the erotic by domesticating it and making it well suited to circulate as an attractive literary commodity.

It seems crucial, though, to explore and imagine other possible uses of the erotic. What Audre Lorde was referring to in her 1978 essay on the 'Uses of the Erotic' was something radically different from what we have just described. According to Lorde, the erotic is a mobile resource that inhabits each woman and 'lies in a deeply female and spiritual plane, firmly rooted in the power of our unexpressed or unrecognized feeling' (Lorde 1984: 53). In other words, it is an assertion of women's living force, a deep awareness of their capacity to suffer and desire. Precisely for this reason, throughout history women 'have been taught to suspect this resource, vilified, abused and devalued within western society', observes Lorde, while superficial eroticism, reduced to trivial sensations and pornography as a stigmatization of female inferiority, has been socially encouraged by men, so as to discourage women from exploring the erotic as a primary source of power (1984: 53).

In Lorde's analysis, the erotic constitutes a tool for self-assertion that works in the opposite direction from the subaltern 'desire to be desired' and from the heteronomous process of eroticization that begins under the other's gaze as a result of the separation of the bodily from the spiritual, of the aesthetic from the political. Conversely, when Lorde suggests that the erotic is the source of women's deepest knowledge, she understands it precisely as a bridge between the emotional and the political.

She writes:

> The erotic is a measure between the beginnings of our sense of self and the chaos of our strongest feelings. It is an internal sense of satisfaction to which, once we have experienced it, we know we can aspire. For having experienced the fullness of this depth of feeling and recognized its power, in honor and self-respect we can require no less of ourselves.
>
> (Lorde 1984: 54)

Here erotic desire combines the full immanence of a self-assertive stance with an element of transcendence, the impetus to go beyond the condition of domination to which women are consigned within neo-colonial and patriarchal hierarchies. For women, then, recognizing the power of the erotic from within themselves can turn into a weapon of resistance for countering both the demeaning of female sexuality and the external injunctions to *jouissance*. In touch with the erotic, Lorde recalls, 'I become less willing to accept powerlessness, or those other supplied states of being which don't naturally belong to us, such as resignation, despair, self-effacement, depression, self-denial' (Lorde 1984: 58). Indeed, if in Lorde's view the erotic reconnects the personal and the political, that is because it doesn't function as a private instrument of empowerment, but, rather, as a collective one. The poet describes it as 'the forerunner for joint concerted actions not possible before' (Lorde 1984: 58).

Lorde's understanding of the erotic thus displays a dual desiring dimension: a reflexive dimension consisting of self-desire (as desire of self-assertion) and an evidently relational dimension that impels the subject to seek a way of sharing. It is here that eroticism combines with language, manifesting a craving for interlocution. As Kaplan remarked in the introduction to *The Erotics of Talk* (1996), feminist writing 'has been taken as a model of "coming to voice" and moving from culturally imposed silence to speech', neglecting and obscuring 'the presence of a competing *topos* in women's literature [...] the search not for a voice, but for a listener capable of hearing that voice and responding appropriately to it' (1996: 15).

Kaplan's project of imagining an *erotics of talk* emphasizes precisely this desiring aspect of narrative. In seeking an appropriate listener, the act of narrating does not express simply an obvious desire for recognition and reconciliation; it also exhibits a conflicting stance vis-à-vis the hegemonic discourse. The choice of the addressee determines the possibility of transforming the register and the forms of interlocution, altering and designifying the current discursive structures.

The allegory of the *erotics of talk*, when applied to the field of postcolonial literature, suggests that to decolonize the symbolic order and to violate its rules, to reconfigure the repertory of icons and images and to invent new codes, one must switch to another interlocutor (Dabashi 2009). The postcolonial narrator is thus asked to renounce the *authority* of the *authentic author* and to reorient her narrative function, shifting from the act of 'speaking for' to the act of 'speaking with' and simultaneously 'speaking against'. Such shift aims to produce an epistemic displacement in order to challenge the sovereignty of the Western 'subject supposed to desire' that governs the series of significances and representations which dominate neo-orientalist textuality. Displacing desires – or rather *rearranging desires*, to borrow Spivak's phrase (2001) – by imagining, sharing and experimenting with alternative scenarios of interlocution, stands thus as crucial imperative for *a postcolonial erotics of talk* yet to be developed.

References

Al Herz, S. (2009) *The Others*, New York: Seven Stories Press.

Al Neimi, S. (2009) *The Proof of the Honey*, New York: Europa Editions; *Borhàn Al 'Asal*, Beirut: Riad El Rayyes, 2007.

Al Sanea, R. (2007) *Girls of Riyadh*, London/New York: Penguin Press.

Boer I. E. (2003) *After Orientalism: Critical Entanglements, Productive Looks*, Amsterdam/New York: Rodopi.
Butler, J. (1993) *Bodies that Matter: On the Discursive Limits of 'Sex'*, London: Routledge.
Caldwell, C. (2009) *Reflections on the Revolution in Europe: Immigration, Islam, and the West*, London: Allen Lane.
Charif, L. (2010) *La maghrébine: du voile à la guépière*, Paris: Éditions Blanche.
—— (2012) *Désirs voilés*, Paris: Pocket.
Dabashi, H. (2009) *Post-Orientalism: Knowledge and Power in Time of Terror*, New Brunswick/London: Transaction Publishers.
Deleuze, G. and Guattari, F. (2004) *Anti-Oedipus: Capitalism and Schizophrenia*, London: Continuum; *Anti-Oedipe. Capitalisme et schizophrénie*, Paris: Éditions de Minuit, 1972.
Dietze, G. (2010) '"Occidentalism", European Identity and Sexual Politics', in H. Brunkhorst and G. Grözinger (eds) *The Study of Europe*, Baden-Baden: Nomos, pp. 87–116.
Fallaci, O. (2001) *La rabbia e l'orgoglio*, Milano: Rizzoli; *The Rage and the Pride*, Milano: Rizzoli, 2002.
—— (2004) *La forza della ragione*, Milano: Rizzoli; *The Force of Reason*, Milano: Rizzoli, 2006.
Flaubert, G. (2002) *Cinq lettres d'Egypte*, Paris: Mille et une nuits.
Foucault, M. (1980) 'What is an Author?', in J. V. Harari (ed.) *Textual Strategies: Perspectives in Post-Structuralist Criticism*, London: Routledge, pp. 141–60; 'Que est-ce qu'un auteur?', in *Dits et écrits 1954–1988*, Paris: Gallimard, 1994, vol. 1, pp. 789–821.
—— (2002) *The Archaeology of Knowledge*, New York/London: Routledge; *L'archéologie du savoir*, Paris: Gallimard 1969.
—— (2004) 'Preface', in G. Deleuze and F. Guattari (2004) *Anti-Oedipus: Capitalism and Schizophrenia*, London: Continuum, pp. xii–xvi; 'Préface à l'édition américaine de *L'Anti-Oedipe*', in *Dits et écrits 1954–1988*, Paris: Gallimard, 1994, vol. 3, pp.134–7.
Gautier, T. (1991) *Constantinople*, Paris: Christian Bourgois Éditeur.
The Guardian (2008) 'From Voyeur's Corner to My First Time: New Magazine Attempts to Life Veil on Arab Taboos'. Available at www.theguardian.com/world/2008/dec/13/lebanon-middleeast-magazine-taboo (accessed 9 December 2014).
Haddad, J. (2010) *I Killed Scheherazade*, London: Saqi Books.
—— (2011) *Le retour de Lilith*, Paris: Actes Sud.
Hammad, S. (2010) 'exotic', in *Born Palestinian, Born Black and the Gaza Suite*, New York: UpSet Press, pp. 64–5.
hooks, b. (1992) 'Eating the Other: Desire and Resistance', in *Black Looks: Race and Representation*, Boston, South End Press, pp. 21–40.
Huggan, G. (2001) *The Postcolonial Exotic: Marketing the Margins*, London: Routledge.
Kaplan, C. (1996) *The Erotics of Talk: Women's Writing and Feminist Paradigms*, Oxford: Oxford University Press.
Levy, B. -H. (2010) *Pièces d'identités*, Paris: Grasset.
Lewis, B. (2002) *What Went Wrong? The Clash between Islam and Modernity in the Middle East*, New York: Oxford University Press.

Lewis, R. (2004) *Rethinking Orientalism: Women, Travel and the Ottoman Harem*, London, New York: IB Tauris.
Lorde, A. (1984) 'Uses of the Erotic: The Erotic as Power', in *Sister Outsider: Essays and Speeches*, Freedom, CA: Crossing Press, pp. 53–9.
Malti-Douglas, F. (1991) *Woman's Body, Woman's Word: Gender and Discourse in Arabo-Islamic writing*, Princeton, NJ: Princeton University Press.
Mernissi, F. (2001) *Scheherazade goes West: Different Cultures, Different Harems*, New York: Washington Square Press.
Mosteghanemi, A. (2004) *Chaos of Senses*, Cairo: American University in Cairo Press.
Nedjma (2005) *The Almond: The Sexual Awakening of a Muslim Woman*, New York: Grove Press; *L'amande*, Paris: Plon, 2004.
—— (2009) *La traversée des sens: conte intime*, Paris: Plon.
Reuters (2009) Europa Editions, Summer 2009. Available at www.europaeditions.com/archivio/articles/europa_editions_attachment_124.pdf (accessed 9 December 2014),
Said, E. (1984) 'Permission to narrate', *London Review of Books* 6(3): 13–17.
—— (1985) 'Orientalism reconsidered', *Cultural Critique* 1: 89–107.
—— (1997) *Covering Islam: How the Media and the Experts Determine How We See the Rest of the World* [1981], New York: Vintage Books.
—— (2003) *Orientalism* [1978], London: Penguin.
Samiei, M. (2010) 'Neo-Orientalism? The Relationship between the West and Islam in our Globalised World', *Third World Quarterly* 31(7): 1145–60.
Sarrazin, T. (2010) *Deutschland schafft sich ab: Wie wir unser Land aufs Spiel setzen*, München: DVA.
Sartre, J. P. (1988) 'What is literature?', in *What is Literature? And Other Essays*, Cambridge, MA: Harvard University Press, pp. 21–246; 'Qu'est-ce que la littérature?', in *Situations II*, Gallimard, 1948, pp. 53–310.
Sobh, A. (2007) *Maryam ou le passé décomposé*, Paris: Gallimard.
Der Spiegel (2008) 'Sexuelle Intifada'. Available at http://magazin.spiegel.de/EpubDelivery/spiegel/pdf/58423290 (accessed 9 December 2014).
Spivak, G. C. (2000) 'The New Subaltern: A Silent Interview', in V. Chaturvedi (ed.) *Mapping Subaltern Studies and the Postcolonial*, London: Verso, pp. 324–40.
—— (2001) 'Righting wrongs', in N. Owen (ed.) *Human Rights, Human Wrongs*, New York: Oxford University Press, pp. 168–227.
Todorov, T. (1994) *On Human Diversity: Nationalism, Racism and Exoticism in French Thought*, Cambridge, MA: Harvard University Press.
Turner B. (1994) *Orientalism, Postmodernism and Globalism*, London: Routledge.
Valassopoulos, A. (2007) *Contemporary Arab Women Writers: Cultural Expression in Context*, London: Routledge.
Yegenoglu, M. (1998) *Colonial Fantasies: Towards a Feminist Critique of Orientalism*, Cambridge: Cambridge University Press.
Younes, I.H. (2008) *Wild Mulberries*, Northampton: Interlink Books.

Chapter 3

The associations of black queer life

Reading and seeing the nineteen-eighties

Roderick A. Ferguson

In an interview which appeared in the 1991 anthology *Brother to Brother: New Writings by Black Gay Men*, the African American poet Essex Hemphill asked the black British filmmaker Isaac Julien what motivated him to create the 1989 film *Looking for Langston*. Julien responded with this:

> Initial ideas came about around a number of things: wanting to do a film about black gay identities that would somehow not be a straightforward film about sexuality, because then to talk about sexuality and black gay experiences, one had to historically anchor it in a space where one would feel at ease in talking about those experiences, or one would feel uncomfortable. [...] In trying to talk about black gay identities without compromise, I didn't want to deal with just gay issues.
>
> (Hemphill 1991: 175)

By way of context, the film is a consideration of Langston Hughes as a black queer[1] cultural icon during the Harlem Renaissance and in nineteen-eighties London. Using archival footage from the nineteen-twenties as well as re-enactments of queer life during the Harlem Renaissance, the film uses the past to provide connections to the urgencies of the nineteen-eighties – homophobic violence, police brutality, homoerotic love between black men, interracial love between black and white men, racism within queer communities, and the formation of black queer male identities. In his remarks, Julien narrates the genesis of *Looking for Langston* as both an interest in addressing 'black gay identities' and an effort to move beyond 'straightforward' issues of sexuality, making the film into a vehicle that would bring the viewer to a variety of destinations – black gay experiences and histories being only one of them.

I am particularly interested in Julien's assertion that to represent black gay sexualities meant veering from a 'straightforward' presentation of sexuality. In this way, the film points to a poignant but underappreciated mode by which many

1 In this chapter, I am focusing on black queers of African descent, all the while reading their formations in dialogue with other racial, ethnic, and cultural formations as well.

black queer artists, activists, and intellectuals of the nineteen-eighties engaged the subject of black queer sexuality, engaged it in such a way as to mark black queer identities and practices as incitements for connecting with issues and urgencies other than sexuality – that is, for breaking sexuality down into other – seemingly – non-related parts. This breaking down of sexuality into ostensibly disparate parts can be seen as resolutely aesthetic practice. For instance, in *Anti-Oedipus: Capitalism and Schizophrenia*, Gilles Deleuze and Félix Guattari advance an argument about how the breaking down of objects is constitutive of artistic work and part of the social production of desire. They write: 'The artist is the master of objects; he puts before us shattered, burned, broken-down objects, converting them into the regime of desiring-machines, breaking down is part of the very functioning of desiring machines' (Deleuze and Guattari 2009: 32).

During the eighties, artists broke black queer sexualities down into a variety of considerations precisely because of the social exigencies that constituted the decade of the eighties. Specifically, the crises around HIV/AIDS, xenophobia, state racism, and upward redistribution produced conditions whereby culture and art took on material significance, especially as the state routed resources away from social services to corporations and to the military, a process that was captured in the work of queer artists in general, white and of color. In other words, art and culture assumed political tasks as the state withdrew – in a neoliberal fashion – from the body politic and refused to represent the various constituencies of that body politic.[2] These social entanglements would help produce the conditions whereby making connections across historical formations would be necessary and desirable in the realms of art, activism, and scholarship. As such, the aesthetic practices of black queer artists in the eighties act as metonyms for activist and critical efforts to connect discussions of black queer sexuality to other social issues.

As an incitement for connecting sexuality to other social formations, black queer sexuality – as a social artifact – is structured like an 'interdisciplinary text'. Here, I mean to reference and extend Roland Barthes' argument about interdisciplinarity. He wrote:

> Interdisciplinary is not the calm of an easy security; it begins effectively [...] when the solidarity of the old disciplines breaks down – perhaps even violently, via the jolts of fashion – in the interests of a new object and a new language neither of which has a place in the field of the sciences that were to be brought peacefully together.
>
> (Barthes 1977: 155)

As interdisciplinary texts and images, black queer sexualities, then, do not provide comfort to any discipline. Instead, they provide constant meditations and

2 For additional discussions about how culture takes on a political function in the midst of state retrenchments, see Lowe 1996; Lowe and Lloyd 1997; Ferguson 2004.

elaborations on how they are eccentric to any and all disciplines. As we will see in the context of black queer visual art in the nineteen-eighties, black queer sexualities were not monolithic sites in any way but ecstatically heterogeneous ones. The visual and literary work of black queer artists in the nineteen-eighties illustrates the interdisciplinary nature of black queer sexual formations.

For instance, given the diversity of media, racial formations, and ethnicities that made up black queer visual culture of that period, we cannot understand, for instance, such classic black gay male texts as Joseph Beam and Essex Hemphill's *Brother to Brother* (Hemphill 1991) and Assotto Saint's *The Road Before Us* (1991) as American texts in any simple way since so many of the contributors were immigrants or the children of immigrants from the Caribbean. In addition, as an artwork constituted from the writings and lives of such past and contemporary literary figures as Hilton Als, James Baldwin, Essex Hemphill, Hughes, and Richard Bruce Nugent, Julien's film revoked the dividing line between the historical and the literary, and designated black sexuality as a formation that respects no such divisions. Julien's film and the anthology *Brother to Brother* also demonstrate an interest in using the subject of black queer sexuality to disrupt easy divisions between African American and Black British identities and histories. By devoting discussions and essays to the cultural and social connections between African American and Black British subjects, the film and the anthology used the topic of black queer formations as a way to observe and theorize connections between historically distinct groups. As objects that are constituted across national and disciplinary boundaries, black queer sexualities are like Barthes' photographs – denoted not simply by the presumed obviousness of queerness but connoted by associations and connections that cannot be exhausted by what is denoted on the screen or on the page.

The interdisciplinary elements of black queer formations

The stakes of black queer sexuality as an interdisciplinary formation are historical in nature. Indeed, the partnerships between literary and visual art by black queers was conceived in the moment of neoliberal emergencies. Indeed, the visual and literary work by black queer intellectuals and artists of the eighties critically comments on the historical formations of that moment – that is, the emergent political and economic processes of that decade. For the study of minority social formations, analyzing the aesthetic work emerging from that period means understanding black queer sexuality as populated by a diversity of communities and interests differentiated in terms of ethnicity, gender, sexuality, religion, nationality, and so on. It also means apprehending how that diversity was thrown into crisis by neoliberal regulation.

We primarily think of African American queer production as a literary exercise. Hence, we recall the landmark anthologies and writing groups that made up the eighties and nineties. In Britain, however, representations of black queer sexuality took place primarily within visual realms. Here we might think of the visual work of such black British artists as Isaac Julien, Rotimi Fani-Kayode, Sonia Boyce, Ingrid Pollard, and Ajamu.

Moreover, it was a moment of diasporic exchanges between black queer intellectuals and artists on both sides of the pond. Indeed, in an unpublished letter that African American poet Essex Hemphill wrote to his friend, the African American writer Joseph Beam, Hemphill said this about his visit to London: 'London truly connects one to other places. What appeals to me most is the sheer diversity of people. Indians, West Indians, Africans, Germans, Italians, Russians ... In the back of my mind, I have made a decision to return here to live.'[3]

The interdisciplinarity of the aesthetic work and the decade is also characterized by an interrogation of the terms of historical narration and representation. Stuart Hall argues that the period is one in which

> the subjects of the local, of the margin, can only come into representation by [...] recovering their own hidden histories [...] History without the majority inside it, history as a minority event [...] The attempt to snatch from the hidden histories another place to stand in, another place to speak from, and that moment is an extremely important moment.
>
> (Hall 1997: 183–4)

Black queer aesthetic formations of the period, like other cultural formations, were historiographical interventions.

For the critique of history, black queer visual art and sexuality jeopardized the status of history as a natural and innocent process. The filmmaker's direction and the photographer's lens exposed history as a discipline with impulses, protocols, agendas, and maneuvers. In addition to the pressures that the work puts on the claims of history, black queer art demonstrates what Saussure famously noted as both the arbitrariness and mutability of the sign, an arbitrariness and mutability that would be exploited in the nineteen-eighties so that black queer sexuality could be fashioned into a technique for connecting to and associating with a variety of issues and historical processes.

If we mobilize the interdisciplinary nature of black queer aesthetic production, we might yield several important observations. Rather than thinking of black queer sexualities as 'disciplined' by a single discipline or genre, we might think of that genre of sexuality as an interdisciplinary venture constituted by a variety of epistemological associations. In addition, juxtaposing the literary and visual components of black queer production helps to illuminate the ethnic and regional heterogeneity of black queer art and life. This juxtaposition helps to illustrate how black queer artistic production in the U.S. and Britain alienated national culture,

3 Essex Hemphill to Joseph Beam, '9 December 1986', Joseph Beam Papers, Schomburg Center for Research in Black Culture, Box 4, Folder 20.

redistributing and aggravating taken-for-granted assumptions about the commonsensical and the moral, and highlighting the global stakes of this disciplinary and interdisciplinary association.

Black queer formations and the dawn of neoliberalism

By way of historical context, the nineteen-eighties were the beginnings of the AIDS epidemic. The disease devastated queer communities and people of all race and class backgrounds. HIV/AIDS was, also, the circumstance and outcome of neoliberal state formations in the U.S., in particular. The Reagan administration, for instance, would cut social services that would have helped individuals and families devastated by HIV/AIDS and channel that money to 'welfare' provisions for corporations.

This was also a moment of migrations to the U.S. from the Caribbean, Latin America, Asia, and Africa. In the nineteen-eighties immigrants accounted for 39 percent of U.S. population growth. This proportion was larger than any decade in the twentieth century, except for the early years of that century from 1901 to 1910. In such a context, black queer formations in the U.S. and Britain would encounter a global diversity due to migration like no other before it. Migrations to the U.S. and Britain would, therefore, help to evolve an already protean and socially eclectic history of race.

The election of Reagan and his British counterpart Margaret Thatcher would, in the words of Lisa Duggan, represent the moment in which the category 'neoliberalism' would be 'retrospectively applied to the "conservative" policies of the Reagan and Thatcher regimes in the U.S. and Great Britain' and '[rocket] to prominence as the brand name for the form of pro-corporate, "free market," anti-"big government" rhetoric shaping Western national policy and dominating international finance institutions since the early 1980s' (Duggan 2003: 10). The rise of neoliberal modes of governance was directly related to the forms of social diversity that achieved visibility in the period of the eighties. As Jodi Melamed goes on to say, neoliberalism was a 'world-historical configuration of economy, governance, biological and social life' (Melamed 2011: 147). No doubt it was the devastations of neoliberalism that led Hemphill to say to his friend Joseph Beam in the aforementioned letter, 'America is rocking us to sleep, Joseph, and while we sleep, America strangles and rapes the world'.[4] Another way of stating this would be to say that neoliberalism was a mode of governance that would apply its measurements and standards to populations and communities diversified by race, gender, class, and sexuality, oftentimes reading those populations and communities as unworthy of a reasonable chance at life.

But even in the midst of government callousness and social catastrophes caused by HIV/AIDS, the nineteen-eighties was also a period of particular intellectual

4 '9 December 1986', Joseph Beam Papers.

richness for interdisciplinary fields such as ethnic studies, women's studies, and gay and lesbian studies. Using Deleuze and Guattari, we might say that the period represented a hegemonic struggle between the desiring-productions of dominant politico-economic regimes and the cultural sites that challenged those regimes. In the U.S., the founding of the Center for Research for Women at Memphis State University, the joint sponsorship of the 'Overdue Partnership Symposium' by the University of Massachusetts's Women's Studies Program and the Afro-American Studies Department at Smith College, the inauguration of the annual Gay and Lesbian Studies Conference, and the international debut of the 'Common Differences: Third World Women and Feminist Perspectives' conference were noteworthy moments in that decade.

The eighties was also an unprecedented moment of intellectual cross-fertilization between the U.S. and Britain. For instance, the nineteen-eighties represented the moment at which Stuart Hall's profound work within cultural studies would impact the American academy, bringing together deliberations on the limitations and possibilities of cultural forms and the maneuvers of aggressive market economies that seemed to be both fetishizing cultural difference as they were causing greater forms of disfranchisement for working-class and non-white folks.

The decade was also a period of interdisciplinary visual engagements with race, sexuality, gender, and class. In 1982, Portsmouth Polytechnic graduate students in fine arts, sociology, and psychology founded the Black Audio Film Collective. The collective would produce such experimental films as *Signs of Empire* in 1983, *Handsworth Songs* in 1986, and *Mysteries of August* in 1991. In 1983, Isaac Julien, then a student at St. Martin's School of Art, founded the Sankofa Film Collective. Its production *The Passion of Remembrance* signaled early on an interest in the possibilities and limits of historical projects.

It is important to note that the emergence of Black Audio Film Collective and Sankofa took place within the contradictions of neoliberalism – that is, the emergence of the state-sponsored Channel 4, which promoted independent and experimental work in television and film *and* the market-driven agendas of the Thatcher administration. Another way of stating this is to say that the emergence of neoliberalism represented the clash of desiring-machines – that is, the machinery of the state and the machinery of social formations like those of black queer aesthetic practices. Seeing the period as a moment of conflicting desiring-machines helps us to reawaken an insight from Deleuze and Guattari: desire doesn't simply bear transgressive potential but socially reproductive capacities as well. Hence, Deleuze and Guattari argue:

> The truth of the matter is that social production is purely and simply desiring-production itself under determinate conditions. We maintain that the social field is immediately invested by desire, that it is the historically determined product of desire, and that the libido has no need of any mediation or sublimation, any psychic operation, any transformation, in order to invade and invest the productive forces and the relations of production. There is only

> desire and the social, and nothing else. Even the most repressive and the most deadly forms of social reproduction are produced by desire.
>
> (Deleuze and Guattari 2009: 29)

In addition to the state's desire to produce repressive and regulatory technologies, we might turn to the history of white gay racism during the period as an example of a desire that helped to reproduce social hierarchies. As Julien and Mercer argue in their article 'True Confessions: A Discourse on Images of Black Male Sexuality':

> As black men we are implicated in the same landscape of stereotypes in the gay subculture, which is dominated by the needs and demands of white males. Black men fit into this territory by being confined to a narrow repertoire of types – the supersexual stud and the sexual savage on the one hand and the delicate and exotic Oriental on the other. The repetition of these stereotypes in sexual representations betrays the circulation of 'colonial fantasy', and traces the way the contours of this landscape have been shaped by mainstream cultural legacies of slavery, empire, and imperialism.
>
> (Julien and Mercer 1991: 170)

Here Julien and Mercer mark white queer desire as an entity that bears the trace of histories of enslavement and imperial conquest, illustrating the ways in which queer desire can also function for the purposes of social reproduction and not simply for the aims of social rupture and transgression.

While deploying Deleuze and Guattari's notion of desire, we cannot forget that their theorization of the category of desire was a way of alienating idealist modes. The idealism that they were attempting to alienate was, of course, that of the Oedipal arrangement in psychoanalysis. As they stated:

> The great discovery of psychoanalysis was that of the production of desire, of the productions of the unconscious. But once Oedipus entered the picture, this discovery was soon buried beneath a new brand of idealism: a classical theater was substituted for the unconscious as a factory; representation was substituted for the units of production of the unconscious; and an unconscious that was capable of nothing but expressing itself – in myth, tragedy, dreams – was substituted for the productive unconscious.
>
> (Deleuze and Guattari 2009: 24)

For Deleuze and Guattari, an idealist conception could only work to suppress an appreciation of the ways in which desire helps to constitute material realities. With this insight in mind, we can understand Julien and Mercer's remarks about hegemonic forms of white desire as an observation about racial hierarchies as desiring-productions that are part of the history of white queer desire. A notion of queer desire as always and already transgressive runs the risk of returning us to an idealism as well as suppressing the very histories that contradict easy pronouncements about the transgressive nature of queerness. As Julien and Mercer suggest, it is a way of forgetting the histories of race. We can indeed say that the emergence of neoliberalism in the U.S. and Britain represented an epochal desire to forget those histories and their reproductions in contemporary moments.

The associations

The social complexity of the nineteen-eighties would be met with what has lately occurred to me as one of the most profound events in the history of ideas and politics, an event that perhaps began with the radical movements of the sixties, but one that was redeployed by women-of-color and queer-of-color formations in the years that came after the sixties. Let us call that event the associative practices of queer-of-color and black-queer critical formations. Here, I mean the complex ways in which queer of color artists and activists, in general, and black queer artists and activists, in particular, used racialized gender and sexuality to connect to and associate with issues that, from many vantage points, seemed to have nothing to do with sexuality. Here's an example: in a conversation between black lesbian feminist activists published in Barbara Smith's classic anthology from 1983 *Home Girls*, Smith referred to a demonstration at the U.N. against nuclear disarmament, saying:

> To me, for somebody to come and present that issue [of nuclear disarmament] to a Black lesbian organization is not disruptive or divisive. But it's up to black lesbians to figure out how do we relate to it in such a way that we make it our issue. I think that's the answer.
>
> (Abdulahad *et al.* 1983: 309).

We might think of the nineteen-eighties as a moment in which black queer artists, activists, and scholars used racialized gender and sexuality to elaborate the associative practices honed by activists in the sixties and seventies. In this sense, the eighties was a moment characterized by the multiplication of associative techniques and exercises. Indeed, as an effort to address various historical and social formations – reproduction, domestic and state violence, sexuality, migration, and the gendered nature of labor – we might also argue that the category 'intersectionality' was the clearest outcome of that multiplication.

By way of history, the category known as 'the associations' was first and most famously theorized in David Hume's 1748 text *An Enquiry Concerning Human Understanding*. In that text, Hume took up the question of the anatomy of human knowledge – where ideas originated, how they came together, and what relationships they bore to facts. Defining the associations in a chapter entitled 'Of the Association of Ideas', Hume begins by stating:

> It is evident that there is a principle of connexion between the different thoughts or ideas of the mind, and that, in their appearance to the memory

> or imagination, they introduce each other with a certain degree of method and regularity.
>
> (Hume 2007: 19)

Here Hume suggests that the associations are the principles of connection between thoughts and ideas. Yet while Hume imagined the associative subject as a canonically and hegemonically rational subject, the associative subjectivities that emerged in the context of women-of-color and queer-of-color formations were historically those folks who were deemed to be rationality's others. As such, we might assume that their associative agendas were very different from the ones enshrined by classical theory and presumably embodied in rational Man.

Indeed, Hume's associational subject is one that can only respond to the irregular and foreign association by rejecting it. As he argues, 'In our more serious thinking or discourse, this is so observable, that any particular thought, which breaks in upon the regular tract or chain of ideas, is immediately remarked or rejected' (Hume 2007: 19). The subjectivities that were emerging in the long post-sixties moment – the ones created and inspired by women-of-color and queer-of-color artists – would instead treat the irregular and the foreign as reasons and opportunities for intellectual, cultural, and political engagement. In this sense, their associations – as opposed to those produced by Hume's rational subjects – would represent desires to connect through non-linearity, irregularity, and difference.

An associative formation with minoritized subjects as its agents – one organized around non-linearity, irregularity, and difference – could, in a sense, only emerge from the political, cultural, and critical contexts produced in the post-sixties period, one characterized by migration as well as political and cultural insurgency. Indeed, one of the contexts for associative practices among black queer artists was diasporic migration. Indeed, the black diaspora that was produced by black queer artists from Britain and the U.S. was one that revised our notions of indigenous and diasporic cultures. One of the ways in which black feminism impacted black queer visual art was by insisting that indigenous culture could and did accommodate homoerotic expressions. Recall, for example, Alexis De Veaux's remarks about Audre Lorde's style after her visit to Ghana, Togo, and Dahomey in 1974:

> The Africa Audre Lorde brought back became the stage upon which her public persona emerged in the late 1970s. She increasingly appeared at readings and in public wearing a dashiki shirt and a gele, the signature head wrap of African women. She was adorned in beads and jewellery.
>
> (De Veaux 2006: 152)

For De Veaux, Lorde's style was a way for Lorde to fashion herself as 'living proof of African foremothers and of their spiritual fusion within her' (De Veaux 2006: 152). That fusion, for Lorde, was achieved through a rearticulation of African indigeneity, a rearticulation that fashioned African cultural practices, beliefs, and aesthetics as in dialogue with homoeroticism.

We can see the ways in which that very idea made its way into the work of Rotimi Fani-Kayode, the queer Nigerian-born British photographer as another meditation on the limits and possibilities of history:

> As an African working in a western medium, I try to bring out the spiritual dimension in my pictures so that concepts of reality become ambiguous and are opened to reinterpretation. This requires what Yoruba priests and artists call a technique of ecstasy.
>
> (Fani-Kayode and Hurst 1996)

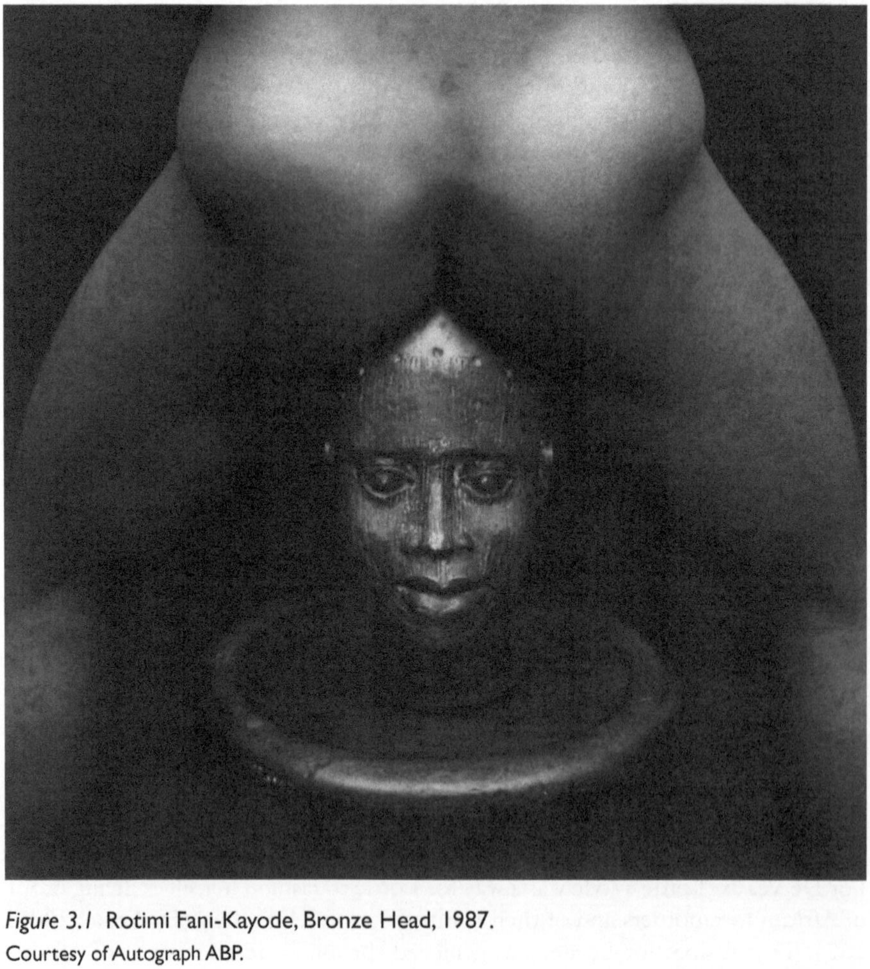

Figure 3.1 Rotimi Fani-Kayode, Bronze Head, 1987.
Courtesy of Autograph ABP.

In this photograph entitled 'Bronze Head' we have a picture of a black man's buttocks astride a Yoruba mask. To some this will look like the defilement of history and tradition – the sacred Yoruba mask symbolizing the central spiritual position that the head and thought have to the body, now taking on the position of excrement or having the function of a dildo. Reading the photograph as a metaphor for Fani-Kayode's desire to 'transform and transgress Yoruba culture', art historian Steve Nelson writes:

> It speaks [...] to the incorporation of an 'Africa' that is a metaphor for the possibility of an erotically charged transformation, one that is spiritual – in the most general sense – and physical. The Ife head here has the capacity not only to enter the body of the model but also to break it apart, to enact an erotic fusion that would, in Bataille's paradigm, dissolve the discontinuity of the individual, making the individual, now released from the prison of the body, one with the world.
>
> (Nelson 2005: 14)

This transformation of the body into an entity that is integrated with 'the world' is also the moment of a transgression. As Nelson argues:

> the photograph's scatological connotations overtly underscore a turbulent relationship between the artist and his culture of origin. In both cases, the combination of head and buttocks is not as much about the Yoruba (or Africa more generally) as it is about making visible the power of the erotic and using that power for other purposes.
>
> (Nelson 2005: 14)

Building upon Nelson's argument, we can read the piece as producing an association between queerness and the non-Western and black sign of 'Africa', an association used to delve into the question of how to negotiate with a history that is both alienating and integral at the same time, a history that is candidate for expulsion as well as the pleasures of penetration and incorporation.

The aforementioned aesthetic practices suggest the emergence of an associative 'campaign' among black queer artists, activists, and intellectuals during the decade of the eighties, a campaign that sought a particular activation of sexuality, one in which sexuality might be used to establish connections across political, cultural, and historical terrains. This particular activation of sexuality, which was simultaneously part of the rearticulation and revalorization of black social formations, is what I would like to engage as 'the erotic', an activation that was born out of the breaking down and the reassembling of sexuality into a mode of difference that could attach itself to other histories, cultures, and struggles. This reassembling was part of the globalizing ethos of the nineteen-eighties. If contemporary globalization, as Hall has argued, was about the management of difference by multinational corporations on the one hand and the reinvention of vernacular histories by marginalized and decolonized groups and peoples on the other (see Hall 1997), then Lorde's writings and Fani-Kayode's photography suggest that contemporary globalization was also about the reinvention of those histories as part of the retheorization of the erotic – that is, how sexuality might be activated for the retelling of indigenous pasts. If neoliberalism, as David Harvey has argued, is a politico-economic theory that valorizes private property rights and entrepreneurial freedoms as the basis of a proposal about human well-being (see Harvey 2005), then the black queer artistic, critical, and political deliberations about the erotic might be seen as rebuttals to neoliberalism's emerging thesis about a good and complete life.

Given the context of devastations wrought by government, capital, and disease, the erotic was also a way of conceiving life's requirements, what a life needs to survive and flourish. There is a part in *The German Ideology* where Marx seems to be getting at this very thing. He writes:

> By producing their means of subsistence men are *indirectly producing their actual material life.*
>
> The way in which men produce their means of subsistence depends first of all on the nature of the actual means of subsistence they find in existence and have to reproduce. This mode of production *must not be considered simply as being the production of the physical existence of the individual.* Rather it is a definite form of activity of these individuals, *a definite form of expressing their life, a definite mode of life on their part.*
>
> (Marx and Engels 1989: 42)

If the erotic denotes those practices that rebutted neoliberalism's thesis about a good and complete life, we might also then say that the erotic designates subsistence as an area of elaboration, particularly the elaboration of life-enhancing associations. Building off this passage, we might read subsistence as a mode of imagination geared toward the clarification of life – what will sustain life and enhance it, something that is, as Marx says, more than *the production of the physical existence of the individual.* As Eva von Redeker argues in her contribution to this volume (Chapter 1): 'As understood by Marx, the concept of need does not just cover anthropological or biological must-haves. As the satisfaction of needs is always socially and culturally mediated, even the basic needs assume particular shapes relative to a given life form and mode of production.' In the period of the nineteen-eighties and in the work of many artists, the erotic named their attempts to change the meaning and contours of actual material life, trying to develop more precise ways for spelling out what a life might need, particularly as that life was threatened by sickness and institutions of power.

As the site of possible counter-theses about the makeup of social life, the history of black queer art demonstrates a signature fact about the relationship between history and aesthetics. Both history and aesthetics are tools for identifying who belongs and who does not, who may participate and who may not. If 'aesthetic practices', according to the French theorist Jacques Rancière, are 'forms of visibility that disclose artistic practices, the place they occupy, what they "do" or "make" from the standpoint of what is common to the community' (Rancière 2006: 13), then historical practices are also forms of visibility that disclose social practices, the place they occupy in a community, what they do or make from the standpoint of what is common to the community, what it needs, and what is tolerable. As an inheritor and extension of black feminist work, black queer sexuality and art of the nineteen-eighties was an effort to call attention to those artistic and social practices that were not understood as being part of 'the community', demonstrating how those practices helped in fact to constitute 'the community'. If seeing is a way of apprehending and locating history, then black queer art can help us see and locate contemporary globalization and neoliberalism as well as the manifold social formations that attempted to challenge them.

The ecstatic and critical possibilities of heterogeneity

As interdisciplinary adventures, black queer sexuality and art were founded by a diverse group of ethnic and racial formations. The history of black queer social formations is not a monosocial history, involving only African Americans or blacks of American parentage. In fact, the visual artwork of the time, in particular, seems to revel in heterogeneity.

Indeed, if we look at not only the visual presentation of the film but the makeup of the crew, we would discover that the production team is made up of black British subjects from a range of ethnicities – Caribbean, African, and Asian – as well as whites. For instance, the South Asian Canadian photographer Sunil Gupta shot the stills for the film. About the collaboration with Julien, Gupta says: 'The quest for a non-white image of gay men and my interest in working with independent gay directors and the films they were making coincided in this particular project.'[5] The question of how to represent queers of color was one shared by several constituencies with various racial formations and histories of migration. Gupta's participation in a British film about an African American poet calls to mind Britain's racial heterogeneity and the potential for collaboration and coalition. In this photographic still, we see the director Isaac Julien as well as the film's protagonists Ben Ellison and Matthew Baidoo with a white lover. Ellison is naked and face down on the bed, taking direction from Julien. Baidoo and the white lover stand across from the bed, their shadows cast prominently on the wall behind.

We see as well the white members of the film crew. In the off-screen of the picture, behind the camera is Gupta himself, symbolizing the ways in which outside the frame of the photograph and the filmic screen is a racial and ethnic heterogeneity that can't be read through the visible presentation of the film alone.

5 www.sunilgupta.net/Langston/langstonfront.html (accessed May 1, 2014).

As an interdisciplinary text, black queer sexuality and black queer visual art, in particular, change the way in which we read other media as well. For instance, we would take note of the ethnic heterogeneity of founding literary texts. Conventionally African American as well as Caribbean-descended subjects made up the black queer male writing collective known as Other Countries. Poet and literary mentor to dozens of black queer writers, Assotto Saint was the child of Haitian immigrants. Writers such as Colin Robinson, Thomas Glave, and G. Winston James hailed from the Caribbean. The ethnic diversity of these black artists belies any uniform pronouncement about the American-ness of black queer literary production within the U.S. and calls for analyses of their work that can illuminate that heterogeneity.

Black queer art and the invention of new forms of life

The final scene from *Looking for Langston* illustrates the reconstruction of the past and the associations that sexuality makes with the Harlem Renaissance, rave cultures, vigilantism, and police repression. In the conclusion of the film, we see a group of thugs and police about to storm a house party inside. The party is made up of black and white men dancing together in tuxedos. The scene is a temporal mix of period attire from the nineteen-twenties, a disco ball, and Royal House's 'Can You Party' in the background. Some of the police officers put on latex gloves, presumably to protect themselves from the infected blood that is certain to flow. Seemingly oblivious to the approaching fag bashers, the boys dance all the same. We might think of the scene in which the boys dance and party to an awaiting mob just a few yards away as analogous to the expulsion of queers of color from their homes by homophobic parents in the nineteen-eighties and the residential segregation that ensued from those expulsions. We also might compare it to the Thatcher government's forced removal of people of color from economically depressed neighborhoods in Britain during that same period. The scene can also be read alongside the vigilante violence waged against queers in Britain during the nineteen-eighties. Talking about such violence, Hemphill informed Beam, 'The National Front, equivalent to our Ku Klux Klan, has issued a pamphlet detailing how to make bombs to blow up homosexual establishments and "smell the stinking faggots burn!!"'[6] Julien himself has said that the scene recalls the closing down of queer clubs in London during the eighties because of state-driven homophobia.

In addition to past scenes of expulsion and pleasure, we can also see the ways in which the clip gestures toward a jeopardized but still possible future. In *The Politics of Aesthetics*, Rancière goes on to write: '[The aesthetic regime] devotes itself to the invention of new forms of life on the basis of an idea of what art *was*, an idea of what art *would have been*' (Rancière 2006: 25). The scene juxtaposes

6 '9 December 1986', Joseph Beam Papers.

several histories and temporalities, imagining what the Harlem Renaissance and techno were as a way to suggest what queer formations were and what they might still be. But the scene is under no delusion that the formation of alternatives will take place without duress. First we see a party, and then we see a baton, which we might read as the subcultures that were being produced in the midst of the violence of a neoliberal age. Given that, we might observe the scene as a gesture towards a future of ecstatic and critical heterogeneities – fragile heterogeneities, to be sure, but ones that can still be ours.

In *The History of Sexuality, Volume 1*, Foucault famously argued that sexuality was not a mode of liberation from power but indeed a relay for power. As he stated: 'The deployment of sexuality has its reason for being, not in reproducing itself, but in proliferating, innovating, annexing, creating, and penetrating bodies in an increasingly comprehensive way [...] [It] is tied to recent devices of power' (Foucault 1990: 107). Indeed, for Foucault, the history of sexuality is a history of power. Without a doubt, those histories of sexuality and power continue to be necessary. But that's not all sexuality is. For instance, if we consider Audre Lorde's definition of the erotic and concentrate, particularly, on those parts of the erotic that she describes as '[making] connections with our similarities and differences' (Lorde 1984: 59), we come away with a sense of sexuality as a critical mode of association rather than simply a technology of power. How interesting it would be to turn our attention as well to sexuality as a relay for new associations and connections, as the dream of a new kind of work. To this end, black queer artists during the nineteen-eighties engaged sexuality as a transmission for a host of issues – migration, indigenous spiritualities, police harassment, state violence, nuclear proliferation, empire, history as a mode power/knowledge, and the list goes on and on. This version of sexuality – one that employs it for the purposes of questionable and unforeseen connections and associations – moves us toward a history of sexuality that is not only an account of hegemonic power but an examination of sexuality's visions for justice, visions that were – in the context of black queer formations in the nineteen-eighties – part of sexuality's erotics.

References

Abdulahad, T., Rogers, G., Smith, J. W., and Waheed, J. (1983) 'Black Lesbian Feminist Organizing: A Conversation', in B. Smith (ed.) *Home Girls: A Black Feminist Anthology*, New York: Kitchen Table Press.

Barthes, R. (1977) *Image, Music, Text*, trans. S. Heath, New York: Hill and Wang.

Deleuze, G. and Guattari, F. (2009) *Anti-Oedipus: Capitalism and Schizophrenia*, trans. R. Hurley, M. Seem, and H. R. Lane, New York: Penguin.

De Veaux, A. (2006) *Warrior Poet: A Biography of Audre Lorde*, New York: W. W. Norton.

Duggan, L. (2003) *The Twilight of Equality: Neoliberalism, Cultural Politics, and the Attack on Democracy*, Boston, MA: Beacon.

Fani-Kayode, R. and Hirst, A. (1996) *Photographs*, London: Autograph ABP.

Ferguson, R. A. (2004) *Aberrations in Black: Toward a Queer of Color Critique*, Minneapolis: University of Minnesota Press.

Foucault, M. (1990) *The History of Sexuality, Volume 1: An Introduction*, trans. R. Hurley, New York: Vintage Books.

Hall, S. (1997) 'The Local and the Global', in A. McClintock, E. Shohat, and A. Mufti (eds) *Dangerous Liaisons: Gender, Nation, and Postcolonial Perspectives*, Minneapolis: University of Minnesota Press, pp. 173–87.

Harvey, D. (2005) *A Brief History of Neoliberalism*, Oxford: Oxford University Press.

Hemphill, E. (1991) 'Looking for Langston: An Interview with Isaac Julien', in E. Hemphill (ed.) *Brother to Brother: New Writings by Black Gay Men*, Boston, MA: Alyson Publications, pp. 174–80.

Hume, D. (2007) *An Enquiry Concerning Human Understanding* [1748], Cambridge: Cambridge University Press.

Julien, I. and Mercer, K. (1991) 'True Confessions: A Discourse on Images of Black Male Sexuality', in E. Hemphill (ed.) *Brother to Brother: New Writings by Black Gay Men*, Boston, MA: Alyson Publications, pp. 167–73.

Lorde, A. (1984) *Sister Outsider: Essays and Speeches*, New York: Quality Paper Backs.

Lowe, L. (1996) *Immigrant Acts: On Asian American Cultural Politics*, Durham, NC: Duke University Press.

Lowe, L. and Lloyd, D. (1997) 'Introduction' in *The Politics of Culture in the Shadow of Capital*, Durham, NC: Duke University Press, pp. 1–32.

Marx, K. and Engels, F. (1989) *The German Ideology: Part One* [1845], New York: International Publishers.

Melamed, J. (2011) *Represent and Destroy: Rationalizing Violence in the New Racial Capitalism*, Minneapolis: University of Minnesota Press.

Nelson, S. (2005) 'Transgressive Transcendence in the Photographs of Rotimi Fani-Kayode', *Art Journal* 64(1): 4–19.

Rancière, J. (2006) *The Politics of Aesthetics*, trans. Gabriel Rockhill, London: Continuum.

Saint, A. (1991) *The Road Before Us: 100 Gay Black Poets*, New York: Galiens Press.

Chapter 4

Queer economic justice

Desire, critique and the practice of knowledge

Margot Weiss

Tim McCaskill, a long-time gay liberation activist, spoke recently in Montreal about the intersections of queer and left, and what might be next for the movement. His talk urged us to build a left analysis of the present situation, one in which, he concluded, radical queers must remember that 'transgression is not transformation': that the sub- or countercultures in which we find community, joy, or love are not the sites from which we might mount the kind of broad-based social transformative action that could change the world. These words left me musing about the ways academia might function, at least for politically motivated academics, as a space of affirmation, without necessarily serving as a launching point for transformative action. Along these lines, I mean in this chapter to explore the ways our objects of study or analysis might stand in for our own political desires, the ways we invest our objects with a politics that, because they substitute for our own, take on certain rigidities that we vigorously defend. But Tim's words also cast into relief a tension intrinsic to late capitalism: radical sexualities and communities serve as sites of semi-permitted *transgression* – not transformation.

My goal in this chapter is to bring these two strands together, to reflect on the political dreams we invest in radical sexualities and to explore why we might want to find liberation, specifically economic justice, in radical sexualities. Part of what I argue is that the desire for sex to be liberatory indexes a more social desire for transformation, and that desire stubbornly persists despite our scholarly analytical moves, even when it challenges their analytical assumptions. Unpacking these claims, in the hope of unsticking certain calcified arguments, is the goal of this chapter.

I suppose I should start with this 'we', which I mean to reference left or progressive academics who are interested in the political possibilities of academic scholarship, in the potential of queerer worlds instantiated through our writing, our thinking, and our conversations. I center my chapter in North America, as that is where I work (as both an academic and an anthropologist), but I suspect readers in other late-capitalist economies will find resonances. And so, first, I must say that this chapter is a reflexive critique of certain conditions of academic labor, conditions that I share. As I am an anthropologist, its primary material is drawn from my ethnographic fieldwork with BDSM (bondage and discipline, domination/submission, sadomasochism) communities in San Francisco, the subject of my book *Techniques of Pleasure* (Weiss 2011), and with queer left activists in New York City, Chicago, and Montreal (the subject of my book in progress, *Visions of Sexual Justice*). But its analytical approach departs from a more traditional ethnographic one when I turn the spotlight toward radical sexual politics in the academy, in a time of ongoing neoliberalization of knowledge, where what might appear to be radical sexual difference is all too easily absorbed into multicultural tolerance. Perhaps it's true to say that it attempts a reflexive reading of queer studies in the academy, or at least of some of the political motivations, modes of analysis, and institutional structures that form and delimit the project of *queering* through scholarship. In other words, this chapter is intended less as a critique of our objects of analysis – those forms of sexuality or desire that we center in our writing – and more as a critique of the politics of the contemporary academy, and especially the ways that we imbue our objects with the political effects we wish or perhaps fantasize for ourselves.

In an essay on faculty activism today, Purnima Bose argues that 'corporatization has radically altered the conditions of work for the professoriate [...] eliminating programs or units [...] ratcheting up standards of productivity, and increasing faculty's general workload in response to the downsizing of academic personnel'. In this 'exhausting', 'frantic', 'unrelenting' context, many faculty, she writes, are left without the 'energy or the desire' necessary for activism (Bose 2012: 816). In queer studies, however, we have not lost the desire. But ironically, as I will suggest, our desires for queer transformation, although laudatory (and, again, these are desires and fantasies that I share), might in the end obscure the conditions of their production, making social transformation less, rather than more, possible. As I will argue, the transfer of the sign of the political onto our objects seems to have had less than ideal effects: creating a situation where we continuously attempt to re-politicize both our objects and ourselves, while simultaneously, necessarily, turning away from the social and political conditions of our analysis. This is a suggestion, a question, not an assertion or a condemnation. But it's one that I think we might wish to consider – even if I'm not sure where it leaves us.

In the end, I will suggest, along with others in this volume, that 'we do not yet have a good understanding of the political economy of sexuality in this neoliberal framework of empire' – especially as we have yet to consider how 'the very questions we know to ask [are] conditioned by the expansive reach of neoliberalism and empire that we deploy them to undermine' (Wesling 2013: 296, 297). Neoliberalism describes not only the conditions that give rise to the sexual politics that we seek to challenge, as Jon Binnie's and Roderick Ferguson's chapters in this volume make clear, but also the social and political conditions of the contemporary academy within which we do our analytical work (the restructuring of the academy in terms of market logics, from a so-called 'marketplace of ideas' to the casualization of labor, to the privatization of public universities). This chapter explores how finding radicality in queer objects can, inadvertently, obscure these shared historical conditions. Taking up the recent turn away from critique in both queer studies and anthropology, I argue that we need critique now more than ever – an immanent critique that implicates both objects and subjects in our shared desire for collective justice.

The queerness of BDSM: transgression as (economic) transformation

I'll start in a place I know best: the political claims made about BDSM. When BDSM is considered within queer studies, it is typically (and perhaps not surprisingly) read as *queer*, even when the players are straight. This is because SM practice is understood to flout, even subvert, gendered norms, disrupting the heterosexual logic that animates sex, gender, and sexuality because roles are chosen and not naturalized based on sexed bodies. Writers drawing on this argument emphasize the ways SM seems to 'play with' norms, enabling BDSM to 'destabilize rigidly identified subjectivities' (MacKendrick 1999: 96) and avoid 'predefined power relations in regard to gender and sexuality' (Bauer 2008: 234). And indeed, contemporary BDSM communities are filled with exciting scenes of genderqueer play that register as queer. But if *queer*, at least in queer studies, has no set content, it does have a political orientation – one that is, in Michael Warner's off-cited phrase, resistant 'to regimes of the normal' (1993: xxvi). For Warner, the regime was heteronormativity; in recent years, the regime has been expanded to include homonormativity, homonationalism, queer liberalism, and more (e.g. Duggan 2002; Puar 2007; Eng 2010). These concepts, and I'm back to Warner again, tend to define queer 'against the normal' and name 'a wide field of normalization [...] as the site of violence' (Warner 1993: xxvi; see also Berlant and Warner 1998). In this logic, BDSM is queer because it is anti-normative.

As generative as this has been for so many of us – myself included – I am taken by a strand of feminist and anti-racist critique that also runs through queer studies' history, a critique that includes the essays of Biddy Martin (1994), Cathy Cohen (1997), and Janet Jakobsen (1998), and has been most recently articulated by Robyn Wiegman (2012). This critique asks after the politics of queer's anti-normativity. Wiegman argues that queer studies' anti-normativity project has, in intervening decades, hardened into an epistemological given, with the effect of removing normativity as a question, or object of inquiry that might generate a historically specific analysis. This can produce 'superficial accounts', as Biddy Martin puts it, where 'to be radical is to locate oneself outside or in a transgressive relation to kinship or community' through a 'romantic celebration of queerness' as 'anti-normativity' (1994: 123). At the same time, *with* queer studies' (albeit partial) institutionalization, anti-normativity has become a political stance that, as Wiegman argues, underwrites queer studies' institutional authority (Wiegman 2012: 308–9, 341–2).[1] In this situation, queer studies' critical authority comes from knowing the difference between queerness and normativity, and always and already being set against that normativity. It comes, in other words, by inscribing our objects with our own aspirational radicality. Wiegman unpacks the irony of the normativity of anti-normativity in queer studies, but I am most concerned with the ways these moves can surrender the explanatory power and critical acumen of queer theory, reifying a queer object whose political valence and meaning is known from the start.[2] In this scenario, we might end up learning what we already know: queer objects are queer, queer analysis critiques normativity, queer objects transgress normativity (see also Boellstorff 2007: 15).

The slide from sexual transgression to radical politics happens, as Elisa Glick argues, when sex-positive critics locate 'political resistance in the transgression of sexual limits' (2000: 26). But this attempt to celebrate or (re)value 'genuinely radical' sexualities (25) often leaves aside 'the political and economic conditions that are responsible for' the violence that befalls queer bodies to begin with, particularly racism and capitalism (26). Glick's concern, and my own, is that idealizing 'the subversive potential of transgressive practices that dislocate and displace the dominant' might prevent us from asking whether or how 'sexually dissident styles' can reproduce 'relations of domination' (24, 28). Such idealization can enable us to forget, as Roderick Ferguson's chapter in this volume notes, that queer 'desire doesn't simply bear transgressive potential but socially reproductive capacities as well'.

Glick provides a broader social context for this idealization: the historical outgrowth of sex liberationist politics that took the 'personal as political' a bit too far, resulting in a vision of the political that is *only* personal. She writes, 'by creating a climate in which *self-transformation is equated with social transformation*', pro-sex theory and activism 'has valorized politics of lifestyle, a personal politics that is centered upon who we are – how we dress or get off – that fails to engage with institutionalized systems of domination' (2000: 31; my emphasis). In these cases, analyzing sexual lifestyle as radical social transformation might not only elide 'institutionalized systems of domination' but also repackage sexual politics so that they are more easily taken up into the very structures we might wish to transform.

So, in the case of BDSM, we might look back on the long history of feminist debates, and, in the end, agree that BDSM is transgressive, in the sense of a

1 See also David Halperin (2003), who argues that queer theory, unlike gay and lesbian studies, is more congenial to institutional normalization. 'Queer', he argues, could be abstracted from historical and social dynamics and turned 'into a generic badge of subversiveness' or oppositionality (341–2).

2 With 'reify', I gesture toward Kevin Floyd (2009) who argues, in a Lukácsian mode, that capitalist sexuality abstracts and reifies desire, objectifying social relationships in the guise of sexual identity.

non-normative sexuality.[3] There are many ways that BDSM's emphasis on exploration and play, along with its creative modes of fantasy and desire, herald new possibilities of intimate connections to others. But while new forms of intimacy or expressions of desire might yield joy, love, and community, as McCaskill argues, such transgression does not guarantee – indeed, such transgression might even work against – broader social transformation.

I am thinking here of claims not only that BDSM is queer (non- or anti-normative), but that it is *resistant to capitalism and the state*. For example, Karmen MacKendrick writes that SM can 'explode our exchange-oriented economic sensibility' because its practices, especially those of pain play and bondage, are 'useless and excessive' (1999: 121, 110). Jeremy Carrette argues that SM is 'a site of resistance because it seeks to reconfigure pleasure in its intensity of exchange rather than through its productive or commercial value' (2005: 23), enabling SM to 'free our gendered bodies from the market of global exploitation' (27). Most recently, Lewis Call argues that practices of consent within BDSM exchanges represent 'a real challenge to the modern state and its political theories' (2011: 134). These claims about BDSM's political effects slide rather too quickly from BDSM as transgressive (of sexual norms) to BDSM as a site of resistance to or even transformation of the state and the global capitalist economy.

And, indeed, it is difficult to sustain these optimistic assertions through ethnography. Take toys as an example. BDSM players in the Bay Area use toys to create new circuits of intimacy; toys extend bodies as graftable prostheses; toys also connect players' bodies through circuits of channeled energy. These new potentialities – transgressions, no doubt – are not, however, resistant to capitalism, non-economic, non-productive, or non-commercial. The marketplace of toys, clothing, and other specialized gear along with the techniques and skills to use them are central components of contemporary BDSM – so much so that the practitioners I spoke with in the Bay Area complain that BDSM has become a 'consumer sexuality', where those who cannot afford the latest or best toys are seen as 'amateurs' or second-class citizens. The structure of the BDSM community, with its educational organizations, enables one to become an expert by taking classes and workshops, mastering a wide range of BDSM techniques, and purchasing a seemingly endless array of specialty toys, clothing, videos, how-to

3 BDSM is somewhat of a hobbyhorse for debates about sex and power. The publication of the anti-BDSM lesbian/radical feminist anthology *Against Sadomasochism* (Linden *et al.* 1982) and the leatherdyke defense from Samois, *Coming to Power* (1981), might be taken as the key texts. On the one hand, radical feminists argued that because BDSM dramatizes real oppression, it must reproduce, validate, or even function as that oppression. On the other hand, leatherdykes, most pro-SM feminists, and, later, queer theorists, argued that BDSM is not a re-enactment but rather a matter of private desires, a consensual game, or a parody, and thus we might view BDSM as legitimate, oppositional, or even transgressive. These two positions have set the parameters for debates over the feminist politics of BDSM since. See Hart (1998: 36–83), Bauer (2008), and Weiss (2011: 143–86) for an analysis of this debate and its contemporary legacy.

books, and other paraphernalia. In this scene – like many others – consuming is a primary means through which practitioners craft identities and secure community belonging.[4]

There is much more to say about all of this – and I say it elsewhere[5] – for these changes have not gone uncontested, nor are they unidirectionally negative; as I've already noted, new toys, for example, open the body to new sensations, pleasures, and forms of connection and exchange. Yet it seems clear that BDSM communities, at least since the mid-1990s, are, like other communities, 'deployed to [...] facilitate the flow of capital' (Joseph 2002: xxxii). Indeed, it seems clear that the BDSM scene of today must be understood in relation not only, and not even primarily, to the transgression of sexual norms, norms that posit, as Gayle Rubin famously put it, that 'good, normal, natural, blessed' sexuality will be heterosexual, marital, monogamous, reproductive, non-commercial, dyadic, adult, and at home, and will never involve pornography, fetish objects, sex toys of any sort, or roles – rules that BDSM quite regularly flouts (1993[1984]: 13). Instead, BDSM must be read in relation to larger shifts in political economy: to the proliferation of sexualities, sexual services, commodities, and purveyors in the US, and to more local transformations of the Bay Area: the growth of informational technology in Silicon Valley, neoliberal class and race dynamics in the city of San Francisco and its suburbs, and the expansion of new sexual-technological industries and consumer-based identities. It is these larger-scale systems, these shared historical conditions that, I fear, go unrecognized when we read sexual transgression *as* social transformation.

If the ethnographic analysis of BDSM reveals, if anything, the *increased* intertwining of capitalism and sexuality, what do we make of the desire, on the part of scholars, to read BDSM in precisely the opposite way? Indeed, one of the more common responses to the argument I just made is that this might be true about *straight* BDSM, but it can't be true about *queer* BDSM. To me, this holds out hope for some true radicalism elsewhere – a pure space of the outside, the *queer* queer. In this, one can see the oppositional condensations – queer versus heteronormative, queer versus homonormative, queer versus *really* queer – that animate this problem. As Kath Weston reminds us, channeling Marx, 'no search is more fruitless than the one that seeks revolutionary forms of social relations which remain "uncontaminated by existing social conditions"' (cited in Boellstorff 2007: 237). Fruitless, perhaps, but sorely tempting.

Tempting even when our scholarly analyses obscure or conceal what BDSM practitioners already know: that it 'takes money to play', that BDSM is part and parcel of late capitalism, that our sexuality cannot be cordoned off from political economy. And again I worry that our scholarly willed ignorance might

4 There is a large archive of work on the role of consumerism in contemporary late-capitalist economies; see, for example, Curtis 2004; Comaroff and Comaroff 2000; and Miller 1995.

5 See Weiss 2011, especially Chapters 2 and 3.

turn us away from the economic, social, and historical conditions that must inform an analysis of sexual politics. If or when it does so, our analysis of the politics of BDSM participates in precisely the dynamics we mean to contest. This misrecognition happens when sex is imagined, as Linda Singer puts it, as 'a mechanism for resistance, transgression, opposition to the sphere of demand', an 'emblem [...] of freedom' from an 'alienating social system' (1993: 36–7). Figuring sex as it is so often understood – as private, deeply personal, individual, psychological, and certainly not economic – is phantasmatic but not inconsequential; this is one way that capitalist social relations are instantiated and validated. Imagining that BDSM transgresses social norms *and therefore* capitalist social relations helps to guarantee the reproduction of the social relations we seek to transform by diverting our attention from the conditions we share – in the name of politicizing sex.

Critique, criticism, complicity: our objects, ourselves

Thus far, I have detailed the misrecognition of the *object of analysis* – of BDSM as an *a priori* radical practice. In this reading, analyzing queer sex as always radical re-entrenches the obfuscation of sexuality as a social relation. In this section I want to refocus this analysis away from our objects, which perhaps we can agree are necessarily complicit with the social world they occupy, and turn this argument back toward ourselves, and the political desires and impasses embedded in our claims and our critiques. How else might we – critics, readers, and analysts of BDSM – evaluate and assert claims about the political value, and, indeed, the conceptual content, of BDSM?

I will suggest that the idealization of queer sex, the slide from transgression to transformation, happens when we project our own political desires onto our objects. As BDSM might teach us, privileging desire as a private realm of self-transformation and individual freedom participates in neoliberal cultural formations that encourage us to see structural inequality as personal dynamics.[6] And here, just as BDSM practitioners are inclined to view the scene as a 'safe space' that exists outside social relations, and just as they mobilize liberal understandings of agency and choice to rationalize and bracket social inequalities, so too do scholars when we imagine that sexuality or desire might exist in a sphere uncontaminated by capitalism, that queer sex or desire might escape our social conditions.

I take inspiration for this move from recent work by Sharon Holland, who diagnoses contemporary queer theory as 'abstracting' desire from history – and particularly histories of racism (2012: 58). As Holland argues, when queer critics

6 As a political rationality, neoliberalism envisions people as autonomous individuals who exercise free choice according to market logics. In this way, neoliberalism works to justify the social inequalities of race, gender, sexuality, disability, etc. produced through its economic operations as a neutral outcome of rational choice (e.g. Harvey 2005; Duggan 2003; Brown 2005).

decouple racism from desire, they tend to consign racism to a '"past" that we would rather not remember', whereas desire holds out hope for the future, containing the 'revolutionary possibilities of queer transgression' (44). This reading draws on Rosemary Hennessy's critique of queer theory's abstraction and reification of desire, so that 'its historical production becomes invisible' (Hennessy 2000: 185–6; Holland 2012: 44). In this way, as Michael Hames-Garcia notes, 'the privileging of desire as a realm of freedom and/or transgression' can 'occlude the collusion of desire with domination and oppression' (2001: 216).[7] The irony here is that abstracting desire in this way, so that it is granted an intrinsic political value (for the future of liberation), not only impedes our ability to analyse the social power we wish to contest but also ensures that our analysis itself replicates the conditions of its production – in this case, through the endless deferral of the material conditions that fuse histories of racism and (queer) desire.

Both queer sexual communities *and* the academic world in which we live and produce our queer analyses share a tendency, as postcolonialist feminist Chandra Talpade Mohanty writes, toward what she labels depoliticization, which 'domesticates power differences, transforming systemic projects of resistance into commodified, private acts of rebellion' (2013: 968). In this situation, it is perhaps not surprising that we are keen to attribute radical sex politics to our objects, politics that might counter capitalism, since it is a struggle to find these politics for ourselves. Indeed, I suspect that it is in part due to the continuous frustrations of political engagement that we look to our objects for a purer, more laudatory form of our own political desires. As I've discussed elsewhere, academics not infrequently fantasize that we are doing politics when we are doing quotidian academic work, writing essays much like this one (Greyser and Weiss 2012). In this situation, I wish to call not only for a deeper engagement with the politics of our objects, but a more reflexive understanding of the way we perform our politics through analysis.

I suspect that these frustrations have played a role in the recent turn in queer studies away from critique. As Wiegman puts it, left (academic) political desire has invested in critique a hope that knowledge practice can 'rescue us from [...] well [...] nearly everything'. Critique, she writes, 'promises to deliver too much' – in the form of knowledge as politics (2012: 34). Instead, recent work in queer studies has pursued forms of Eve Sedgwick's (2003) reparative reading practices, emphasizing affect, archive, and description. These threads, diverse as they are, have in common a desire to locate the critic within the object, to resist a kind of masterful, from-above gaze in favor of being alongside, or attuning to, or

7 Related arguments about queer studies' analytical abstractions have been made by critics working within Marxist traditions; Rosemary Hennessy's contributions (2000, 1994) are essential, alongside newer work in queer Marxism (Floyd 2009; Sears 2005) and queer of color critique (Ferguson 2004).

dwelling with one's object.[8] For example, Heather Love describes her method in *Feeling Backward* as 'a move away from the central methodology of cultural criticism: ideology critique, or lifting the veil of mystification to reveal the truth of social processes'. Instead, and following Sedgwick, her approach 'tends toward the descriptive rather than the critical [...]. I tend to think *with* them (the authors and critics in my study) rather than *against* them' (Love 2007: 23). Love does not reject the critical in toto; but, still, I want to pause on the suggestion that critique requires the critic to be positioned 'against' one's objects, rather than 'with' them.

I am sympathetic to reconsidering queer alignments with objects, to articulating modes of analysis that might depart from prior assumptions, and to challenging taken-for-granted ways of knowing and the power such ways cohere. Yet I remain suspicious, too, suspicious of the ways a turn away from critique seems to offer a pure place of politics – at least for the critic. Love notes that Sedgwick describes reparative reading practices with words like 'surprise [...] creativity, and love' and paranoid (critical) readings as 'rigid, grim [...] contemptuous, sneering [...] cruel, monopolistic, and terrible'. 'Look,' Love writes, 'you don't have to tell me twice' – not only a better method, reparative reading appears to be a superior ethical and political stance too (2010: 372). *Critique*, then, becomes *criticizing*: a moralistic judgment served from on high. Yet, ironically, rejecting critique does not seem, at least to me, to align the critic with the object, and thus resist knowledge-as-mastery (an impossibility in any case). Instead, it seems – perhaps counter-intuitively and certainly unintentionally – to affirm a distance between critics and objects that fosters a misrecognition of the political conditions both critic and object share (Weiss 2012).[9]

Anthropologist Tom Boellstorff describes the rejection of criticism from the other direction, cautioning against queer theory's transcendental and abstracted claims in favor of ethnography's immanent and contradictory critique (2007: 15, 17–18). Anthropologists have long embraced what we call 'cultural critique', by which we usually mean the deconstruction of the taken-for-granted through strategies such as juxtaposition, cultural comparison, and defamiliarization. From *Anthropology as Cultural Critique* (Marcus and Fischer 1986) to today, cultural critique in anthropology has merged a critique of ideology (a project of demystification) with the analysis of the generative contradictions of social life. This is how I would frame my own work, in which I read BDSM as a late-capitalist sexual

8 These terms come from the keynote lectures and discussions at Duke University's 2013 Feminist Theory Workshop, but I take them as representative of new work in queer studies that seeks to move away from critique as mastery. For critical reviews of this turn in, especially, literary criticism, see Weed 2012 and Wiegman 2014. Although no queer theorist, Bruno Latour (2004) might be taken as the limit case of the argument that critique is a mode of punishing, humiliating domination/mastery from above.

9 These general dynamics are the subject of the essays in my co-edited special forum of *American Quarterly* on 'Academia and Activism' (Greyser and Weiss 2012).

culture, situated within the vicissitudes of neoliberal rationalities. To me, a turning away from this kind of critique (to try to avoid knowledge-mastery-power) inadvertently abstracts our objects and our analysis from the social world. In the case of BDSM, this blocks an analysis of the social conditions central to both BDSM and the contemporary academy – neoliberal cultural formations such as color-blind understandings of tolerance or diversity; a post-sexism, post-racial fantasy world; a reliance on commodities as signs of identity; and the fantasy that sexuality is (still) the truth of the self and thus the sign of an individual's freedom from social norms – when such an analysis might instead prompt a political intervention in BDSM communities, the academy, and elsewhere. In other words, the cost of giving in to the temptation to celebrate BDSM cultures as transgressive, as existing *outside* those political, social, and economic dynamics we might dislike for our objects and for ourselves, might be precisely the obfuscation of the way those dynamics operate in our shared historical moment.

It is ironic, then, that some anthropologists have called for a turn away from critique, claiming, in terms that parallel literary queer theorists, that critique relies on *distance*. Charles Hale, for example, advocates a turn away from cultural critique and toward activist or engaged anthropology.[10] For Hale, cultural critique, while politically progressive and de-essentializing, establishes its politics through distancing. Activist anthropology, in contrast, affirms closeness, 'collaboration, dialogue', and 'accountability' to 'the principles and practices of people who struggle outside the academic setting' (Hale 2006: 104).

For Hale, activist commitments might produce innovative theories and methods, and new forms of knowledge, bound to the struggles on which they are centered. I do not dispute this – indeed, this has been the case in my own research with queer activists (and BDSM practitioners, too) – but I do question the dichotomy between cultural critique and activist research framed in terms of distance. As Setha Low and Sally Engle Merry write:

> In practice, academic and activist endeavors are never autonomous, despite our analytical assumptions of separateness [...]. As anthropologists move into new fields of research such as human rights, they encounter subjects who themselves employ anthropological concepts and engage in theoretical debates about what they mean [...]. *They are self-reflective, analytical, and participate in the same intellectual world as anthropologists.*
>
> (2012: s211; my emphasis)

These dichotomies imagine a separation between academic (as intellectual or theoretical) and activist (as practical or political), a separation that seems to locate politics out there, on the ground, in the field, rather than in the academy, or in the spaces we inhabit together. Imagining this putative separation between what

10 See Checker 2009 and Low and Merry 2010 for reviews of activist or engaged anthropology.

are, in actuality, shared worlds and linked historical situations, as I have been suggesting, turns us away from the grounds on which we produce knowledge, encouraging us to locate politics in places other and separate from those in which we do our work. In this case, there is a second irony: academics can imagine that writing about activists is activism, perhaps especially when our analysis avoids the forms of cultural critique that might challenge the underlying contexts that demand activist and academic intervention, both.

I have space for only one brief example of the ways the queer left activists with whom I've been working unsettle conceptual dichotomies between activist and academic ways of knowing, between closeness and distance as modes of critique. Part of my project entailed working with Queers for Economic Justice (QEJ), a progressive non-profit organization based in New York City that sought to 'challenge and change the systems that create poverty and economic injustice in our communities' while advancing sexual and gender liberation.[11] Their work focused on the lived experiences and expressed needs of queer people in poverty. As such, they were an organization that centralized the concepts of 'economic justice' and 'queerness' in their work.

In much of the literature on activist anthropology, activists are those interested in usable, even commodifiable, concepts and practical ends. Because of this commitment, activist research is seen as contradictory to, even compromised by, 'the inevitable negotiations and contradictions that these broader political struggles entail' (Hale 2006: 100). In contrast, ethnographic cultural critique, Hale argues, is characterized by 'analytical complexity and sophistication' and the 'energetic deconstruction of powerful ideas, institutions, and practices' (101, 102), by a striving toward 'intellectual production uncompromised' by politics (100). In Hale's binary, cultural critique is distant, knowing, and unencumbered; activism, by contrast, is close, pragmatic, and compromised by social realities.

Based on this dichotomy, one might imagine that methodologically, as an anthropologist, I have a choice: either to do cultural criticism or to do activism. The former, like paranoid reading, would entail deconstructing QEJ's understandings of 'economic justice'; the latter would entail surrendering any such powerful critiques to more pressing political exigencies. Yet there is a third choice, one that is, as Elizabeth Weed makes clear, already part of the purportedly paranoid practice of critique (2012). QEJ members produced cultural critiques of 'economic justice' that were both intellectual and activist; they were already doing activism as cultural critique. The 'analytical complexity and sophistication' of critique, and its efforts to develop concepts and modes of analysis are intrinsic to the everyday work of an organization like QEJ: during a staff meeting devoted to figuring out how to best deal with police harassment of homeless transwomen of color, given the current political climate, or while drafting an overarching vision

11 A victim of the non-profit industrial complex, Queers for Economic Justice was forced to close its doors in January 2014: their radical agenda did not attract stable funding.

statement on the impact of the 2008 economic recession on queer and trans people.[12] This critical intellectual work parallels the everyday work of an academic (especially, perhaps, an anthropologist): building concepts from everyday details, re-scaling and focusing analysis, deconstructing and scrutinizing a multiplicity of claims.[13] Throughout, critique is crucial for consciousness-raising, to share ideas and analysis, to link up multiple segments of the struggle, and to build a stronger movement.

Such critique is also, necessarily, compromised. Indeed, QEJ was to some extent founded on the competing and contradictory demands to ameliorate the suffering of poor queers in New York City and at the same time to transform the economic structures that necessitate such programs. As one of QEJ's founders explained to me, QEJ was always pulled in multiple directions, simultaneously working on economic justice in terms of class and union politics, building social services for poor queers, and crafting a queer critique of capitalism. One of its central components – organizing support groups for queer and trans people within NYC shelters, and advocating for queer and trans homeless people – fits uneasily into a deeper critique of capitalism. Yet analyzing how these multiple dimensions might fit together is an ongoing and open question, and one that not only informed QEJ's contingent politics but also served, in some ways, as the central dynamic of their struggle.

In my reading, this intellectual work resonates with Robin D. G. Kelley's point that activists 'generate new knowledge, new theories, new questions. The most radical ideas often grow out of a concrete intellectual engagement with the problems of aggrieved populations confronting systems of oppression' (2002: 8). Charles Hale agrees that activists produce new forms of knowledge, yet argues that activists 'rarely have the resources and other means available to choose the language and conditions of their own struggles', and so might 'partly reproduce the very systems of inequality that oppress them' (2006: 109). This logic suggests that, unlike activists, academic critics *can* choose the conditions of their own struggles, and can, thus, escape from the systems of inequality within which they work. And so, ironically, the call to turn away from the masterful, distant mode of critique not only ends up reinforcing a dichotomy between critique and activism, intellectual work and practical orientations, but leads to the untenable, if unintended, assumption that activists *alone* are contaminated by contingency, or compromise. Gayatri Spivak opens 'Can the Subaltern Speak?' (1988) with a critique

12 The latter example comes from my participation in a working group on 'Queer Survival Economies', which aims to document the connections between queerness and labour (especially low-wage and non-unionized labour), and use such knowledge to organize queer and trans economic justice campaigns in a context where gay and lesbian organizing rarely addresses class, economics, or poverty, and labour organizations rarely address queerness, gender, or sexuality. This work continues today.

13 In this sense, the critical intellectual work of the activist is akin to Antonio Gramsci's (1971) 'organic intellectual', against the abstracted critical distance of the 'traditional intellectual'.

of Michel Foucault and Gilles Deleuze's analysis of the role of the intellectual. In their dialogue, she writes, they valorize 'the concrete experience of the oppressed' while remaining 'uncritical about the historical role of the intellectual' (in helping to 'consolidate the international division of labor'). This slip produces an unrecognized contradiction that generates what she sees as a rather self-congratulatory intellectualism in the name of politics (274–5). I see much the same dynamic in the turn away from critique and the valorization of activist anthropology.

It is at this point that I think we might return to what Robyn Wiegman has diagnosed as an over-attachment to one's object in identity knowledge fields such as queer studies. For if queer studies' normative analytical move is to find transgression in its objects, it does so as a way to reflect those politics back at us as a measure of our own and our field's political worth. In this way, when queer academics locate in our objects the radical politics we wish for ourselves, we install distance between the conditions that give rise to our objects and our own analysis of them. Finding, in queer practices, resistance to capitalism or triumph over global exploitation or autonomous desire allows us to bypass our own embeddedness in global capitalism, in neoliberalism, in structures that condition our analytical work. Yet when we seek to overcome that distance between our objects and ourselves by surrendering critique and, instead, identifying with or as our object, we end up affirming that very distance, a distance that disguises the conditions of its production even as it locates such complicity elsewhere. In the end, the turn away from critique seems a false humility that might unintentionally bolster the superiority of the academic while simultaneously refusing the political power of immanent cultural critique.

Conclusion: desiring a queerer world

Meg Wesling, building on Kevin Floyd's queer Marxist critique, has suggested that 'the conditions of neoliberalism are evidenced not only in the privatization of rights to which privileged queer subjects now aspire' (a homonationalism and broader dynamic of sexual neoliberalism), 'but also in the very critical identities and capacities we might want to occupy to critique those desires'. This is, then, a dialectic: 'queer studies' focus on anti-normativity as a disciplinary model and political desire is itself produced in relation to neoliberalism, not solely in contestation of it' (2013: 299). In this situation, the queer sexual cultures we aim to explore can become a 'commodity to be consumed' through critical reading practices that, unmoored from emancipatory knowledges, circulate instead 'as a sign of prestige in an elitist, neoliberal landscape' (Mohanty 2013: 972; see also Hennessy 2000). In the marketplace of ideas, queer difference and desire are easily absorbed through an embrace of multicultural diversity that re-entrenches, rather than unseats, the everyday workings of the neoliberal university (see Ferguson 2012; also Ahmed 2012).

The irony I have been tracing in this chapter is that such circulations arise precisely because of scholars' desires to find emancipatory politics in our objects, rather than in the contradictions of the historical conditions we share. As long as queer studies scholars locate politics in individual style or personal desire (as in the case of sexual practices such as BDSM), we risk taking transgression for (social) transformation. Desiring to be with or on the side of the object, this critical work instead reaffirms a division between intellectual labor and activism or politics, ignoring activists' intellectual critique and, more crucially for my argument here, the complicit – because located – politics of intellectual labor. As I've been arguing, the desire for queer sex to stand against capitalism, to serve as a form of economic justice, might not be a new queer analysis of sexuality, but rather a symptom of our own inhabitation of the conditions of late capitalism we seek to transform.

And so, finally, we arrive at desire. In my analysis, critique is falsely opposed to desire: critique is autonomous, dominating, mastering, while desire is compromised, affective, utopic. But what if we see critique as a form of desire? Might we be able to recognize our desires for social transformation, for justice, for something better as complicit without giving up on the necessity of politics? I am inclined to agree with Nancy Fraser that 'no one has yet improved on Marx's 1843 definition of Critical Theory as the "the self-clarification of the struggles and wishes of the age"' (1985: 97). To my mind, this means that critique already entails the desire for collective transformation.

In a political landscape defined by the seamless proliferation of difference and desire, we need, I think, more rigorously social and historical ways of apprehending sexuality that can challenge the radically individualist understandings that characterize neoliberal sexual politics. We cannot imagine that investing objects with radical politics will guard against commodification, since such work seems, in the end, to bolster our own fantasized departure from the conditions that produce our work. But we can't surrender our political dreams, either, as complicit as those might be. Instead, I think we must risk critique that recognizes that we are not above our 'objects' but rather participants in the social fields we are attempting to transform. If we take for granted that we are already enmeshed with our objects, that we can't do critique from elsewhere, might we imagine, as Johannes Fabian writes, knowledge as 'activity or practice' rather than a state or a possession (2012: 444)? Could we then see knowledge as 'pragmatic and dialectical' (447), as political, as changing 'the knower as well as the known' (449)? Might we see this as the very definition of critique?

I don't have the answers to these questions, but I suspect that, as long as we valorize the transgressive, we will move away from the dialectical – thereby shoring up or reifying forms of power we mean to unseat. And, alongside others in this volume, I'd like us instead to work toward a reading of sexual and economic justice that might marshal critique not as a hollow gesture, but rather as the work of creating possibilities for contesting social power now, for all of us. In this context, we might be able to build a critical practice that resists the false divisions between theory and politics, academic and activist, distance and closeness, objectivity and complicity – that might enable transformation of ourselves and the academy as much as the objects of our knowledge.

References

Ahmed, S. (2012) *On Being Included: Racism and Diversity in Institutional Life*, Durham, NC: Duke University Press.

Bauer, R. (2008) 'Transgressive and Transformative Gendered Sexual Practices and White Privileges: The Case of the Dyke/Trans BDSM Communities', *WSQ: Women's Studies Quarterly* 36(3–4): 233–53.

Berlant, L. and Warner, M. (1998) 'Sex in Public', *Critical Inquiry* 24(2): 547–66.

Boellstorff, T. (2007) *A Coincidence Of Desires: Anthropology, Queer Studies, Indonesia*, Durham, NC: Duke University Press.

Bose, P. (2012) 'Faculty Activism and the Corporatization of the University', *American Quarterly* 64(4): 815–18.

Brown, W. (2005) 'Neoliberalism and the End of Liberal Democracy', in *Edgework: Critical Essays on Knowledge and Politics*, Princeton, NJ: Princeton University Press, pp. 37–59.

Call, L. (2011) 'Structures of Desire: Post-Anarchist Kink in the Speculative Fiction of Octavia Butler and Samuel Delany', in J. Heckert and R. Cleminson (eds) *Anarchism and Sexuality: Ethics, Relationships and Power*, Abingdon: Routledge, pp. 131–53.

Carrette, J. R. (2005) 'Intense Exchange: Sadomasochism, Theology and the Politics of Late Capitalism', *Theology and Sexuality* 11(2): 11–30.

Checker, M. (2009) 'Anthropology in the Public Sphere, 2008: Emerging Trends and Significant Impacts', *American Anthropologist* 111: 162–70.

Cohen, C. (1997) 'Punks, Bulldaggers, and Welfare Queens', *GLQ: A Journal of Lesbian and Gay Studies* 3: 437–65.

Comaroff, J. and Comaroff, J. L. (2000) 'Millennial Capitalism: First Thoughts on a Second Coming', *Public Culture* 12(2): 291–343.

Curtis, D. (2004) 'Commodities and Sexual Subjectivities: A Look at Capitalism and its Desires', *Cultural Anthropology* 19(1): 95–121.

Duggan, L. (2002) 'The New Homonormativity: The Sexual Politics of Neoliberalism', in R. Castronovo and D. D. Nelson (eds) *Materializing Democracy: Toward a Revitalized Cultural Politics*, Durham, NC: Duke University Press, pp. 175–94.

—— (2003) *The Twilight of Equality? Neoliberalism, Cultural Politics, and the Attack on Democracy*, Boston, MA: Beacon Press.

Eng, D. L. (2010) *The Feeling of Kinship: Queer Liberalism and the Racialization of Intimacy*, Durham, NC: Duke University Press.

Fabian, J. (2012) 'Cultural Anthropology and the Question of Knowledge', *Journal of the Royal Anthropological Institute* 18: 439–53.

Ferguson, R. A. (2004) *Aberrations in Black: Toward a Queer of Color Critique*, Minneapolis: University of Minnesota Press.

—— (2012) *The Reorder of Things: The University and its Pedagogies of Minority Difference*, Minneapolis: University of Minnesota Press.

Floyd, K. (2009) *The Reification of Desire: Toward a Queer Marxism*, Minneapolis: University of Minnesota Press.

Fraser, N. (1985) 'What's Critical about Critical Theory? The Case of Habermas and Gender', *New German Critique* 35: 97–131.

Glick, E. (2000) 'Sex Positive: Feminism, Queer Theory, and the Politics of Transgression', *Feminist Review* 64: 19–45.

Gramsci, A. (1971) *Selections from the Prison Notebooks of Antonio Gramsci*, New York: International Publishers.
Greyser, N. and Weiss, M. (2012) 'Introduction: Left Intellectuals and the Neoliberal University', *American Quarterly* 64(4): 787–93.
Hale, C. R. (2006) 'Activist Research v. Cultural Critique: Indigenous Land Rights and the Contradictions of Politically Engaged Anthropology', *Cultural Anthropology* 21(1): 96–120.
Halperin, D. (2003) 'The Normalization of Queer Theory', *Journal of Homosexuality* 45(2–4): 339–43.
Hames-Garcia, M. (2001) 'Can Queer Theory Be Critical Theory?', in W. S. Wilkerson and J. Paris (eds) *New Critical Theory: Essays on Liberation*, Lanham, MD: Rowman & Littlefield Publishers, pp. 201–22.
Hart, L. (1998) *Between the Body and the Flesh: Performing Sadomasochism*, New York: Columbia University Press.
Harvey, D. (2005) *A Brief History of Neoliberalism*, Oxford: Oxford University Press.
Hennessy, R. (1994) 'Queer Theory, Left Politics', *Rethinking Marxism* 7(3): 85–111.
—— (2000) *Profit and Pleasure: Sexual Identities in Late Capitalism*, New York: Routledge.
Holland, S. P. (2012) *The Erotic Life of Racism*, Durham, NC: Duke University Press.
Jakobsen, J.R. (1998) 'Queer is? Queer does? Normativity and the Problem of Resistance', *GLQ: A Journal of Lesbian and Gay Studies* 4(4): 511–36.
Joseph, M. (2002) *Against the Romance of Community*, Minneapolis: University of Minnesota Press.
Kelley, R. D. G. (2002) *Freedom Dreams: The Black Radical Imagination*, Boston, MA: Beacon Press.
Latour, B. (2004) 'Why Has Critique Run out of Steam? From Matters of Fact to Matters of Concern', *Critical Inquiry* 30(2): 225–48.
Linden, R. R., Pagano, D. R., Russell, D. E. H., and Star, S. L. (1982) *Against Sadomasochism: A Radical Feminist Analysis*, East Palo Alto, CA: Frog in the Well.
Love, H. (2010) 'Truth and Consequences: On Paranoid Reading and Reparative Reading', *Criticism* 52(2): 235–41.
—— (2007) *Feeling Backward: Loss and the Politics of Queer History*, Cambridge, MA: Harvard University Press.
Low, S. and Merry, S. (2010) 'Engaged Anthropology: Diversity and Dilemmas', *Current Anthropology* 51(S2): 203–26.
MacKendrick, K. (1999) *Counterpleasures*, Albany: State University of New York Press.
Marcus, G. and Fischer, M. F. (1986) *Anthropology as Cultural Critique: An Experimental Moment in the Human Sciences*, Chicago, IL: University of Chicago Press.
Martin, B. (1994) 'Extraordinary Homosexuals and the Fear of Being Ordinary', *Differences: A Journal of Feminist Cultural Studies* 6(2–3): 100–26.
Miller, D. (1995) *Acknowledging Consumption*, New York: Routledge.
Mohanty, C. T. (2013) 'Transnational Feminist Crossings: On Neoliberalism and Radical Critique', *Signs* 38(4): 967–91.
Puar, J. K. (2007) *Terrorist Assemblages: Homonationalism in Queer Times*, Durham, NC: Duke University Press.
Rubin, G. (1993[1984]) 'Thinking Sex: Notes for a Radical Theory of the Politics of Sexuality', in H. Abelove, M. Barale, and D. Halperin (eds) *The Lesbian and Gay Studies Reader*, New York: Routledge, pp. 3–44.

Samois (1981) *Coming to Power: Writings and Graphics on Lesbian S/M*, Boston, MA: Alyson Publications.
Sears, A. (2005) 'Queer Anti-Capitalism: What's Left of Lesbian and Gay Liberation?', *Science and Society* 69(1): 92–112.
Sedgwick, E. K. (2003) 'Paranoid Reading and Reparative Reading, or, You're So Paranoid, You Probably Think This Essay Is About You', in *Touching Feeling: Affect, Pedagogy, Performativity*, Durham, NC: Duke University Press, pp. 123–52.
Singer, L. (1993) *Erotic Welfare: Sexual Theory and Politics in the Age of Epidemic*, London: Routledge.
Spivak, G. C. (1988) 'Can the Subaltern Speak?', in C. Nelson and C. Grossberg (eds) *Marxism and the Interpretation of Culture*, Urbana: University of Illinois Press, pp. 271–313.
Warner, M. (1993) 'Introduction', in *Fear of a Queer Planet: Queer Politics and Social Theory*, Minneapolis: University of Minnesota Press.
Weed, E. (2012) 'The Way We Read Now', *History of the Present* 2(1): 95–106.
Weiss, M. (2011) *Techniques of Pleasure: BDSM and the Circuits of Sexuality*, Durham, NC: Duke University Press.
—— (2012) '"Reinvigorating the Queer Political Imagination": A Roundtable with Ryan Conrad, Yasmin Nair, and Karma Chávez of Against Equality', *American Quarterly* 64(4): 845–9.
Wesling, M. (2013) 'Epistemologies of Empire: Sexuality and Knowledge within the Neoliberal Academy', *American Quarterly* 65(2): 291–302.
Wiegman, R. (2014) 'The Times We're In: Queer Feminist Criticism and the Reparative "Turn"', *Feminist Theory* 15(1): 4–25.
—— (2012) *Object Lessons*, Durham, NC: Duke University Press.

Part II

Intersections of sexual and economic justice

Chapter 5

The instrumentalization of sexual diversity in a civilizational frame of cosmopolitanism and tolerance

Randi Gressgård

Sexual and cultural diversity is increasingly made an ally of capitalism. As the city has become a strategic site for economic growth and global competitiveness, tolerance to sexual and cultural diversity is seen by urban strategists as an index of a city's financial success (Florida 2002). The promotion of sub-cultural spaces, such as 'gay villages' and 'cultural quarters', has become an important instrument to attract tourists, investors, businesses and creative people looking for jobs. Margit Mayer (2012: 76) notes that '[t]he new "creative" policies make use of (sub) cultural milieus in their branding strategies and harness them as location-specific assets in the intensifying interurban competition'. However, the instrumentalization of urban diversity, sexual diversity in particular, is not an issue of prosperity in a straightforwardly economic sense. Visible queer subcultures are made into desirable objects not only by reason of their market value, but also as markers of civilizational progress and justice, in opposition to non-progressive 'others'. When sexual minorities' rights and freedoms are taken as a measure of a country's successful development and modernization, sexual diversity can be discursively deployed to mark a difference between civilized and non-civilized nations and internal minority populations – without tarring the 'civilized' status of the aggressor (Brown 2006; Donald *et al.* 2009; Puar 2007; Stella 2013).

The present chapter draws attention to how marketing strategies and civilizational discourses are converging in the instrumentalization of sexual minorities in urban governance, especially in the global North. Focus of attention is on how tolerance to sexual diversity gains momentum in urban politics when it operates to reinforce social and financial success in a homogenous, linear timeframe of succession – a discursive frame of civilizational progress. While some sexual minorities are identified with success(ion), other sexual dissidents are deemed as improper and backward; and while some cities and nations are identified as economically and socially progressive, others are constituted as traditional and lagging behind. This temporal binary is, in turn, transversed in spatial imaginations of cosmopolitanism versus parochialism. The central task in the following discussion is to elucidate how these split geo-temporal imaginations are intrinsic to the language of cosmopolitanism and tolerance, and how the link between cosmopolitanism and the economic sphere in urban politics recodes social divisions as an opposition between advanced, desirable and backward, non-desirable urban diversity.[1] This raises questions about social justice in queer theory and politics. The compelling question is how to conceptualize social justice in a critical, rather than an affirmative, relationship to the geo-temporal coordinates that foster instrumentalization of sexual diversity in a civilizational frame. I shall argue that the discursive splitting that characterizes instrumentalization of urban sexual diversity – and its pernicious social effects – urges critical queer theory to focus attention on the level of representation when discussing social justice.

Conceptualizing instrumentalization of sexual diversity

One way of looking at the convergence of market values (identified with economic development) and normative values (identified with social progress) would be to assert that market politics works in tandem with socio-cultural politics to secure the health and reproduction of the nation (see e.g. Miller and Rose 2008: 40). From this point of view, instrumentalization of sexual diversity involves a governmental fabrication of 'homonormative' subjects who are willing to submit to and agree with the task of reproducing the nation, economically as well as normatively (Ahmed 2012: 163). What Lisa Duggan (2002: 179) has termed *homonormativity* denotes 'a politics that does not contest dominant heteronormative assumptions and institutions, but upholds and sustains them, while promising the possibility of a demobilized gay constituency and a privatized, depoliticized gay culture anchored in domesticity and consumption' (see Binnie, Chapter 8 in this volume).

Another, and yet not entirely different, way of looking at the relationship between market values and normative values would be to argue, in accord with Wendy Brown (2005: 46–47, 51), that the cost–benefit rationality of neoliberalism has facilitated (neoconservative) strategies of national security and imperial world politics, couched in a liberal-democratic language. Viewed from this perspective, instrumentalization of urban sexual diversity is a combined economic and national–political strategy by which economic success is intertwined with ideas of civilizational progress (associated with cosmopolitanism and liberal tolerance). Conversely, lack of economic growth potential amounts to backwardness within a civilizational frame which serves to vindicate – but also hide from view – coercive politics targeting undesirable (internal as well as external) 'others' (see e.g. Floyd 2009; Lamble 2013; Manalansan 2005; see also Kapur's discussion in Chapter 6 of this volume of how some desires are desirable while other desires are not).

1 Sara Ahmed (2012: 69) argues that diversity is a success factor as long as it is associated with desire: something valuable that can be celebrated, consumed, shared and make people feel good. Diversity is desirable to the extent that it attests to a vibrant, dynamic and tolerant atmosphere, identified with cosmopolitan localities.

In my discussion of instrumentalization of urban sexual diversity, these two approaches convene in cases where governing through individual freedom, rights and responsibility (i.e. the neoliberal formation of homonormative subjects) is accompanied by displacement and containment of non-profitable, non-normative bodies configured as backward and stationary within a geo-temporal civilizational frame. Instead of seeing cosmopolitanism as an antidote against coercive management of undesirable urban populations, I shall – in my critical review of existing studies from a predominantly Western context – depict it as a conduit of coercive power.

Urban cosmopolitan and progressive, or rural and backward

Hiram Perez (2005) deploys the term *cosmopolitan* to designate the privileged subject position associated with mobility and consumption. He notes that cosmopolitan tourism and being gay have become inextricably linked; being 'gay' requires some kind of travel (actual or imagined), and this, in turn, evokes the notion of mobility: gay becomes premised on mobility, in contrast to the stationary. In so far as the cosmopolitan subject position originates with a white, urban, leisure-class gay male, the mobility of the gay subject is enabled by privileges of class, race, citizenship and quite often also gender (185). Social acceptance, signalled by greater access to mobility for 'the good homosexual', Jasbir Puar (2002: 126) remarks, is contingent on 'queer others' who fall outside normative parameters of consumption practices, legal recognition and citizenship (see also Ossome, Chapter 7 in this volume). In a similar vein, Jon Binnie and Beverley Skeggs (2004: 43–4) argue that gay cosmopolitan discourse tends to reinforce homophobic discourses of Western gay men as hyper-mobile, affluent and privileged consumers, while reinforcing ethnocentricity and reducing indigenous cultures and discourses to specific commercial spaces. Another case in point is Gustav Visser's (2003) study of the gay-friendly space De Waterkant in Cape Town in South Africa which shows how this neighbourhood is 'cleaned up' to become racially white and profitable, even as it is branded as inclusive and tolerant (cf. Waitt *et al.* 2008: 791; see also e.g. Bell and Binnie 2004; Binnie 2004; Casey 2009; Elder 2004; Kosnick 2009a, 2009b; Puar 2002; Rushbrook 2002; Visser 2003; Woltersdorff 2011).

The above examples indicate that the nexus of mobility and consumption articulates with a linear progressive notion of time pertaining to cosmopolitanism and liberal tolerance – a timeline of civilizational and individual development (Mehta 1990). Elizabeth Freeman (2005: 57) notes that bourgeois–liberal entities from nations to individuals are defined within a narrow chronopolitics of development at once racialized, gendered and sexualized. In many cases, she argues, the neoliberal project continues to reconstruct time like the colonial state as it 'develops' new regions and depends on the idea of capital's movement as itself an inexorable progress that will eventually accommodate select women, people of colour and queers (57–8). While some queer subcultures are accommodated by way of tolerance and capitalized upon according to prevailing norms of success(ion), others are marked as backward (Halberstam 2011). It is also worth noting that the normative centre is almost always figured as metropolitan. Judith Halberstam (2005) calls into question this dynamics of queer time and place when inquiring into how rural USA is constructed as backward and gender-conservative, in contrast to urban, gender-flexible and modern environments. Whereas flexible, urban queers serve as markers of political modernity, rural queers conjure up notions of anachronism (see Halberstam 2005: 37; 2011: 94f.; cf. Love 2007). The discursive production of non-urban sexualities as 'traditional' tends to be conflated with 'non-Western' and 'uncivilized' (Halberstam 2005: 34), assigning the rural queers a place 'elsewhere' (akin to what Johannes Fabian (2002) terms 'the denial of coevalness'). Although the metropolitan gay model can be found in many cities around the world, it is, as Halberstam (2005) points out, almost always constituted in relation to non-urban, non-modern gender and sexuality models. We may deduce from this that 'urban' acts as shorthand for modern and progressive, whereas rural connotes traditional and stationary, and there seems to be a substantive interconnection – not merely a parallel – between the instrumentalization of urban sexual diversity and (neo)colonial formations of otherness: a geo-temporal splitting between 'us' and 'others', 'civilization' and 'barbarism (Gregory 2004; Halberstam 2011).

Pinkwashing and pinkwatching

An eloquent example of how instrumentalization of sexual diversity invokes a geo-temporal splitting between 'us' and 'others' is the campaign 'Brand Israel', launched in 2005 by the Israeli Foreign Ministry, the Prime Minister's Office and the Finance Ministry. This composition of sponsors signals a joint national–political and economic effort to re-brand Israel as successful and modern through the promotion of Tel Aviv as a cosmopolitan, gay-friendly city. In an interview with *The Jewish Chronicle Online*, the campaign leader, Ido Aharoni, conveys the following message to the diaspora: 'Help us celebrate Israel's success. [...] In today's world, which is highly competitive, it is no less important for Israel to be attractive than to be right' (JC.com 2010). Some queer activists and critical scholars have described this branding campaign in terms of 'pinkwashing': 'a deliberate strategy to conceal the continuing violations of Palestinians' human rights behind an image of modernity signified by Israeli gay life' (Schulman 2011).

The critique of pinkwashing shares an affinity with Puar's (2007) analysis of 'homonationalism' (informed by Duggan's concept of homonormativity), which suggests that the right to – or quality of – sovereignty is now being evaluated by how a nation treats its homosexuals. The practice of pinkwashing could be seen as a manifestation of homonationalism, and Puar has herself contributed significantly to the public debate on pinkwashing (see e.g. Puar 2010). At the same time, Puar and Maya Mikdashi (2012) caution against what has come to be known as 'pinkwatching'. They note that many of the same assumptions that animate the discourses of pinkwashing are unwittingly and sometimes intentionally reproduced in the pinkwatching efforts to challenge the basis of pinkwashing, thus reproducing a discourse of homonationalism. This is an important intervention which urges us to draw attention to the level of representation when analysing instrumentalization of sexual diversity. What concerns us here is how the campaign represents Tel Aviv as a modern, cosmopolitan and gay-friendly city, in opposition to the traditional, parochial and homophobic 'other', associated with the Palestinian population. The campaign illustrates how the issue of economic success (recalling Aharoni's message to the diaspora) is coupled with civilizational progress: urban sexual diversity is instrumentalized to accumulate capital, while at the same time creating a progressive image of the nation (even as it continues to oppress its Palestinian 'others' and discursively obliterates Palestinian queers). In this regard, the branding campaign epitomizes the interweaving of economic rationality and colonial formations described above, underpinned by liberal-democratic values associated with cosmopolitan tolerance and humanism (cf. Sabsay's argument in Chapter 10 of this volume on the colonial othering logic that continues to be central to the organization of Western sexual imaginaries). The example suggests that the polarizing geo-temporal representations are integral to – and not merely contingently bound up with – cosmopolitan humanism, which makes illiberal treatment of 'others', including colonial conquest, seem like an obvious curse of action (see e.g. El-Tayeb 2011).

Some would perhaps respond to this critique of the language of cosmopolitanism by referring to a variety of conceptions that counter the above outline. For instance, Pheng Cheah (2006: 487) distinguishes between popular notions of cosmopolitanism associated with rootlessness and a philosophical usage of the term. What is imagined in the philosophical usage, he notes, is a universal circle of belonging that involves the transcendence of the particularistic and blindly given ties of kinship and country. Provided that the cosmopolitan's universal circle of belonging embraces the whole of humanity, he goes on to argue, the popular view of cosmopolitanism as an elite form of rootlessness and a state of detachment and nomadic non-belonging is mistaken (487). By the same token, Seyla Benhabib (2004: 23–4) opposes the conflation of cosmopolitanism with detachment and non-belonging when asserting that cosmopolitan citizenship is the reclaiming and the repositioning of the universal within the framework of the local, the regional or other sites of democratic activism and engagement. Others, such as Phina Werbner (2006), advocate a so-called vernacular cosmopolitanism, arguing that 'vernacular ethnic rootedness does not negate openness to cultural difference or the fostering of a universalist civic consciousness and a sense of moral responsibility beyond the local' (Werbner 2006: 497). The latter position converges on several points with what some refer to as 'cosmopolitanism-from-below', which highlights the historical contingency of universality and reflects the standpoint of excluded 'others' (see e.g. Gilroy 2004; Mignolo 2000; Mendieta 2009). Nevertheless, I would argue that these conceptualizations of cosmopolitanism, where rootedness and otherness are regarded as central components of the term (rather than signalling a living tradition that is rooted in the past), remain entrenched in the component concepts of cosmopolitan/parochial and their geo-temporal underpinnings (see e.g. Donald *et al.* 2009; El-Tayeb 2011). As Tariq Jazeel (2011: 84f.) points out, the cosmopolitan idiom cannot avoid offering 'cosmos' as the geographical motif for living together: cosmos as aspiration to universalism and as container for difference, and hence as foundation for justice.

Cosmopolitanism and historicism

Jazeel (2011: 76f.) maintains that the central and shared tenet of disparate strands of cosmopolitan thinking is that all people, regardless of their particular affiliations, do or can belong to a single, universal community of human beings that should be cultivated: championed over and above the parochialism of the nation-state and cultural belongings associated with fixity and closure. As he sees it, the desire for some kind of world citizenship involves a 'planetary yearning' which assumes that the planet is the ground that unites humankind, but one that can only be glimpsed through moments of willing transcendence of that ground in terms of a cosmopolitan vision (79f.). It is this vision – and the accompanying ideas of escaping the shackles of time – that writes the planet as completion and universality, as cosmos (81): '[A] certain normalization of cosmopolitanism as *the* mechanic for achieving just modes of alterity in a common present fixes a particular kind of planetary space as that which gives us ways of glimpsing universal humanity and, importantly, vice versa' (Jazeel 2011: 85). Another way of putting this would be that the geographical imagination of cosmos becomes *the* evaluative standard through which differences are registered: the one, single model for social justice (84f.).

Although Jazeel does not provide us with an elaborate account of how the spatial imaginations of cosmopolitanism are connected with ideas of escaping the shackles of time, he hints at a historicist configuration by reference to Dipesh Chakrabarty's (2000) book *Provincialzing Europe*. Chakrabarty's point of departure is the argument that imaginations of socially just futures for humans usually take the idea of a single, homogenous and secular historical time for granted (15). In order to conceptualize justice beyond this universalized conception of time, it is necessary to denaturalize modern historicism, defined as objectivation of a past in the observer's time. When we act as if we could reduce the past to a nullity, Chakrabary argues, we produce what Paul de Man once called 'the true present' in terms of a *tabula rasa*, or a *terra nullius*: an expression of 'the desire of the modern political subject to practice, in pursuit of the goal of social justice, a certain degree of freedom with respect to the past' (244). Historicism promises to the human subject a degree of autonomy with respect to history, in combination with a 'decisionist' disposition that allows the autonomous subject to treat the past as a resource to draw on when criticizing the present and choosing the most wise – and just – future for humanity (247). Importantly for purposes of our argument, freedom from cultural–historical bindings is conflated with cosmopolitan transcendence of particularistic and given ties of kinship and country. And this transcendence is conceived as freedom to respect the aspects of cultural 'tradition' considered useful to building the desirable future (244, 247). Conversely, that which is considered as mired in tradition might be condemned as intolerable by virtue of being a despised throwback to an antiquated era, as opposed to a desirable object of choice. Cosmopolitan tolerance inevitably constructs 'the traditional' as an anachronistic relic of another time.

This brings us to Brown's (2006: 167f.) assertion that tolerance discourse casts culture as an external attribute to individuality and as a recourse from which the modern, autonomous individual can 'choose', in opposition to that which is given (identified with traditionalism). We could, accordingly, conceive of instrumentalization of diversity as a strategic deployment of tolerance to convert given identitarian differences – such as cultural traditions – into privatized choice and 'cool' loyalties (Nash 2009), thereby turning 'problems' into 'recourses' that can be shared and exchanged as assets. By means of tolerance, select queer subjectivities can be made compatible with norms of individual autonomy and the universalist civic consciousness associated with cosmopolitanism, while also marking the limits of tolerance vis-à-vis backward, uncivilized 'others' (cf. Jazeel 2011: 85; see also Gressgård and Jacobsen 2008).[2] This, in turn, gives legitimacy to coercive management of urban populations that are deemed outside the purview of tolerance through, for instance, spatial displacement and security measures.

The above discussion has emphasized the combined role of market forces and ideas of social progress in instrumentalization of urban sexual diversity. But the geo-temporal representations that prompt the instrumentalization of sexual diversity are far from restricted to the strategic field of urban governance. As indicated above with regard to pinkwatching and philosophical conceptualizations of cosmopolitanism, the polarizing geo-temporal representations are also prevalent in – and derive legitimacy from – scholarly literature. A case in point is a piece by Steven Seidman (2012) on the neighbourhood Hamra in Beirut which illustrates quite well how tolerance to sexual diversity is constituted in academic work as a defining feature of cosmopolitanism, in contrast to parochial otherness.

2 The autonomous subject becomes incorporated in the universal subject – as a carrier of universal subjectivity (Gressgård 2010). Individual autonomy should in this context be understood as a combination of (positive) freedom to self-fulfilment and personal identity formation on the one hand, and (negative) freedom from external obstacles to self-guided choice and action on the other (see Mahmood 2001: 207). However, while explicitly promoting individual choice and autonomy, tolerance requires and reproduces the essentualized identitarian differences it purports to overcome. This paradox lies at the heart of tolerance discourse (Brown 2006).

Cosmopolitan tolerance in civilizational discourse

Based on his empirical observations of Hamra, which is known for its public culture, Seidman (2012: 12) argues that a robust urban cosmopolitanism is characterized by the spirit of empathy and openness, cultural exchange and mixing, thus inferring that a culture of diversity and dynamic innovation would not be possible without tolerance. Seidman seems to view cosmopolitan tolerance as an index of dynamic innovation, which unwittingly paves the way for instrumentalization of urban sexual diversity. Most significantly, the cosmopolitan tolerance that Seidman (2012) identifies in Hamra is pitted against the surrounding Arab world: 'Lebanon's experiment has often been championed as a bold alternative to an Arab world otherwise mired in tradition, tribalism, and patrimonialism' (28). Recalling the historicist understanding of tradition, Seidman (10) contends that Hamra's street culture holds out the promise of some release from customary rule. These statements, which serve to constitute cosmopolitan queer culture in relation to non-urban, non-modern gender and sexuality practices, are further underscored by his geo-temporal interlinking of Hamra and Western, homo-friendly urban areas, contrasted to the Arab parts of Beirut. He writes: 'Hamra's ethno-national diversity and culture bears a closer affinity with Manhattan's East Village or East London's "Spitalfields" than to the rest of Beirut' (27). In a footnote to the latter remark, Seidman concedes that the polarizing contrast drawn between the modernity and cosmopolitanism of Hamra and the traditionalism and provincialism of other Beirut neighbourhoods is misleading to the extent that it ignores the social diversity that exists in many of Beirut's other neighbourhoods (32, n1). This attempt at modifying the polarized image can only go so far, however, since it is limited to the level of social practice. His suggestion that the contrast belies the more diverse empirical realities – which suggests that other areas of the city might also have cosmopolitan qualities – ratifies rather than dismantles the representations that animate civilizational discourses of cosmopolitanism and tolerance. I would argue that the conceptual foundation of modern historicism is reified in Seidman's attempt to give a nuance to the picture in so far as it constitutes Hamra as a normative model to all Beirut neighbourhoods, although it still has a way to go before it catches up with the cosmopolitan, gay-friendly areas of Western metropols (premised on the temporality of one-trajectory development) (cf. Chakrabarty 2000; Massad 2008; see also Sabsay's and Mascat's respective discussions in this volume of revitalized colonial and Orientalist representations, as well as Kapur's discussion of how tolerance is used to demonize the Muslim 'other').

I will linger over this subject because Seidman's account is particularly instructive as to how tolerance and cosmopolitanism are intertwined in a civilizational discourse that universalizes specific Western criteria of judgment (Jazeel 2011: 78). Brown (2006: 43f.) notes that while the original Enlightenment meaning of liberal tolerance – as formulated by John Locke and others at the end of the seventeenth century – concerned conflicts of meaning and religious belief, present-day liberal tolerance concerns identitarian differences. Tolerance is invoked when the ascriptive identities harbour orders of belief, practices or desire cast as significant enough to provoke the rejection or hostility that makes tolerance necessary. Seidman (2012: 22), for his part, does not seem to take into account this cultural specificity and historicity of identity-based models and the liberal concept of tolerance. Instead, he sees the absence of visual sexual identity communities in Beirut as an expression of a *resistance* to identity-based models of self and politics. 'This is hardly surprising', he comments, 'in a nation in which kin and sect impose enveloping and inflexible identities on all individuals' (ibid.). Evidently, the absence of visual sexual identity communities in Beirut is seen – through a historicist lens – as expression of an immature form of tolerance, circumscribed by ties of kinship and Arabic culture. Tolerance in Beirut is, according to Seidman, restricted to religious diversity and attitudes towards the West, in contrast to the counter-spaces of Hamra where 'multiple differences and a robust culture of tolerance provide a place of belonging for all sorts of dissidents who might elsewhere be less welcomed' (25). As Brown (2006: 6, 179) reminds us, liberal tolerance emerges as part of a civilizational discourse that marks an opposition and a hierarchy between a cosmopolitan 'us' and its putatively fundamentalist 'other'. And, crucially, the operations of tolerance discourse in a civilizational frame serve to legitimate liberal polities' illiberal treatment of those who are deemed outside the order for tolerance. This raises the question of how social justice can be conceptualized beyond the geo-temporal imaginations of cosmopolitan tolerance. The salient question, to paraphrase Jazeel (2011: 94), is how to conceptualize justice in a way that challenges cosmopolitanism's own injustices.

When social justice is understood as tolerant inclusion of marginalized populations (be they sexual dissidents or other minorities, in Beirut or elsewhere) into the narratives of cosmopolitan success or, alternatively, achieving 'true' cosmopolitanism by freeing the concept from its market success connotations, then the framing is given rather than politicized, and it remains intact (see Young 1990: 16). As the above discussion has suggested, however, injustice has less to do with being expelled from the narrative of success than being constituted as the undesirable 'others' upon which the success narrative is premised. From a critical queer perspective, the inhospitality experienced by undesirable minorities in the segregated city cannot be eased by policies of inclusive tolerance which expand prevalent norms rather than questioning normativity. In the following section, I shall argue that social justice involves contestation of representations that, through repetition, become ever more self-evident and normalized. It is important to mark in this context that the critique of prevalent representations is not made from the basis of some previously discovered universal ideas of the good and the just, but – as Iris Young (1990: 6) puts it – from the desiring negation that action brings to what is given: 'Each social reality presents its own unrealized possibilities, experienced as lack and desires [...] it does not have to be this way, it could be otherwise'. It is therefore of primary importance to interrogate 'the given'.

Social justice and the given

Focusing on the concept of hospitality, as deployed by Jacques Derrida (2000), Mustafa Dikeç *et al.* (2009) discuss the possibility for encounters that do not involve inclusion of 'others' into a host society or community in terms of a given social body that accommodates and tolerates the 'arrivants'. As they see it, hospitable encounters do not occur *in* space (understood as container for social life), but are themselves generative of space: 'If we think of space not only in terms of positioning or movement, but as the relations that give us our bearings [...] then there is indeed a terrain *which is given*' (12). The spatially given is precisely that which is *not* given in advance. Since we do not know yet who and what will come, the opening is an intrinsic part of the notion of hospitality (Dikeç 2002: 230). As Dikeç sees it, hospitality is a refusal to conceive of the host and the guest as pre-constituted: 'It is about the recognition that they are mutually constitutive of each other, and thus, relational and shifting' (Dikeç 2002: 239; see also Dikeç 2001). Hospitality entails a genuinely relational approach to space which emphasizes the subjects' inter-dependency and, at the same time, their heterogeneous irreducibility to unity (Massey 2005). Because relational thought dismisses the idea of space as a given unity, it throws open for question the spatial totalities and fixities woven into notions of cosmopolitanism – the logic of an overarching unity (see Hutchings 2008: 72; Jazeel 2011: 93). In this regard, the dismissal of the idea of space as a given unity does not involve cosmopolitan transcendence of given identities or ties, and mobility of space does not mean human freedom of movement within space, but signifies instead a process of becoming and continuous production whereby diverse relations make and remake different spaces.

As for temporality, Dikeç *et al.* argue – still by reference to Derrida (2000: 76) – that every act of hospitality gives time, just as it gives space. Hospitality as temporization means 'not just an event that takes place *in* time, but one that actually generates or *gives* time [...] "Time" is what the arrival of the other opens up' (Dikeç *et al.* 2009: 11). Transposed to our conceptual framework, the temporal modality in which we encounter the unknown would denounce the chronopolitics of development and the conditional incorporation of sexual diversity into the normative order by way of tolerance.[3] With respect to queer intervention,

3 Derrida (2000) conceives of tolerance as conditional hospitality, like a welcome that presupposes invitation (i.e. tolerance is extended to a guest whose identity is pre-given, which leaves no room for surprise). It should also be noted that Derrida (2001) uses the term *cosmopolitanism* to address issues of justice. However, as Jazeel (2011: 94) points out, Derrida's deployment of cosmopolitanism gestures towards its own undoing (see also Dikeç 2002). As for justice, Derrida (1992: 26) refuses to assign an ontological content to the concept, maintaining instead that the call of justice can be heard in the failure to do justice by way of force of law. Yet, as Clive Barnett (2005) points out, the ethical relation of hospitality, which involves a temporality of the unanticipated event (i.e. the surprise), does not negate the relations of justice (i.e. aligning multiple subjects and claims into a relation of identity and comparison), but exists in a parasitical–supplementary relationship to it. That is to say,

Freeman (2005: 59) maintains that 'various queer practices [...] produce form(s) of time consciousness, even historical consciousness, that can intervene upon the material damage done in the name of development'. Queer social justice could be conceived as a mode of critique that refuses 'those developmental narratives that know in advance in what a just view of human flourishing consists' (Butler 2008: 20).

Against this background, I take social justice to mean a critical practice that questions the given, homogenous time of historicism and brings to light the contingency of the given socio-spatial order. When viewed as a critical practice, social justice entails bringing the content of normative judgment under discussion – politicizing it – in order to intervene in the ideological and material conditions that create social divisions along lines such as race, class, gender and sexuality (Young 1990; see also Sabsay's discussion of critique in Chapter 10 of this volume). Criticizing normativity does not amount to dismissing any norms, regulations or principles, however; it is a matter of identifying the alterity within the norm (the otherness that is constitutive of the norm) so as to throw the normative order open to contestation and possible transfiguration (Butler 1990, 2000; Foucault 1997a, 1997b).[4]

---

an organized infrastructure of laws, rights, regulations, border and boundaries is necessary to avoid installing indifference and abstract principles of tolerance into the understanding of hospitality and responsible action. The condition of possibility for responsible action thus lies in the divisibility of borders and the finitude of boundaries, not their erasure (Derrida cited in Barnett 2005: 16). This view is reflected in the discussion below of queer critique of normativity (see also Gressgård 2010).

4 At this juncture it should be noted that even though the above review has lent support to Harvey's (2005) concept of 'accumulation by dispossession', my perspective differs in significant ways from his approach to cosmopolitanism and social justice (see Harvey 2009a). For one, Harvey (2009b) re-embraces the idea of cosmopolitanism, and could thus be criticized, as does Jazeel (2011), for reaffirming the geographical imaginations that cosmopolitanism implicates. Second, as Halberstam (2005) points out, Harvey leaves out gender and sexuality in his (materialist) approach to flexible capitalism and its implication for social justice. Similarly, Edward Soja (2010) and the authors of *Searching for the Just City* (Marcuse *et al.* 2009) focus mainly on the material conditions of urban justice. The latter volume is based on a conference that explores Susan Fainstein's work. Some commentators are critical of her argument that we have to seek social and economic just cities within the parameters of the existing economic system (e.g. Harvey, Marcuse), but none of her critics seem to question the orthodox distinction she makes between 'desires' and 'needs', which tactically leaves out sexual struggles from her reflexions on urban justice. This is most particularly the case in her latest book, *The Just City* (Fainstein 2010). Marcuse's (2012) distinction between the 'deprived' and the 'discontented' invokes a similar division between the material and the cultural, which unwittingly relegates queer struggles to the sphere of the 'merely cultural' (see Butler 1997: 36, 38). Much of the literature that draws on Henri Lefebvre's (1996) concept of the 'right to the city' considers material inequality to be in the forefront of urban (in)justice. This leads many critical scholars to call for economic redistribution and alternative institutionalizations of democratic rights without questioning rights and justice per se (cf. Young 1990: 198). One notable exception is Dikeç (2001).

Concluding remarks

Rather than shoring up my argument, I shall in conclusion point to some possible misapprehensions pertaining to the above outline. My account of the instrumentalization of sexual diversity in a civilizational frame of cosmopolitanism and tolerance runs the risk of reproducing the problem it purports to address by re-appropriating the conceptual binaries and imaginations of Western modernity. For instance, the distinction I make between 'us' and 'others' risks fortifying existing stereotypes and social hierarchies, and the mobility–freedom–progress nexus risks lending support to perspectives that conceive of spatial boundaries as impediments to freedom of movement in terms of individual mobility (see e.g. Reed 2003: 437). On that account, some would perhaps argue that my outline gestures towards a concept of justice premised on individual freedom from constraints, in accord with – rather than opposed to – the historicist scheme criticized above (akin to how pinkwatching risks reproducing the representations of pinkwashing). There are two interrelated responses to this reading. First, while I do believe that social justice requires freedom of movement for sexual minorities, as opposed to spatial containment and displacement, my discussion of instrumentalization of urban sexual diversity draws critical attention to the racialized, Eurocentric underpinnings of individual autonomy and mobility. Second, while my account does point towards a tension between mobility and containment, the present analysis underscores their constitutive interconnection rather than assuming a contradiction between displacement (materialized in the 'cleaning up' of city-spaces) on the one hand and cosmopolitanism associated with the city's civic character on the other. The above discussion suggests that the growing displacement of certain categories of people – whose discreteness is defined in practices of governance – is part and parcel of cosmopolitanism rather than supplanting cosmopolitanism (see e.g. Sassen 2010: 37). Among other things, the discussion has elucidated how the planetary geographical imagination of 'cosmos' invokes a set of normative criteria of judgment that normalizes universality as an extension of Eurocentric modernity (Jazeel 2011: 78). A queer mode of critique, on the other hand, means politicizing the content of normative judgment in order to counter oppressive effects of hegemonic representations. This form of critique entails a non-determinative notion of social justice, and it is precisely the lack of pre-given criteria of justice that gives counter-public queer world making – to paraphrase Lauren Berlant and Michael Warner (1998) – its critical force.

Acknowledgement

I would like to thank the volume editors, especially Volker Woltersdorff, for valuable feedback. I am also grateful to series editor Sarah Lamble for giving helpful comments.

References

Ahmed, S. (2012) *On Being Included: Racism and Diversity in Institutional Life*, Durham, NC: Duke University Press.

Barnett, C. (2005) 'Ways of Relating: Hospitality and the Acknowledgement of Otherness', *Progress in Human Geography* 29(5): 5–21.

Bell, D. and Binnie, J. (2004) 'Authenticating Queer Space: Citizenship Urbanism and Governance', *Urban Studies* 41(9): 1807–20.

Benhabib, S. (2004) *The Rights of Others: Aliens, Residents and Citizens*, Cambridge: Cambridge University Press.

Berlant, L. and Warner, M. (1998) 'Sex in Public', *Critical Inquiry* 24(2): 547–66.

Binnie, J. (2004) *The Globalization of Sexuality*, London: Sage.

Binnie, J. and Skeggs, B. (2004) 'Cosmopolitan Knowledge and the Production and Consumption of Sexualized Space: Manchester's Gay Village', *Sociological Review* 52: 39–61.

Brown, W. (2005) 'Neoliberalism and the End of Liberal Democracy', in *Edgework: Critical Essays on Knowledge and Politics*, Princeton, NJ: Princeton University Press, pp. 37–59.

—— (2006) *Regulating Aversion: Tolerance in the Age of Identity and Empire*, Princeton, NJ: Princeton University Press.

Butler, J. (1990) *Gender Trouble: Feminism and the Subversion of Identity*, New York: Routledge.

—— (1997): 'Merely Cultural', *Social Text* 52/53: 265–77.

—— (2000): 'What is Critique? An Essay on Foucault's Virtue', Cambridge University Raymond Williams Lecture; longer version reprinted in D. Ingram (ed.) (2002) *The Political: Readings in Continental Philosophy*, London: Blackwell. Available online at www.egs.edu/faculty/judith-butler/articles/what-is-critique (accessed 24 November 2014).

—— (2008) 'Sexual Politics, Torture, and Secular Time', *British Journal of Sociology* 59(1): 1–23.

Casey, M. (2009) 'The Queer Unwanted and Their Undesirable "Otherness"', in K. Browne, J. Lim and G. Brown (eds) *Geographies of Sexualities: Theory, Practices and Politics*, Farnham: Ashgate, pp. 125–36.

Chakrabarty, D. (2000) *Provincializing Europe: Postcolonial Thought and Historical Difference*, Princeton, NJ: Princeton University Press.

Cheah, P. (2006) 'Cosmopolitanism', *Theory, Culture and Society* 23(2–3): 486–96.

Derrida, J. (1992) 'Force of Law: The "Mystical Foundation of Authority"', in D. Cornell, M. Rosenfeld and D. G. Carlson (eds) *Deconstruction and the Possibility of Justice*, New York: Routledge, pp. 3–67.

—— (2000) *Of Hospitality*, trans. R. Bowlby, Stanford, CA: Stanford University Press.

—— (2001) *On Cosmopolitanism and Forgiveness*, trans. M. Dooley and M. Hughes, London: Routledge.

Dikeç, M. (2001) 'Justice and the Spatial Imagination', *Environment and Planning A* 33(10): 1785–805.

—— (2002) 'Pera Peras Poros: Longings for Space of Hospitality', *Theory, Culture and Society* 19(1–2): 227–47.

Dikeç, M., Clark, N. and Barnett, C. (2009) 'Extending Hospitality: Giving Space, Taking Time', *Paragraph* 32(1): 1–14.

Donald, S. H., Kofman, E. and Kevin, C. (2009) 'Introduction: Processes of Cosmopolitanism and Parochialism', in S. H. Donald, E. Kofman and C. Kevin (eds) *Branding Cities: Cosmopolitanism, Parochialism, and Social Change*, New York: Routledge, pp. 1–13.

Duggan, L. (2002) 'The New Homonormativity: The Sexual Politics of Neoliberalism', in R. Castronovo and D. D. Nelson (eds) *Materializing Democracy: Toward a Revitalized Cultural Politics*, Durham, NC: Duke University Press, pp. 175–94.

Elder, G. S. (2004) 'Love for Sale: Marketing Gay Male P/leisure Space in Contemporary Cape Town, South Africa', in L. Nelson and J. Seager (eds) *A Companion to Feminist Geography*, Malder, MA: Blackwell, pp. 578–89.

El-Tayeb, F. (2011) *European Others: Queering Ethnicity in Postnational Europe*, Minneapolis: University of Minnesota Press.

Fabian, J. (2002/1983) *Time and the Other: How Anthropology Makes its Objects*, New York: Columbia University Press.

Fainstein, S. (2010) *The Just City*, Ithaca, NY: Cornell University Press.

Florida, R. (2002) *The Rise of the Creative Class*, New York: Basic Books.

Floyd, K. (2009) *The Reification of Desire: Toward a Queer Marxism*, Minneapolis: University of Minnesota Press.

Foucault, M. (1997a) 'What Is Enlightenment?', in L. Hochroth and S. Lotringer (eds) *The Politics of Truth*, Los Angeles, CA: Semiotext(e), pp. 101–34.

—— (1997b) 'What Is Critique?', in L. Hochroth and S. Lotringer (eds) *The Politics of Truth*, Los Angeles, CA: Semiotext(e), pp. 23–82.

Freeman, E. (2005) 'Time Binds, or, Erotohistoriography', *Social Text* 23(3–4): 57–68.

Gilroy, P. (2004) *After Empire: Multiculture or Postcolonial Melancholia*, London: Routledge.

Gregory, D. (2004) *The Colonial Present*, Oxford: Blackwell.

Gressgård, R. (2010) *Multicultural Dialogue: Dilemmas, Paradoxes, Conflicts*, New York: Berghahn Books.

Gressgård, R. and Jacobsen, C. (2008) 'Krevende toleranse: Islam og homoseksualitet' [Demanding tolerance: Islam and homosexuality], *Tidsskrift for kjønnsforskning* 32(2): 22–39.

Halberstam, J. (2005) *In a Queer Time and Space: Transgender Bodies, Subcultural Lives*, New York: New York University Press.

—— (2011) *The Queer Art of Failure*, Durham, NC: Duke University Press.

Harvey, D. (2005) *The New Imperialism*, Oxford: Oxford University Press.

—— (2009a) *Social Justice and the City*, revised edition, London: University of Georgia Press.

—— (2009b) *Cosmopolitanism and the Geographies of Freedom*, New York: Columbia University Press.

Hutchings, K. (2008) *Time and World Politics: Thinking the Present*, Manchester: Manchester University Press.

Jazeel T. (2011) 'Spatializing Difference beyond Cosmopolitanism: Rethinking Planetary Futures', *Theory, Culture and Society* 28(5): 75–97.

JC.com (2010) 'Diplomat's Bid to "Re-brand" Israel'. *The Jewish Chronicle Online*. Available online at www.thejc.com/news/israel-news/33195/diplomats-bid-re-brand-israel (accessed 24 November 2014).

Kosnick, K. (2009a) 'Cosmopolitan Capital or Multicultural Community? Reflections on the Production and Management of Differential Mobilities in Germany's Capital

City', in M. Nowicka and M. Rovisco (eds) *Cosmopolitanism in Practice*, Farnham: Ashgate, pp. 161–80.
—— (2009b) 'Conflicting Mobilities: Cultural Diversity and City Branding in Berlin', in S. H. Donald, E. Kofman and C. Kevin (eds) *Branding Cities: Cosmopolitanism, Parochialism, and Social Change*, New York: Routledge, pp. 28–44.
Lamble, S. (2013) 'Queer Necropolitics and the Expanding Carceral State: Interrogating Sexual Investments in Punishment', *Law Critique* 24(3): 229–53.
Lefebvre, H. (1996/1969) *Writing on Cities*, trans. and ed. E. Kofman and E. Lebas, Oxford: Blackwell.
Love, H. (2007) *Feeling Backward: Loss and the Politics of Queer History*, Cambridge, MA: Harvard University Press.
Mahmood, S. (2001) 'Feminist Theory, Embodiment, and the Docile Agent: Some Reflections on the Egyptian Islamic Revival', *Cultural Anthropology* 16(2): 202–36.
Manalansan, M. (2005) 'Race, Violence, and Neoliberal Spatial Politics in the Global City', *Social Text* 23(3–4): 141–55.
Marcuse, P. (2012) 'Whose Right(s) to What City?', in N. Brenner, P. Marcuse and M. Mayer (eds) *Cities for People, Not for Profit: Critical Urban Theory and the Right to the City*, New York: Routledge, pp. 24–41.
Marcuse, P., Connolly, J., Novy, J., Olivo, I., Potter, C. and Steil, J. (eds) (2009) *Searching for the Just City: Debates in Urban Theory and Practice*, New York: Routledge.
Massad, J. (2008) *Desiring Arabs*, Chicago, IL: University of Chicago Press.
Massey, D. (2005) *For Space*, London: Sage.
Mayer, M. (2012) 'The "Right to the City" in Urban Social Movements', in N. Brenner, P. Marcuse and M. Mayer (eds) *Cities for People, Not for Profit: Critical Urban Theory and the Right to the City*, New York: Routledge.
Mehta, U. (1990) 'Liberal Strategies of Exclusion', *Politics and Society* 18(4): 427–54.
Mendieta, E. (2009) 'From Imperial to Dialogical Cosmopolitanism', *Ethics and Global Politics* 2(3): 241–58.
Mignolo, W. (2000) 'The Many Faces of Cosmo-polis: Border Thinking and Critical Cosmopolitanism', *Public Culture* 12(3): 721–48.
Miller, P. and Rose, N. (2008) *Governing the Present: Administering Economic, Social and Personal Life*, Cambridge: Polity Press.
Nash, K. (2009) 'Between Citizenship and Human Rights', *Sociology* 43(6): 1067–83.
Perez, H. (2005) 'You Can Have My Brown Body and Eat It, Too!', *Social Text* 23(3–4): 171–91.
Puar, J. (2002) 'Circuits of Queer Mobility Tourism, Travel, and Globalization', *GLQ: A Journal of Lesbian and Gay Studies* 8(1–2): 101–37.
—— (2007) *Terrorist Assemblages: Homonationalism in Queer Times*, Durham, NC: Duke University Press.
—— (2010) 'Israel's Gay Propaganda War', *The Guardian*. Available online at www.guardian.co.uk/commentisfree/2010/jul/01/israels-gay-propaganda-war/print (accessed 24 November 2014).
Puar, J. and Mikdashi, M. (2012) 'Pinkwatching and Pinkwashing: Interpretation and Its Discontents', *Jadalyya*. Available online at www.jadaliyya.com/pages/index/6774 (accessed 24 November 2014).
Reed, C. (2003) 'We're from Oz: Marking Ethnic and Sexual Identity in Chicago', *Environment and Planning D: Society and Space* 21: 425–40.

Rushbrook, D. (2002) 'Cities, Queer Space, and the Cosmopolitan Tourist', *GLQ: A Journal of Lesbian and Gay Studies* 8(1–2): 183–206.
Sassen, S. (2010) 'When the City Itself Becomes a Technology of War', *Theory, Culture and Society* 27(6): 33–50.
Schulman (2011) 'A Documentary Guide to Pinkwashing', *Pretty Queer*. Available online at http://recapsmagazine.com/rethink/pink-washing-a-documentary-guide-by-sarah-schulman (accessed 10 December 2014).
Seidman, S. (2012) 'The Politics of Cosmopolitan Beirut: From the Stranger to the Other', *Theory, Culture and Society* 29(3): 3–36.
Soja, E. (2010) *Seeking Spatial Justice*, Minneapolis: University of Minnesota Press.
Stella, F. (2013) 'Queer Space, Pride and Shame in Moscow', *Slavic Review* 72(3): 458–80.
Visser, G. (2003) 'Gay Men, Tourism and Urban Space: Reflections on Africa's "Gay Capital"', *Tourism Geographies* 5(2): 168–89.
Waitt, G., Markwell, K. and Gorman-Murray, A. (2008) 'Challenging Heteronormativity in Tourism Studies: Locating Progress', *Progress in Human Geography* 32(6): 781–800.
Werbner, P. (2006) 'Vernacular Cosmopolitanism', *Theory, Culture and Society* 23(2–3): 496–8.
Woltersdorff, V. (2011) 'Paradoxes of Precarious Sexualities', *Cultural Studies* 25(2): 164–82.
Young, I.M. (1990) *Justice and the Politics of Difference*, Princeton, NJ: Princeton University Press.

Chapter 6

Unruly desires, gay governance and the makeover of sexuality in postcolonial India

Ratna Kapur

The contemporary moment in queer activism in postcolonial India is marked by two contradictory events. The first is the 2009 historic victory in the Naz Foundation decision where the Delhi High Court decided to read down the provisions of section 377 of the Indian Penal Code, 1860, that criminalizes sodomy, holding that it was inapplicable to consensual adult sexual relationships.[1] There was jubilation in the courtroom and celebration in the streets. In the days following the High Court's pronouncement, gays and lesbians around India openly declared their sexuality and interpreted the victory as enabling marriage. Couples began to take vows and exchange garlands in a ritual that marked their passage into acceptance and legitimacy.

At one level there seemed little to critique about the decision – homosexuality was finally out of the closet. However, within a short period various social and religious conservative groups expressed disapproval and disappointment over the decision. And some filed an appeal against the decision to the Supreme Court of India, arguing that the High Court's verdict eroded Indian cultural values and undermined governing sexual norms that are tethered to the very identity of the Indian nation (Kapur 2005b; Chatterjee 1989; Mondal 2002). In December 2013, the Supreme Court reversed the High Court decision, holding not only that was there insufficient evidence that the provision was used to target homosexuals, but that the community constituted a 'miniscule fraction' of the population, implicitly suggesting that it was therefore undeserving of either constitutional protection or serious consideration given the small number of prosecutions under the provision. The recurrent references to 'unnatural sex' and 'unnatural means' in relation to sex scattered throughout the decision, which was producing in the Court's words a 'sexual crisis', reveal the normative assumptions about sex and sexuality on which the decision was based. The Court held that any change in the law was to be brought about by Parliament and not the courts. In the process, the Court re-criminalized homosexuals, putting a powerful

1 *Naz Foundation v Government of the National Capital Territory of Delhi and Others*, Delhi High Court, July 2, 2009, MANU/DE/0869/2009.

tool of discrimination back into the hands of the law enforcement agencies. The precariousness of unruly desires is reflected in this process of re-criminalization by the judiciary, where a liveable life is one that includes legal recognition and the juridical entitlements that flow from such recognition (Butler 2004, 2009). However, outside the courtroom battles, representations of queer sexuality have continued to proliferate – in academic scholarship and public debates, in cinema, on the streets and in popular culture.

The varied responses to unruly desires have compelled a deeper interrogation of understandings of justice. Is the legal domain the primary site through which justice can be secured? What role do non-legal sites such as the market, family, culture, and religion play in the pursuit of justice? How do we know whether the justice sought has been secured? Through the acquisition of rights? Social and cultural recognition and acceptability? Participation in the market as legitimate consumer subjects? Is normative acquiescence a primary condition for securing justice? How does normative sexuality operate to produce a hierarchy of citizens – those who belong and those who do not, or who are designated as lesser citizens entitled to fewer rights or denied access to justice altogether (Cossman 2007; Bell and Binnie 2005)? Does justice rest in excavating normative sexuality and unmasking its exclusionary boundaries and fixed understandings of male/female, masculine/feminine, against which it operates? The celebration following the 2009 *Naz Foundation* judgment, contrasted with the displays of anguish and disappoint after the 2013 reversal, seemed to acknowledge the law as emblematic of justice for sexual minorities. Yet what exactly was 'won' or 'lost' remains contested.

The opening up of the market in postcolonial India has witnessed a proliferation of sexual representations in celluloid and the public space. Representation in and through the market may be offering one of a number of competing sites for securing justice that sits in contrast to the one offered in and through law. But the move towards the market has its risks. In the search for greater public displays of non-normative sexuality and sexual identities comes the pull away from the state, greater reliance on self-governance and responsibility, together with a de-politicization and privatization of non-normative sexualities (D'Emelio 1993; Joshi 2012: 431–8). As Jamila Mascat argues in Chapter 2 of this volume, consumption and commodification of the sexual and racial 'other' may lead to the disempowerment of the erotic. Gays and lesbians are moving towards a new normativity that is not necessarily disruptive or transformative, nor is it generative of a counter-public sphere.

The story of sexuality in contemporary India needs to be framed within the logic of the colonial encounter and contemporary economic processes. I discuss how this framing helps in understanding the issue of homosexuality within a postcolonial context, namely India, and the tensions produced in the area of queer desire between the potentially liberating influences of the market in the public arena and the continued constraints imposed by dominant cultural, sexual, and familial norms that inform the legal regulation of sexual subjectivity. The modern state has its antecedents in the colonial encounter, which was not structurally designed to secure justice for the colonial subject, but to govern the subject in a specific way (Haldar 2007: 1–17). Its civilizing zeal was tied to a notion of justice that was linked to the capacity to reason and civilizational maturity that complied with a Eurocentric understanding of the rational subject (Mehta 1999; Goswami 2004).

This chapter analyses whether queer desire has been liberated from the postcolonial closet and, if so, how the processes of the market and law have been implicated in bringing about the emergence and legibility of queer desire. I explore the understanding of justice that informs such processes and how these processes have produced equivocal victories in terms of bringing justice to highly stigmatized identities and the practices associated with them. While the re-criminalization of homosexuality exposes the precariousness of the sexual subject and unruly desires, I discuss how victory in the courtroom and greater visibility in and through the market are results that cannot necessarily be understood within the discourse of emancipation or liberation. They have resulted in instantiating queer desire into a linear, regulatory framework – designed to cabin and confine, rather than to liberate or emancipate. In both instances, justice operates to restrain homosexuals to the borders of heteronormativity. This restraint is partly produced in and through the discourse of tolerance in law combined with the makeover of homosexuality produced in and through the consumptive market.

This chapter is divided into three parts. In the first part, I briefly set out the various discursive framings of counter-heteronormative unruly desires in postcolonial India, through a distinct set of terms: LGBT (lesbian, gay, bisexual, transgender), queer, and sexual subaltern. The discussion sets out some of the conceptual tangles encountered in discussions about desire through the terminology and argues in favour of the adoption of more critical framings for the purposes of conceptual clarity and pursuing the subversive possibilities of unruly desires. In the second part, I briefly discuss the proliferation of homoerotic imagery, sexual representations, and sex talk that has occurred with the opening up of the market as well as the various legal challenges pursued in and through counter-heteronormative desire in postcolonial India (John 2008: 560–6; Vanita and Kidwai 2000; Bose and Bhattacharyya 2007). I argue that these processes at one level provide a liberating moment for the emergence of queer sexualities, while at another level operate to contain and confine such desires within governing norms. In the third part of the chapter I draw attention to some of the contradictory results produced in the sexual subjects' engagements with the market and law. I argue that the market, with its focus on self-governance and responsibility, and the focus on tolerance in legal advocacy as well as the ever-present fear of re-recriminalization combine to regulate and discipline rather than liberate sexual desire or bring about justice in terms of securing legibility on the same terms as non-queers. While the possibility of full legibility continues to exist, it can only be achieved through what Lisa Duggan has described as the new homonormativity (2002: 179). According to Duggan, this possibility is secured through compliance with heteronormative assumptions and institutions, and participation in the market as consumers. The result is the de-politicization, privatization, and domestication of the gay constituency, rather than the production of a transformative understanding of justice (Bell and Binnie 2004; Halberstam 2005).

LGBT, sexual subalterns, or queer desire

A distinct set of terms has framed contemporary debates on non-normative sexualities: LGBT, queer, and sexual subaltern. In this section, I argue how the terms adopted are implicitly linked to a particular vision of justice. During the course of the 1980s and 1990s there was a good deal of writing on homosexuality, mostly in the form of anthologies, memoirs, and fictions designed to validate the existence of lesbians and gays in Indian history and Indian culture through the mode of excavation (Rati 1993; Vanita 2002; Sukthankar 1999; Pattanaik 2002).[2] Ensuring that homosexuality emerged as legitimate, familiar, and respectable required excavation work and a tracing of this subject in some long-lost ancient Indian cultural past. The work of Ruth Vanita and Salim Kidwai was foremost in locating lesbian and gay identity within the historical context of India, drawing on what they describe as a 2000-year-old tradition of homosexuality. The authors consciously chose not to deploy the term 'queer' in their work because it was too wide, included behaviour 'from fetishism to exhibitionism' and also associated with unconventional or strange sexual behaviour (Vanita and Kidwai 2001: xxi). Their work focused on identity and the recuperation of lesbian and gay identities within the context of Indian culture as something that was admirable and respectable.

A central underlying impulse informing the mode of cultural excavations of same-sex desire in India is the effort to disassociate or delink homosexuality from its Western moorings and situate it within the national and historical consciousness of postcolonial India (Puri 1999: 176–83). Homosexuality is not a Western contaminant, but the phobias associated with homosexuality are Western imports introduced through legal codes and medical texts as well as a Victorian sensibility (Puri 1999: 184). This mode of recovery is located within a heterosexual/homosexual binary, and seeks to recuperate a distinct homosexual voice within the historical narrative of the Indian nation.

However, in the contemporary moment a politics and scholarship based on the mode of recovery is confronted with the challenge of hegemonic Euro-American signifiers for same-sex love/non-heterosexual desire that are fast becoming the prescribed blueprint across the world. Massad refers to this move as the production of the 'gay international' (Massad 2002: 361). The prescriptive gay subject is

2 See, however, one exception in the Rati edited collection by Nayan Shah, who challenges an excavation mode of engagement with the colonial archives as a way to legitimize the existence of homosexuality in India (Shah 1993: 113–32, at 122–4).

based on a specific assumption including the idea that this subject exists in opposition to heterosexuality and that the fulfilment of same-sex desire and identity can be found through public visibility and a departure from the heteronormative structures and patriarchal institutions of the family. This powerful articulation of the end goals of same-sex desire marginalizes and de-legitimates other articulations and subjectivities in non-Euro American contexts (Rao 2011: 43–66). The ultimate performance of this identity rests in an 'out of the closet' LGBT identity pursued by LGBT human rights advocates that is prescribed as the antidote for all Third World settings. A strategy based on the recovery of same-sex desire is not necessarily up to the task of countering the newly emerging hegemonic, colonizing queer. Its quest for a gay subject may serve to legitimate homosexual identity within the national narrative. While this perspective is culturally positioned against Eurocentricism, it is unable to distinguish itself from the prescriptive gay international that is framing the conversation on same-sex desire in the international legal arena. It is both distinct and not.

The term 'sexual subaltern' seeks to capture understandings of counter-heteronormative desire in a postcolonial context (Kapur 2005a: 20–8). The subaltern is a theoretical device derived from subaltern studies, which is a particular form of historiography that has emerged in South Asia, and gives voice to those who have been left outside historical narratives produced by colonial or nationalist writers (Sarkar 1997: 82–108; Guha 1982). The project, as it emerged in India, was initially based on the position and location of the subaltern subject and of writing history from below (Guha 1982: vii–viii; Sarkar 1985). In the 1980s a new focus sought to challenge all traditions and disciplines defined within the logic and rationale of the Enlightenment project, including unmasking the universal subject of liberal rights discourse (Chakrabarty and Bhabha 2002; Chakrabarty 1995; O'Hanlon 2000; Mignolo 2000; Bhabha 1994: 171–97).

The term 'sexual subaltern' as situated within this later tradition is intended to bring together the disparate range of sexual minorities within postcolonial India without suggesting that it is either a homogenized or stable category. The term is at one level intended to capture the extraordinary range and diversity of the counter-heteronormative movement in India, which includes a vast array of non-LGBT sexual identities: *kush*, queer, *hijra*, *kothis*, *panthis*, and many more (Sherry 2005; Khan 2001). It also includes sexual practices and behaviours such as adult and consensual pre-marital, extra-marital, non-marital, auto-erotic/masturbatory, promiscuous, and paid-for sex, as well as MSM (men who have sex with men). This fluidity and diversity of identities and practices cannot be captured within an LGBT framework based on fixed and essentialized identities. The sexual subaltern performs a normatively disruptive role and brings into crisis the architecture of normalized and naturalized sexuality, exposing its contingency in a postcolonial context.

Similarly, the term 'queer', which has its origins primarily in Western scholarship, has been used in a number of complex and contradictory ways (Sedgwick

1990; Butler 1990; Rubin 1993: 3–44).[3] Its use has become increasingly visible and prominent in legal advocacy as well as in a number of postcolonial scholarly and theoretical texts. In India, there is no consistent meaning ascribed to the term 'queer'. For example, Narrain and Gupta present an argument for recovering 'queer' voices from a putatively more tolerant pre-colonial era when it was ostensibly not subject to official disciplinary regulation. They deploy the term interchangeably with LGBT, which is associated with fixed notions of identity (Narrain and Gupta 2011: xi–lvi; Narrain 2011b: 253–7). At the same time, these scholars also invoke the term 'queer' in ways that are intended to perform a more critical function – through queer intersections – where queer aligns with other excluded subaltern voices (Narrain and Bhan 2005: 3–6; Narrain 2011a: 1–25, at 15–17, 21–22). Queer is thus delinked from the subject and is viewed in practices that seek out alternative ways of living, without subjectivity being expressive of an internal preference or orientation, or a political programme that advocates on how to live (Sedgwick 1993; Giffney 2004). The critical capacities of queer have relevance within a postcolonial context as its critical guise is closely aligned with postcolonial theory and the subaltern project. It is the critical features of queer as a politics of love transgressing social norms and dominant heteronormativity that inscribe it with disruptive and transformative possibilities.

The critical capacities of the terms 'sexual subaltern' and 'queer' reflect a rejection of the mode of 'recovery' or 'excavation' in the literature. As a number of scholars have argued, the mode of recovery fails to engage with the complexities of nationalist as well as the neo-colonizing moves that enact erasure of same-sex desire in the postcolonial context. Arondekar's work on the search for the voice of the sexual subject in the official archives argues that such retrieval is impossible (Arondekar 2009). Gayatri Gopinath also dislodges the fixed, prescriptive understandings of same-sex desire using a 'queer diaspora' framework and her specific focus on queer female diasporic subjectivity in popular culture (Gopinath 2005: 6–7). She deploys queer to disrupt homonormative imaginings and prescriptions of same-sex desire or the 'Rainbow Flag' worldview, which erase possibilities of understanding the relationship between the diaspora, nationalism, and the processes of transnational capitalism. She illustrates how such formations are both capable of migrating and pollinating other cultural spaces in ways that do not fit within a homosexual/heterosexual, male/female binary and an uninterrogated, identity-centred LGBT politics.

Similarly, Jasbir Puar's work also complicates the deployment of queer in relation to assemblages as opposed to binaries or excavations. Puar tracks how queer can be deployed in ways that are complicit in dominant formations of sexuality

3 For example, Judith Butler discusses how *queer* has historically been deployed as a homophobic expression for the purposes of shaming. She interrogates *queer*'s capacity to be taken up and reclaimed, and critiques the ways in which the term ends up enforcing overlapping divisions between who is entitled to use the term and with what meaning (Butler 1993).

(Puar 2010: 121–2). She proposes the term 'queer assemblages', both heteronormative and homonormative, for analysing the indoctrination of the sexual subject into the belief in the superiority and exceptionalism of the US as a nation and a culture. Puar moves away from understanding the construction of postcolonial sexual subjectivities as based on a thesis of sexual repression versus sexual liberation.

The contributions of these scholars mark important interventions in how queer has been and can be deployed in a critical manner in a postcolonial context. They trace the ways in which the techniques of gender and sexuality operate within the matrix of power arrangements and use a queer lens to understand the work that is being done by these techniques. In the remainder of this chapter I use the terms 'queer' and 'sexual subaltern' in their critical guises. These terms offer possibilities for framing desire in ways that are provocative and disruptive, while also complicating our understandings of justice beyond a pursuit of more law and more rights for sexual minorities.

Representing unruly desires

Within postcolonial India, sexuality and sexual desire have also always been a site of cultural contests. Culture and sexuality have both been sutured together as a result of the colonial encounter. In the nineteenth century, nationalists safeguarded women's sexual purity and confined it to the home, opposing any attempts by the colonial power to intervene in this space. The home and women's sexuality represented the purity of Indian culture and was constitutive of the emerging Indian nation (Chatterjee 1989: 233–53; Mani 1989: 117–48; Sarkar 1997). This backdrop informs the contemporary controversies and explains why sexual controversies invariably also erupt as cultural controversies.

In the 1990s, as India began pursuing a package of neo-liberal reforms to become a global player, there was heightened anxiety over the emerging and proliferating discourses of sexual desire and agency that implicated the very identity of the Indian nation and its distinction from the West. The Hindu nationalists, who seek to reconstitute India as a Hindu state, routinely attacked heterosexual couples celebrating Valentine's Day or stores selling Valentine's Day cards for being Western contaminants. Police raided the new culture of cyber cafes for clients surfing for pornography, or routinely launched 'clean-up' operations in parks visited by heterosexual couples in large urban centres as well as to harass gays. There were attacks against public displays of affection and celluloid representations of the 'kiss' sequence (which has displaced the wedding as the climactic moment in Bollywood cinema), as well as increased surveillance of female sexual conduct in public (*India Today* 2009; Garg 2009). The Hindu nationalists, key players in the movement to purge India and Indians of sexual agency and sex talk, are intent on degrading sexuality and banishing any overt expression of it outside the model of the good Hindu wife and heteronormative arrangements. In the process, they have projected outward expressions of this degraded sexuality onto its 'others', such as Muslims, sex workers, migrants and homosexuals (Bacchetta 1999). And they have used the legal provisions of obscenity, and the constitutional restriction on the right to free speech and expression that involves offending public morality to pursue their agenda.

Sex per se invites cries of 'Indian culture being in danger or under threat of extinction', especially when it comes to women. One well-known example involved the public controversy in 1998 over the diasporic film *Fire*, which rendered same-sex desire intelligible through the performance of queer femininity between two women married to two utterly resistible and undesirable men in the postcolonial domestic space (Gopinath 2005: 155). The film cleared the Censor Board without any cuts, but the mobs of the Hindu Right disrupted screenings in a number of major cities in India through an alarming destruction of the property of cinema houses where the film was screened as well as attacks against members of the viewing audiences (Jain and Rawal 1998; Swami 1998/1999; Gopinath 1998). Despite judicial intervention, many cinemas did not subsequently screen the film for fear of inviting further destruction of their property or harm to their patrons.

Celluloid and popular culture remain an important site on which queer desire has emerged to challenge some of the dominant sexual, familial, and cultural norms that have defined the borders of sexual legitimacy as well as to counter some of the state and non-state efforts that seek to confine or censor alternative sexual expression and representations. Some serious representations include *My Brother Nikhil* (2005), a small-budget film sympathetically depicting the discrimination and homophobia experienced by an HIV patient in contemporary Indian society as well as *Phir Milenge* (*We Will Meet Again*), a 2004 Bollywood portrayal of a single woman who contracts HIV after a one-night stand of unprotected sex.

In 2008 the Bollywood blockbuster *Dostana* (*Male Friendship*) pulled gay sexuality from its erratic margins and served up a full-frontal gay performance. We witnessed the makeover of two of the hottest superstars in Bollywood cinema – Abhishek Bachchan and John Abraham – into the most unlikely 'queer folk'. In the film, Sameer and Kunal, two straight guys, present themselves as a gay couple in order to secure a lease in a penthouse apartment in downtown Miami, which they share with the hot, ambitious, and high-powered editor of a glossy high-end fashion magazine – Neha, played by Priyanka Chopra, who oozes the confident sexuality of the '*desi* (Indian) girl' or the 'new Indian woman' in the global market. They also learn that their gay façade makes them eligible to be fast-tracked through the US immigration process and claim that ever-coveted green card. Through a series of twists, this queering of the Bollywood hunks receives its ultimate seal of approval from Ama, Sameer's mother, who, after much hand wringing expressed in the song 'Mama's boy has gotten spoilt', blesses the relationship in a Hindu wedding choreographed through one of Bollywood's signature song and dance sequences. While inclusion and assimilation appeared to be the end goal for the two superstars, the pursuit of these goals involves a complete makeover of heterosexuality during the course of the film.

Throughout the film the two actors are on the frontlines of defending masculinity. Beef and brawn are on display for the heroine and no doubt also for the spectator, male and female. These men are not sexual strangers in this celluloid universe. Their sexuality is centred on screen, as familiar, loveable, and even desirable. Ultimately they are forced to confess their betrayal and reveal their 'true' sexuality credentials to Neha. She forgives them only after they perform a very public thirty-second lip-locking kiss sequence with one another. The film closes with a pleasurable recollection of the kiss by both heroes, putting into question the certainty of their heterosexual status.

The explosion in sexual imagery has been accompanied by a simultaneous proliferation of rights talk in favour of greater sexual expression in public, as well as recognition of more heterogeneous sexual identities. In 2009 the Delhi High Court stayed criminal proceedings against a young married heterosexual couple charged with criminal obscenity for kissing in public, holding that such conduct amounted to nothing more than an 'expression of love' (Garg 2009). Attacks by right-wing activists on women drinking in bars gave rise to an internet-driven pink *chaddi* (underwear) campaign, calling on women of all ages, class, and religious and sexual dispositions to inundate the headquarters of the Hindu Right with pink underwear (Kapur 2012).[4] In 2014 transgendered persons were recognized by the Indian Supreme Court as equal citizens entitles to the same human and fundamental rights. And in 2009, gay and lesbian groups successfully challenged the scope of section 377 which criminalized sodomy, limiting its application only to non-consensual sex.[5] While the Supreme Court reversal of the 2009 decision has diminished the legal rights of gays and lesbians by continuing to subject them to the surveillance mechanisms of the criminal law, the intellectual, cultural, and representational spaces continue to proliferate.

These moments have shifted the goal posts on what constitutes good sex and bad sex, legitimate and illegitimate desire (Rubin 1993: 3–44). Eroticism and unruly desires are claiming a space in law, celluloid, and on the streets, and efforts to eliminate or incarcerate these are being seriously challenged as violations of human rights. The question is whether sexual subalterns in India are getting closer to realizing the promise of justice – a goal that seemed unrealizable only a decade ago? Yet this teleological progressive reading of how sexual subalterns are in the process of becoming full and equal members of the Indian polity in the process of globalization makes invisible the heavy costs inflicted in securing membership, including at the expense of transgression as well as the precariousness

4 See '"Pink Panty" Women Target Extremist Right Wing Indian Leader', 9 February 2009. Available online at www.foxnews.com/story/0,2933,490690,00.html (accessed 12 January 2012).

5 Section 377 states as follows: *Unnatural sexual offences:* Whoever voluntarily has carnal intercourse against the order of nature with any man, woman or animal, shall be punished with imprisonment [...] Which may extend to ten years, and shall also be liable to fine. Explanation – Penetration is sufficient to constitute the carnal intercourse necessary to the offence described in this section.

of legal victories. In the remainder of this chapter, I revisit and unpack these moments to trace the complex trajectory of justice in relation to unruly desires and examine what work justice does and the terms on which it is secured.

Gay governance

The question arises whether the legal challenges, rights advocacy, civil dissidence, and increased sex talk have actually furthered the cause of sexual subalterns. Are unruly desires being liberated through such recognition or are they being subjected to greater self-regulation, self-discipline, and responsibility through the market that is re-privatizing the domestic arena and calling for greater self-governance and responsibility as legible subjects or citizens (Cossman 2007: 14–20)?

This model of governance was on display in *Dostana*. The apartment that Sameer and Kunal shared with Neha was exquisitely modern, adorned with all the accoutrements of stylish living. They drove a flaming-pink vintage Chevrolet convertible, owned Harley-Davidson motorbikes, and their clothes and cell phones were all branded, luxurious, and exquisite. Almost all the characters in this film were rich and consumption-oriented. These gay men and women inhabited the universe of private enterprise: from the glitzy bars to the fashion magazine offices or the swimwear shoots where Kunal clicks away as a fashion photographer. The gay subject emerges as a privatized consumer of all these spaces and services.

In many ways the film was a performance of the emerging consumer citizen in India, encouraging the queer subject to participate in a shopping spree of luxury brand names, latest gadgets, and haute couture fashion styles. The marketized space produces the status and identity of each of the participants, where consumption rather than performance of a subversive sexuality is the core feature. Those who critiqued the film for reinforcing gay stereotypes missed the broader discursive significance of the film and the new models of citizenship that it represents – that is, the perfect queering of gay desire in the neo-liberal moment, as tamed, well groomed, reliable, and responsible. And this form of representation is partly brought about by an LGBT politics that, as Binnie discusses in Chapter 8 of this volume, has focused on an assimilationist politics that has ignored the economic component of sexuality and sold out to the market (Chasin 2000: xiv).

The critical capacities of the queer are lost in the translation of this potentially disruptive sexual subject into a consumer citizen and the conversion of gayness into a consumer lifestyle (Sender 2004: 240). It reflects a homonormative pursuit where success is assessed not necessarily by one's sexual location but by wealth accumulation and the practices of responsible citizenship. The metamorphosis of the rogue sexual subject into the neo-liberal market order represents perhaps justice for those who are perpetually relegated to the fringe. It is simultaneously part of the project of disciplinarity that is a technique of modern power and a condition for legibility (Foucault: 1995). In this process, the sexual subject is relocated into a universe designed to push economic and social responsibility away from the state and onto the private arena.

In contrast to the market, the law is producing less legible and more cabined sexual subjects. A critical look at the 2009 High Court ruling in the *Naz Foundation* case reveals that it cannot be claimed as an unequivocal victory. The actual decision was less of an outright victory than a grudging tolerance of consensual sexual conduct between homosexuals. The decision read down the sodomy provision under the Indian Penal Code as inapplicable to consenting adults. While it eloquently set out the need to recognize the fundamental rights of gays and lesbians, these rights were not conferred as a result of the reading down of the impugned provision. The decision fell short of conferring juridical entitlements on a fully legible subject. While the government accepted the decision, there was no subsequent move on its part to confer greater recognition on gays and lesbians. This position of tolerance is a cause for concern as it serves as a device for social and political control, rather than empowering the groups being tolerated. The implicit outcome of the 2009 decision was to bring about a resolution by deploying the discourse of tolerance to recognize the entry of homosexuality into the public domain, while also seeking to cabin and contain it.

In India, the discourse of tolerance has operated as a way of reinforcing dominant norms, while at the same time sustaining an antagonistic posture towards difference and sustaining the perception of that difference as contaminating, uncivilized, threatening, or toxic. This discursive aspect of tolerance challenges the normally benign understanding of tolerance as a universal transnational norm or tool to protect the weak against the strong. An example of the working of this concept in India can be seen in relation to the treatment of religious minorities. Tolerance in India has had a deeply religious mooring (Cossman and Kapur 2001: 117–35). The judicial and constitutional discourse as well as the propaganda of the Hindu nationalists have emphasized that the principle of tolerance is derived from the cultural traditions of Indian society – cultural traditions that more often than not are equated with Hindu traditions and Hinduism. Thus tolerance has been informed by a majoritarian sensibility that is used to cast Muslims as intolerant either because of their treatment of women or because of their propensity to proselytize. Hinduism in contrast is cast as truly tolerant because unlike other traditions it does not proselytize and also because it is committed to promoting gender equality where Muslim women are to be treated the same as Hindu women, omitting any argument in favour of treating all women equal to Hindu men. Tolerance is both communalized and also used to demonize the Muslim 'other', while keeping dominant religious, gender, and sexual norms in place.

The legal interventions of the sexual subalterns have attempted to delink tolerance from its religious and majoritarian moorings through a concept of political tolerance, which begins from the most basic premise of accepting people and their practices despite our disagreements and disapproval. Yet this approach does not get the sexual subject out of the trap of Indian culture and normative sexuality that police the borders of tolerance. It is the inability to disrupt the gravitational pull of normative sexuality on which tolerance is based that ultimately de-radicalizes the subversive potential of rights claims by sexual subalterns.

In the context of sexual desire and sexual subalterns, tolerance becomes a supplement to equality, a tool for handling that difference that formal equality is unable to accommodate or address. It operates as a compromise as it permits membership into society even though this acceptance is just barely able to contain its revulsion at the difference. Tolerance does not operate to dissolve or resolve the hatred (Brown 2006: 28). It plays no counter-hegemonic role. It is depoliticized and does not offer any vision of transformation.

It may be that tolerance is the best that can be hoped for in the current political and cultural climate in India, and it certainly seems to be better than the move towards re-criminalization. The *Naz* case can be read as a case of what Spivak has called 'strategic essentialism', where the subjectivities pursued in the legal proceedings were intended to be tactical rather than disruptive (Spivak 2006: 63). Locating sexual subjects within the trajectory of a linear, ancient, and glorious history, in some instances, provides potential for social and legal recognition. In the Supreme Court, the bench repeatedly called for evidence of the scriptural recognition of sexual alterity, implying that it was a critical consideration in deciding upon legal recognition. At the same time, there is a risk attending such a strategy that results in essentializing sexual difference as freakish and abnormal (Govindan and Vaudevan 2011: 84–112).

A number of counsel representing the different sexual minorities in the *Naz Foundation* case before the Supreme Court argued precisely from this essentialist position that homosexuals cannot help themselves and hence should not be penalized for what is for them a natural orientation. The unruly desires as well as complex choices that inform the lives of the sexual other risk erasure as their legal claims reduce them to essentially abnormal and deviant subjects who need to be drawn into the sphere of state regulation and discipline. This process of harnessing deviancy without conferring full citizenship rights produces a de-radicalized, de-politicized subject.

Conclusions: becoming desires

Both inclusion and exclusion take a toll. Involving identities once excluded by law or from the public domain brings about a reconstitution of those once-excluded identities into newly inscribed regimes of governance. At the same time, while exclusion can remain somewhat subversive, it also has its costs in respect of the continuous process of struggle that accompanies living on such terms. As Brenda Cossman argues, to understand and focus on the process of 'becoming' introduces a politics that cannot be captured in terms of assimilation or transgression, exclusion or inclusion, but, rather, focuses on the spaces somewhere in between (Cossman 2007: 9). It is never either/or.

I adopt the proposal to stop thinking in terms of normalizing or transgressing, integrating or transforming. This chapter highlights how normalization and subversion go hand in hand. Focusing on how legitimate or illegitimate sexual subjects come into being, on how some desires are desirable, while other desires are not, draws us into the messiness of desire production. We can understand the transformation that takes place by focusing on the process of becoming.

So what does a strategy that focuses on the process of becoming require? Tracing desire and how it subverts while in the process of becoming, and also how it is normalized in the process of subverting, provides a more complicated understanding of how desire operates and what work it seeks to accomplish. While *Dostana* at one level represents how subject constitution occurs in and through the processes of the market, it also reveals that sexual subjectivity is incapable of being wholly disciplined. It is disorderly, chaotic, and messy. When *Dostana* ends, both heroes daydream about the kiss, recollecting it with some pleasure and delight. Their heterosexual credentials remain troubled – remember that they are after all married. The process of becoming is incomplete, uneven, and bumpy. But it is nevertheless underway.

Similarly, the challenge to section 377 in the Delhi High Court weakened, albeit minimally, the heteronormative logic. Post the 2009 decision, the public discourse on the part of many gays and lesbians not only claimed that homosexuality was not illegal, but promptly plunged them into discussions about same-sex marriage, and many even married before deities, priests, or through the exchange of garlands. The sexual subaltern was transcending the disciplinary limits of the decision. Yet is the objective of sexual subalterns primarily to acquire respectability and participate in the rituals of familial domesticity? Through becoming desires, do sexual subalterns want to pursue everything that straight people have in order to prove their own humanity and sense of belonging? Perhaps we need to give greater acknowledgement to the moments of disruption rather than focus on the slippery slopes that constitute the boundaries of the precipice where these moments are enacted. It is after all in these small moments, in the minutiae of everyday life, where power is bureaucratized and most immediately exercised and felt.

The implications of marriage, adoption, or consensual sodomy can be disruptive. Two men or women who perform the cultural rituals of marriage while not legally recognized are mimicking marriage and gesturing towards assimilation. At the same time they are also disrupting the normative understandings of marriage. The 2009 decision became a mechanism for triggering performances of marriage. As Cossman argues, the subversive and intimate erotics of sodomy becomes the basis of the claim for marriage and the performance of 'sodomy as consummation' unravels the tight seams of what constitutes marriage legally and culturally (Cossman 2007: 165). Justice can perhaps then be traced to such disruptive moments rather than exclusively to either a victory or loss in the courtroom.

But the legal challenge is fragile and uneven. The courts have to grapple with the idea of who and what constitutes a citizen subject in India entitled to rights. The criminalized sodomite became a tolerated subject – an unbecoming outlaw – only to become a criminalized sodomite again.[6] In both situations this subject is

6 The outrage expressed over the Supreme Court decision by all sectors of the media and in intellectual and activist spaces speaks to the seismic shift that has occurred over the years in favour of LGBT recognition. This shift has not emanated from a single source, but from multiple arenas including the market and popular culture and facilitated by the 2009 Delhi High

not quite a fully fledged sexual citizen. The borders managing these seismic shifts are continuously policed. Crossing over from criminality needs to be managed and these subjects will ultimately be subject to the same regulatory norms that govern private domestic relationships.

The line between good sex and bad sex has shifted but has not been demolished. There is an expanded space for the representation of sexual subaltern relationships and unruly desires which are at times challenging the boundaries of normative sex and desires. And there remain spaces available for the expression of unruly desires outside the discourses of governance discussed in this chapter. They reside in the frenzied trances of the transgendered persons who wed the god Iravan once a year under the full moon in May in a south Indian state. Or in the homoerotic desires expressed in Sufi poetry or music, an immanent as well as transcendent experience of desire between the subject and her inner self. The potential of such spaces calls for a more robust and engaged conversation that can produce more imaginative and creative possibilities for desire than have hitherto been either permissible or possible.

Acknowledgments

I am grateful to the participants at the international conference on Desiring Just Economies/Just Economies of Desire, in Berlin, 24–26 June 2010, for their inputs on an earlier version of this chapter as well as to the editors for their feedback. Thanks to Apurva Tripathi and Darshan Datar for their very able research assistance.

References

Arondekar, A. (2009) *For the Record: On Sexuality and the Colonial Archive in India*, Durham, NC: Duke University Press.

Bacchetta, P. (1999) 'When the (Hindu) Nation Exiles its Queers', *Social Text* 17(4): 141–66.

Bell, D. and Binnie, J. (2004) *The Sexual Citizen: Queer Politics and Beyond*, Oxford: Polity Press.

Bhabha, H. (1994) *The Location of Culture*, London: Routledge.

Bose, B. and Bhattacharyya, S. (eds) (2007) *The Phobic and the Erotic: The Politics of Sexualities in Contemporary India*, London: Seagull Books.

Court decision. It is also not de-linked from the global processes, which demonstrates that the recognition of LGBT rights is being pulled in different directions: either in the direction of homonormativity or in the direction of increased criminalization. LGBT rights in India stand in the centre of this tension. The re-criminalization of homosexuality by the Supreme Court in 2013 is now the subject matter of a 'curative' petition. This process enables parties to file such a petition when the Court has failed to take into account changed societal perceptions and hence has resulted in a gross miscarriage of justice. The Court has the power to correct the holding in the interests of due process and 'to do justice' between the parties.

Butler, J. (1990) *Gender Trouble: Feminism and the Subversion of Identity*, New York: Routledge.
—— (1993) 'Critically Queer', *GLQ: A Journal of Lesbian and Gay Studies* 1(1): 17.
—— (2004) *Precarious Life: The Power of Mourning and Violence*, New York: Verso.
—— (2009) *Frames of War: When is Life Grievable?*, New York: Verso.
Chakrabarty, D. (1995) 'Radical Histories and Questions of Enlightenment Rationalism: Some Recent Critiques of Subaltern Studies', *Economic and Political Weekly* 30(14): 751–9; reprinted in V. Chaturvedi (ed.) (2000) *Mapping Subaltern Studies and the Postcolonial*, London: Verso.
Chakrabarty, D. and Bhabha, H. (2002) *Habitations in Modernity: Essays in the Wake of Subaltern Studies*, Chicago, IL: University of Chicago Press.
Chasin, A. (2000) *Selling Out: The Gay and Lesbian Movement Goes to the Market*, Basingstoke/New York: Palgrave Macmillan.
Chatterjee, P. (1989) 'The Nationalist Resolution of the Women's Question', in K. Sanghariand and S. Vaid (eds) *Recasting Women: Essays in Colonial History*, New Delhi: Kali for Women, pp. 233–53.
Cossman, B. (2007) *Sexual Citizens: The Legal and Cultural Regulation of Sex and Belonging*, Stanford, CA: Stanford University Press.
Cossman, B. and Kapur, R. (2001) *Secularism's Last Sight? Hindutva and the (Mis) Rule of Law*, Delhi/London: Oxford University Press.
D'Emelio, J. (1993) 'Capitalism and Gay Identity', in H. Abelove, M. A. Barale and D. M. Halperin (eds) *The Lesbian and Gay Studies Reader*, New York/London: Routledge, pp. 467–76.
Duggan, L. (2002) 'The New Homonormativity: The Sexual Politics of Neoliberalism', in R. Castronovo and D. Nelson (eds) *Materializing Democracy: Toward a Revitalized Cultural Politics*, Durham, NC/London: Duke University Press, pp. 175–94.
Foucault, M. (1995) *Discipline and Punish: The Birth of the Prison*, trans. Alan Sheridan, New York: Vintage.
Garg, A. (2009) 'Kissing in Public by Married Couples not Obscene', *Times of India*, 2 February. Available online at http://timesofindia.indiatimes.com/city/delhi/Kissing-in-public-by-married-couple-not-obscene-HC/articleshow/4066941.cms (accessed 10 December 2014).
Giffney, N. (2004) 'Denormatizing Queer Theory: More Than (Simply) Lesbian and Gay Studies', *Feminist Theory* 5(1): 73–8.
Gopinath, G. (1998) 'On Fire', *GLQ: A Journal of Lesbian and Gay Studies* 4(4): 631–6.
—— (2005) *Impossible Desires: Queer Diasporas and South Asian Public Cultures*, Durham, NC: Duke University Press.
Goswami, M. (2004) *Producing India: From Colonial Economy to National Space*, Chicago, IL: University of Chicago Press.
Govindan, P. and Vasudevan, A. (2011) 'The Razor's Edge of Oppositionality', in A. Narrain and A. Gupta (eds) *Law Like Love: Queer Perspectives on Law*, Calcutta: Yoda Press, pp. 84–112.
Guha, R. (ed.) (1982) *Subaltern Studies I: Writings on South Asian History and Society*, Delhi: Oxford University Press.
Halberstam, J. (2005) *In a Queer Time and Place: Transgender Bodies, Subcultural Lives*, New York: New York University Press.

Haldar, P. (2007) *Law, Orientalism and Postcolonialism: Jurisdiction of the Lotus Eaters*, London: Routledge.

India Today (2009) 'Pub Culture Against Indian Ethos, Must Stop: Ramdoss', 30 January. Available online at http://timesofindia.indiatimes.com/india/Pub-culture-against-Indian-ethos-must-stop-Ramadoss/articleshow/4054517.cms (accessed 28 November 2014).

Jain, M. and Rawal, S. (1998) 'Ire over Fire', *India Today*, 21 December. Available online at www.india-today.com/itoday/21121998/cinema.html (accessed 28 November 2014).

John, M. (2008) *Women's Studies in India: A Reader*, New Delhi: Penguin Books.

Joshi, Y. (2012) 'Respectable Queerness', *Columbia Human Rights Law Review* 43(2): 415–67.

Kapur, R. (2005a) *Erotic Justice: Law and the New Politics of Postcolonialism*, London: Cavendish.

—— (2005b) 'A Love Song to Our Mongrel Selves', *Social and Legal Studies: An International Journal* 8(3): 353–63.

—— (2012) 'Pink Chaddis and Slutwalk Couture: The Postcolonial Politics of Feminism Lite', *Feminist Legal Studies* 20: 1–20.

Khan, S. (2001) 'Culture, Sexualities, and Identities: Men Who Have Sex with Men in India', *Journal of Homosexuality* 40(3–4): 99–115.

Mani, L. (1989) 'Contentious Traditions: The Debate on Sati in Colonial India', in K. Sangari and S. Vaid (eds) *Recasting Women: Essays in Colonial History*, New Delhi: Kali for Women, pp. 88–126.

Massad, J. (2002) 'Re-orienting Desire: The Gay International in the Arab World', *Public Culture* 14(2): 361–86.

Mehta, U. (1999) *Liberalism and Empire: A Study in Nineteenth-Century British Liberal Thought*, Chicago, IL: University of Chicago Press.

Mondal, A. (2002) 'The Emblematics of Gender and Sexuality in Indian Nationalist Discourse', *Modern Asian Studies* 36(4): 913–36.

Mignolo, W. (2000) *Local Histories/Global Designs*, Princeton, NJ: Princeton University Press.

Narrain, A. (2011a) 'Queering Democracy: The Politics of Erotic Love', in A. Narrain and A. Gupta (eds) *Law Like Love: Queer Perspectives on Law*, Calcutta: Yoda Press, pp. 3–23.

—— (2011b) 'A New Language of Morality: From the Trial of Nowshirwan to the Judgment in Naz Foundation', in A. Narrain and A. Gupta (eds) *Law Like Love: Queer Perspectives on Law*, Calcutta: Yoda Press, pp. 253–77.

Narrain, A. and Bhan, G. (2005) 'Introduction' in A. Narrain and G. Bhan (eds) *Because I have a Voice: Queer Politics in India*, Calcutta: Yoda Press.

Narrain, A. and Gupta, A. (2011) 'Introduction', in A. Narrain and A. Gupta (eds) *Law Like Love: Queer Perspectives on Law*, Calcutta: Yoda Press, pp. xi–lvi.

O'Hanlon, R. (2000) 'Recovering the Subject: Subaltern Studies and Histories of Resistance in Colonial South Asia', in V. Chaturvedi (ed.) *Mapping Subaltern Studies and the Postcolonial*, New York: Verso Books, pp. 72–115.

Pattanaik, D. (2002) *The Man Who Was a Woman and Other Queer Tales of Hindu Lore*, London: Haworth Press.

Puar, J. (2010) *Terrorist Assemblages: Homonationalism in Queer Times*, Durham, NC: Duke University Press.

Puri, J. (1999) *Women, Body, Desire in Post-Colonial India: Narratives of Gender and Sexuality*, New York: Routledge.
Rao, R. (2011) 'Queer in the Time of Terror', in A. Narrain and A. Gupta (eds) *Law Like Love: Queer Perspectives on Law*, Calcutta: Yoda Press, pp. 43–66.
Rati, R. (1993) *Lotus of Another Colour: An Unfolding of the South Asian Gay and Lesbian Experience*, London: Alyson Publications.
Rubin, G. (1993) 'Thinking Sex: Notes for a Radical Theory of the Politics of Sexuality', in H. Abelove, M. Aina Barale and D. M. Halperin (eds) *The Lesbian and Gay Studies Reader*, New York: Routledge, pp. 3–44.
Sarkar, S. (1985) *A Critique of Colonial India*, Calcutta: Papyrus.
—— (1997) *Writing Social History*, Delhi: Oxford University Press.
Sarkar, T. (1986) 'Colonial Lawmaking and Lives/Deaths of India Women: Different Readings of Law and Community', in R. Kapur (ed.) *Feminist Terrains in Legal Domains: Interdisciplinary Essays on Women and Law*, New Delhi: Kali for Women, pp. 210–42.
Sedgwick, E. K. (1990) *Epistemology of the Closet*, Berkeley: University of California Press.
—— (1993) *Tendencies*, Durham, NC: Duke University Press.
Sender, K. (2004) *Business, Not Politics: The Making of the Gay Market*, New York: Columbia University Press.
Shah, N. (1993) 'Sexuality, Identity and the Uses of History', in R. Rati (ed.) *Lotus of Another Colour: An Unfolding of the South Asian Gay and Lesbian Experience*, London: Alyson Publications, pp. 481–90.
Sherry, J. (2005) *Social Work Practice and Men Who Have Sex with Men*, London: Sage Publications.
Spivak, G. (1985) 'The Rani of Sirmur: An Essay in Reading the Archives', *History and Theory* 24(3): 247–72.
—— (1995) 'Can the Subaltern Speak?', in B. Ashcroft, G. Griffiths and H. Tiffin (eds) *The Post-Colonial Studies Reader*, Oxford: Routledge, pp. 28–37.
Sukthankar, A. (ed.) (1999) *Facing the Mirror: Lesbian Writing from India*, New Delhi: Penguin Books.
Swami, P. (1998/1999) 'Furore over a Film', *Frontline* 15(26), 19 December 1998–1 January 1999. Available online at www.frontline.in/static/html/fl1526/15260430.htm (accessed 28 November 2014).
Thadani, G. (1996) *Sakhiyani: Lesbian Desire in Ancient and Modern India*, London: Cassell.
Vance, C. (1989) 'Pleasure and Danger: Toward a Politics of Sexuality', in C. Vance (ed.) *Pleasure and Danger: Exploring Female Sexuality*, London: Routledge and Kegan Paul, pp. 1–27.
Vanita, R. (2002) 'Introduction', in R. Vanita (ed.) *Queering India: Same-Sex Love and Eroticism in India Culture and Society*, New York: Routledge, pp. 1–14.
Vanita, R. and Kidwai, S. (2001) *Same-Sex Love in India: Readings from Literature and History*, New York: Palgrave-MacMillan.

Chapter 7

Integrating Sexual and Economic Justice

Challenges for queer feminist activism against sexual violence in South Africa

Lyn Ossome

Postcoloniality, queer desires and justice

South Africa's 1996 Interim Constitution[1] was the first anywhere explicitly to include sexual orientation in an enumerated list of constitutional equality guarantees (Stychin 1996). The Equality Act, passed in 2000, specifically outlaws 'hate crimes', where people are targeted based on their identification as part of a group. At around the same time, discourses around 'corrective' rape emerged in strong reaction to its disarticulation from the broad concepts of what was considered to constitute a hate crime. To a large extent, activists began to highlight the fact that rape that targeted lesbians in order to 'cure' them of their 'aberrant' sexuality or gender non-conformity was specific and ought to be criminalized as being a hate crime, a distinction which no existing legislation made at the time. Increasingly, 'curative' rapes were seen as being synonymous with hate crimes (Muholi 2004). Nonetheless, the use of this term within the framework of hate crimes legislation is not unproblematic: 'corrective' rapes have a specific purpose, which is both captured (from the point of view of the perpetrator) and not captured (from the point of view of the survivor) in the language of 'corrective/curative' (Matebeni 2011).[2] Conflating corrective rapes and hate crimes thus carries the risk of rendering invisible the subject (black lesbians) and nature of injustice(s) experienced by them. Critically, too, there has emerged a strong need to ensure that hate crime legislation is not be used as a cover to avoid systemic change, concern with the fact that hate crime legislation ought to be created for the protection of the most marginalized groups in society, and recognition that it was in fact these groups

1 The Interim Constitution was replaced by the permanent Constitution following general elections in 1999.

2 As Matebeni (2011) has argued, even though the strategic implications of the use of 'corrective/ curative' rape may be beneficial for activists in lobbying for hate crime laws, a critical reading of the language of 'curative/corrective' rape can be ambiguous for some, and the use of such terms as analytical tools can produce problems. Such language suggests an elevated status of the perpetrator who is seen as 'curing'/'correcting' for the good of the dominant culture while stigmatizing and branding the survivor; and can imply or shift blame from perpetrator to victim, seen as having 'transgressed' societal norms.

who struggle to exercise their rights and to access justice and resources. In other words, without broader social and political transformation, hate crime legislation would have little benefit for those marginalized on the basis of class, race, sexual orientation or citizenship status (Pizzale 2011).

These are some of the contentions informing queer feminist debates in the post-apartheid period, which was marked by an intensified demand for liberties, and which in turn surfaced a complex dialectic of claims. At the same time as it facilitated and legitimated LGBTI (lesbian, gay, bisexual, trans(gender/sexual), intersexual) rights, this period also stirred a conservative discourse that re-articulated these rights as being 'a legacy of colonialism and a means of facilitating a new identity form that threaten[ed] national values [...] a relic of the colonial past that [had to] be transcended and/or a sign of the transnational figure that [had to] be feared' (Hoad 1999: 561–2). As well as mobilizing a variety of contestations over meanings of the 'post-colonial', post-apartheid identity politics foregrounded the question of whether the law could, out of the dominant heteronormative regime, produce intelligible and viable subjects, and whether the normative frame of a progressive constitution could afford to gays and lesbians freedom from all forms of discrimination, accord them justice and protect their enjoyment of full citizenship rights enshrined in this document. In other words, could queer desires be adequately read within the liberal discourses of constitutionalism and human rights, out of which they were being translated? Could justice for homosexuals, as Kapur too enquires in Chapter 6 of this volume, function beyond the borders of heteronormativity?

The 'complexities and re-stagings' (Hall 2001: 248) of oppressions in the post-apartheid state have taken many forms, one of which could be argued to be the hierarchization of bodies, the violent inscription of gendered norms expressed through the rape and murder of black lesbian women. Whether or not deliberate, the term 'corrective rape' that is associated with these acts of sexual violence itself endorses the notion of an *acceptable* and valid way of being. Its normative use, conveyed through activist discursive spaces in civil society and academia with the ostensible intention of criminalizing such violence against lesbian women, problematically fixates the 'normative gaze' upon lesbians as being deviant, filthy, ugly and unclean.[3] Iris Young is especially suspicious of such subliminal normativity, arguing that averse or anxious reactions to the bodily presence of others are usually unconscious, often exhibited by liberal-minded people who intend to treat everyone with equal respect. And because moral theories tend to focus on deliberate action for which they seek means of justification, they usually do not bring unintended social sources of oppression under judgement (1990: 11). Another observation is the differentiated treatment of oppressions in the public discourse,

3 See Iris Young's (1990: 122–55) discussion of modern society's denigration of the body, in which she critiques the location of bodies on a single aesthetic scale that constructs some kinds of bodies as ugly, disgusting or degenerate.

which lends less concerted attention to certain harms, particularly those linked to the cultural valuation of people's lives and activities, than it does to those harms understood to be the result of prevailing political and economic arrangements in South Africa. Such dichotomization is not unlike the one Nancy Fraser maintains between injustices, claiming them to occur either when cultural norms that are unfairly biased against some are institutionalized in the state and the economy, or occurring due to economic disadvantage which impedes equal participation in the making of culture, in public spheres and in everyday life (Fraser 2008: 16). The hermeneutically persuasive analytical framework through which she derives this distinction nonetheless fails to account for injustices that are subject to more than just the cultural location of queer groups (see Butler 2008). Fraser's binary logic of oppressions leaves unchallenged her own question regarding the sorts of mutual interferences that can arise when claims for both redistribution, aimed at redressing economic injustice, and recognition, aimed at addressing cultural injustice, are made simultaneously (2008: 18). The discussion throughout this chapter locates queer feminist activists in South Africa – delimited by a social justice space that inadvertently binds queer claims to purely identity politics – at this delicate conjuncture.

Scholarly critiques are divided over the usefulness of dichotomizing injustices, a paradigm that retains ambiguities as well as introducing unnecessary conflicts. Fraser, for example, even when she shifts from the extremes of cultural injustices on the one hand, and economic injustices on the other, to consider collectivities located in the middle of the conceptual spectrum, those that combine features of the exploited class with features of the despised sexuality – so-called 'bivalent' collectivities such as gender and 'race' (2008: 23) – does not resolve questions of hierarchization of oppression as her analysis remains limited by the dual-paradigmatic analysis of justice. Her insistence that harms deriving from cultural-valuational differentiation are injustices of recognition, relatively independent of the political economy (ibid.: 24) forcefully excludes and subordinates questions of sexuality and race, marking them as secondary to the 'real' business of politics (Butler 2008: 47). The real business of politics is defined precisely by that which it accepts against that which is eschews – the latter setting the discursive limits of the former. Or, following Butler, difference is not simply the external differences between movements, but rather the *self-difference of movement itself*, a constitutive rupture that makes movements possible on non-identitarian grounds, that installs a certain mobilizing conflict as the basis of politicization; difference is the condition of possibility of identity or, rather, its constitutive limit (2008: 47). Queer desires may thus appear to stand in extreme opposition to those claims for justice made by mainstream movements, yet the argument may be made that a constant dialectically subversive process is at work (between the two spaces) that enables the articulation and counter-articulation of claims in the broad social justice sphere. It is out of normative discourses defining just economies that queer groups derive, subvert and re-articulate their desires in ways that also inform broader discourses.[4] Indeed, as Jagose (1996: 98) has argued, queerness partly stems from an exclusionary heterosexual citizenship that ignores the fact that queer represents a resistance to anything that is socially defined as normal, and in that sense queer may exclude some gay and lesbian practices that have a 'normative perspective', or may include other experiences that are not explicitly sexual. Livermon asserts this point in reference to scholarship which has focused on the ways in which black queer South Africans, when confronted with new social and political identities both nationally and internationally, came to understand themselves as 'gay' or 'lesbian', and how, through such subversions, black queerness could both become visible and destabilize forms of black identity based on heteronormativity (2012: 310–11). From a political perspective, the impact that queer activism has had in African and the diasporan post-liberation evolution is one area that has received scant attention in post-colonial discourses.[5]

Social justice spaces thus appear as contested arenas within which competing discourses find resonance variedly and at different moments depending on the interests and arrangements seeking articulation and fulfilment. The post-apartheid moment in South Africa was that period that enabled not just the insertion of a queer discourse into the nationalist political territory, due mostly to the

4 The manifesto of the Johannesburg People's Pride (JPP) is an illustration of some of the ways in which queers are taking up economic discourses and subversively asserting these questions in spaces of queer organizing. The JPP initiative brings together individuals from diverse backgrounds with the common aim of organizing a series of events and actions leading up to the annual LGBTIAQ Pride Day on 5 October 2013. The events and actions organized by the initiative have the aim of advancing the rights and visibility of lesbian, gay, bisexual, transgender, intersex, asexual, queer and questioning (LGBTIAQ) individuals and communities; increasing social integration of LGBTIAQ individuals by dispelling stereotypes about sexual orientation and gender identity; generating spaces for learning and dialogue between LGBTIAQ communities, other civil society groups and the larger public; and contributing towards greater social cohesion across divisions of class, nationality, race and ethnicity, ability, age, health status, gender, sexual orientation and profession. See http://peoplespride.blogspot.com (accessed 26 September 2013).

5 Its contribution to studies related to gender and sexuality as well as violence and representation remains under-theorized or altogether ignored on the continent. One significant contribution relates to the rise of HIV/AIDS and its links to Haiti and Africa. In the early discovery of the epidemic, the scapegoating of Haitians and, later, Africans brought a certain diaspora consciousness and sensibility into at least one encounter with the disease – the twinning of anti-racist activism and queer activism occurred (Walcott 2007: 30). From the early 1990s, the multidirectional pressures which the AIDS epidemic placed on categories of identification, power and knowledge, and necessitating and nurturing new forms of political organization, education and theorizing were largely produced under the rubric of queer theory. Notably, this contribution spanned the coalition politics of much AIDS activism that rethinks identity in terms of affinity rather than essence (Saalfield and Navarro 1991) and therefore includes not only lesbians and gay men but also bisexuals, transsexuals, sex workers, PWAs (People with AIDS), health workers, and parents and friends of gays; and the rethinking of traditional understandings of the workings of power in cross-hatched struggles over epidemiology, scientific research, public health, and immigration policy (Halperin 1995: 28).

visible contributions that gay and lesbian activists made to the anti-apartheid struggle; reclaiming a queer discourse, long critiqued for undermining class, race and gender differences in this country, also made it possible to maintain, in the 'post-liberation' period, discussions around economic justice among groups whose ostensible freedom had been guaranteed by a progressive new constitution. Queer voices were among those that emboldened other oppressed groups to voice their own varied subjugated positions, and the latter are at present in perpetual negotiation and conflict with the state, their claims legitimized through a revival, in the past decade, of class politics.

Yet locating LGBTI groups within this emerging discourse has become a much more exigent task, as, more and more, LGBTI groups appear defenceless against accusations of being privileged by race, class and gender. Part of this is due to the effect of the South African constitution, which, Livermon observes, cannot in its very nature define rights on the basis of unnamed queerness (2012: 314). LGBTI visibility has thus emerged formally in response to what society considers as being cultural forms of injustices, which for various reasons, including political expediency, are disarticulated from political economic injustices in the broader spaces of social struggles. For LGBTI groups in South Africa, this silencing is subsumed within the classical struggle between progressive social movements and nationalist hegemonies, especially conservative political parties and ruling elites, to control popular support and retain power in the face of global economic and social challenges. Social movements exist primarily as a counterweight to bureaucratic excesses: as an alternative voice they appeal to a conscious majority that is marginalized economically, politically, socially and culturally by dominant individuals, institutions and processes within society. Yet at the same time social movements respond to and articulate their demands through means that are (necessarily) tactical and may be exclusionary if expedient. As groups in constant vigilance of shifts in global priorities, in constant conversation with and interrogation of national prerogatives for development, and in perpetual search for mass appeal, social movements are bound to eschew, albeit tacitly, themes and contestations that might compromise their critical broad reach and dilute their effectiveness. Inevitably, too, the thematic issues defining struggles are bound to be swayed by hegemonic notions of 'good' or 'bad' as they instinctively react to mainstream coding (Ossome 2013). The discussion that follows draws from narratives of sexual violence directed towards black lesbians in poor townships in South Africa, using this to reflect on questions of economic subjectivity and exclusion of queer groups in the post-apartheid state. In Iris Young's (2008) conception of justice where oppressions are simultaneous, we are urged to consider justice beyond a dichotomy of political economy/cultural valuational, and to ask, in addition, who the rule-makers are, the ways in which cultural attitudes about sexuality are formed, who defines certain bodily harms as injustice, and whether dominant frameworks of redress can adequately respond to these injustices, or indeed correctly identify violations specific to certain groups as being unjustly reproduced within the political and economic contexts in operation. This is in essence a critique of the social forces that separate sexuality from the rest of social production, and an analysis of sexuality that recognizes 'the mutual interdependence of sexuality, economics, and politics without underestimating the full significance of each in human society' (Rubin 1975: 210).[6] The basis of a theory that captures this interdependence is perhaps to be found in Charlotte Bunch's conclusion, that while it is necessity which moves (lesbians) in the cultural task of creating their own world, the impetus is economic: *the expression of necessity is always material* (Bunch 1997: 57; my italics).

Liberalism and queering the post-apartheid state

> Considered inessential to what is most pressing in material life, queer politics is regularly figured by the orthodoxy as the cultural extreme of politicization.
>
> (Butler 2008: 48)

The repressive and heteronormative regulation of sexuality in South Africa historically served paranoid state interests throughout the apartheid years. Fundamental to the apartheid project,[7] it was affected both formally and informally within the boundaries of race and gender. Posel (2005) observes that, particularly obsessive in its determination to prohibit sex across racial boundaries and driven by typically colonial anxieties about rapacious black sexuality, the apartheid state accumulated an extensive armoury of regulations and prohibitions to control the practice and transaction of sex, its public presentation and performance. Within these political and legislative strictures, sex within the domestic domain was deemed a 'private matter' – with no sense of the contradiction entailed. So sexual violence (particularly within 'the home') was typically not a site of political concern, unless the perpetrator was black and the victim was white, in which case the public outrage was virulent. Sex across the black–white racial divide was forbidden, and miscegenation intensely stigmatized.[8] Reinforced by laws that stigmatized homosexuality, a deep-seated and widespread homophobia deterred the open expression or assertion of any sexualities deemed transgressive (Posel 2005: 128). Post-1994, there has been a veritable explosion of sexual imagery, display and debate. Yet

6 Hennessy (2000: 184) points out that although Rubin has now forsaken this strand in her thinking, it nonetheless provides a useful starting point for such a project.

7 Inherent in the call for 'white supremacy' was a zealous drive to preserve the 'purity' of the 'white race', by preventing the sexual sullying of the white body. Powerful imagery of the black mass, and the ever immanent threat of its overwhelming the far smaller number of whites, fanned fears of black 'overpopulation' and the imperative of controlling black fertility (Posel 2005: 128).

8 Reference is made here to the ways in which the history of capital accumulation relied on a political economy of race, including ideologies of racism to justify and structure labour and state power, kinship and sexuality.

these changes are by no means either wholesale or uncontested. Issues of sexuality have an extraordinary prominence, but not in ways which indicate widespread comfort or acceptance of their profile or substance. Indeed, the anxieties, denials and stigma that persist in the midst of new and unprecedented declarations of sexuality – often provoked directly by them – contribute directly to the new sites and intensities of the politicization of sexuality (ibid.: 129).

Partly these anxieties are born of contradictions inherent in the liberal discourse through which sexuality has been mediated. Post-1994, sexuality has become the sight of *right* in a number of ways – with enormously profound consequences. One apparent contradiction, Livermon argues, is the fact that black queer South Africans are not able to enjoy fully the privileges encoded in the South African constitution as *black* and *queer*, because cultural politics consistently mark the black queer body as the constitutive outside of blackness and the queer body is subsequently racialized as white. This creates a conundrum for black queers who are caught outside both the representational (cultural) and the material realities of queerness (2012: 314f.), Fraser's so-called 'bivalent' collectivities (2008: 23). The new Bill of Rights affirmed, among others, the right of sexual preference and the right to gender equality, along with the right to 'freedom and security of the person', including the right to 'be free from all forms of violence from either public or private sources' (Posel 2005: 129). The long raft of social, political and economic rights guaranteed by the state was the lever with which a placated public was expected to re-negotiate its freedom after decades of struggle. Yet liberally thrusting rights into the public domain, at the exact post-colonial moment as the 'liberated' public begins to internalize the idea of freedom and, out of their struggles, to define their own conception of needs and desires, may be viewed as a latent interruption of conscientization that exerts influence on the ways in which publics internalize or express their notions of various forms of justice.[9] Rather, what is apparent in the case of post-apartheid South Africa is that, to experience freedom, the black queer body must enter either a deracinated queerness or a blackness divorced from sexuality (Livermon 2012: 315). Rosemary Hennessy's assertion that the invocation of 'rights' is not an obvious or universal standpoint is, here, critical: it is rather, she argues, a way of making sense of social actors that binds the subject to accompanying notions of property, individuality, legal power and citizenship – in short, to a history of modernity (2000: 182). And problematically so.

As well as political and socio-economic rights, the rights of LGBTI groups acquired symbolic weight as part of the said interruption. But it is, within the South African capitalist project, the queer interruption that especially threatened not only the codes of exchange between state and society but also the modes of production and exchange within the family and kinship system, and it is the

9 Recall, for instance, the Fanonian submission that it is at the heart of national consciousness that international consciousness lives and grows, and that this two-fold emerging is ultimately the source of all culture (Fanon 1965).

assumed autonomy of queer women that most threatened the social (re)production practice of the male (giver) and the female (gift) (Mauss 2000).[10] Within such a formation, 'corrective' raping of black lesbian women may be understood as functioning heteronormatively to reinforce existing hierarchical economic relations. Accompanying this threat is the discursive thrust to separate or distinguish the claims made by queer groups from those made by 'everyone' else. This desire is visible especially in the silencing of LGBTI claims within broader movements for social justice in the country. On this point, significant contrast can be drawn between different African countries regarding processes of insertion of concepts of justice. For instance, between a country such as South Africa where the constitutional insertion of LGBTI rights is expected to have justly accounted for and, in effect, withdrawn injustices suffered by sexual minority groups from the public discourse, and the trend in other countries in Africa, for example Uganda, which is at present steeped in a deeply polemical struggle between right wing, religious and ultra-conservative groups and liberal rights groups over the issue of homosexuality. Albeit contentious, a rich discursive space has emerged in Uganda around the 'Kill the Gays' bill that is politically nuanced and suffused with the possibility of engendering more critically engaged activist spaces. The shock of the bill, Tavia Nyong'o argues, is a strange attractor of global affect which could be parlayed into a more sustained, deeply historical knowledge of the situation in Uganda (2012: 50f.). As Ekine (2010) too observes, the increased visibility of LGBTI activists there has led to public discussion in the media and an easier access to information, and it has forced people to think about the effect of exclusionary right in their society.[11] In South Africa, on the other hand, the space for

10 Levi-Strauss, in his appropriation of the theory of the gift, showed that this relation of exchange was not only cultural and economic at once, but also made the distinction inappropriate and unstable: exchange produces a set of social relations, communicates a cultural or symbolic value, and secures routes of distribution and consumption (see Butler 2008: 55).

11 Ekine highlights the ways in which activists have utilized institutional mechanisms to influence public discourse: 'One of the ways in which LGBTI people have increased their visibility is through the formation of national and Pan-African organizations working at grassroots level in the struggle for decriminalization and sensitizing their respective communities. Organizations such as SMUG (Sexual Minorities Uganda) and the CAL (Coalition of African Lesbians) have been at the forefront of the campaign for LGBTI rights in Uganda and in preventing the passing of the Ugandan "Anti-Homosexuality Bill". One particular high-profile case took place in Uganda in 2005 when the home of Ugandan activist and founder of SMUG, Victor Mukasa, was raided by the police and documents removed from the house. Victor chose to fight the case and sued the Attorney General of Uganda. In December 2008, after three and half years of being in hiding, repeated disappointments, limited funds and at much detriment to his physical and emotional health, Victor won his case against the Ugandan Attorney General. The judge in the case stated that the actions of the police were "unconstitutional, inhuman, and should be condemned, and said it was important to respect Human Rights laws and protect them in the spirit of brotherhood and sisterhood". From the momentum created by the Ugandan LGBTI Human Rights Court Case, the numbers of people involved in advocating for the protection of the basic human rights of LGBTI people have continued to grow in Uganda' (Ekine 2010).

critical public debate remains foreclosed, the discussion one that de-links sex, sexuality and violence from broader political, social and economic questions.

The critical value that activism continues to play in South Africa cannot be gainsaid. Yet, at the same time, activists in South Africa *are* compliant in celebrating the neoliberal project of constitutional triumphalism, with minimalist demands on the state to 'issue steeper sentencing to corrective rape offenders', or to 'recognise corrective rape as a hate crime'. The case of Zoliswa Nkonyana, a 19-year-old lesbian who was stabbed and stoned to death in February 2006, illustrates this point well. The recognition by court ruling in October 2011 that homophobia and hatred were motivating forces for her murder was a significant victory. Yet hers was not necessarily a case of corrective rape – little or no evidence exists that ties the fact of her sexual identity to the crime of her murder. In asserting that this crime had been 'corrective', the possibilities of broadening the reach of justice for LGBTI persons also stood foreclosed. The tendency among LGBTI activists to deduce all forms of violence experienced by lesbian women as being 'corrective' rape bars a more extended critique of the spectrum of homophobic violence and 'narrows the field of legitimate discussion to single issue politics' (Nyong'o 2012: 44). What we are left to ponder, then, are the inherent possibilities of political and queer activist work that is willing to elaborate alternative considerations of violence beyond notions of the 'merely cultural' that inadvertently disarticulate hate crimes from other forms of social injustices that may be political or economic in nature. In affirming the liberal notion of rights as capable of resolving all social problems, activists also displace or limit any alternative discourses of justice, including those that subject democratic theory to critical analysis, or those that altogether refuse co-optation into discourses that reaffirm the morality of justice while refusing to acknowledge the breadth of political, social, cultural and economic influences that reproduce injustices and out of which different moral claims emerge. Gressgård's critique of tolerance to sexual and cultural diversity in Chapter 5 of this volume is significant in pointing out that, while explicitly promoting individual choice and autonomy, tolerance requires and reproduces the essentialized identitarian differences it purports to overcome. The tolerable are instrumentally reconstituted as modern, 'autonomous' individuals, freed from the burden of backwardness and incivility – a discursive split Gressgård argues, that has pernicious social effects. The liberal discourse of justice succeeds in excluding lesbian women from the surplus value nexus of social production, affirming the anachronism of 'justice within capitalism', and ignoring literature demonstrating the ways in which the regulation of sexuality was systematically tied to the mode of production proper to the functioning of political economy (Butler 2008: 51). This literature challenges Fraser's claim that homophobia has no roots in political economy because, she argues, homosexuals occupy no distinctive position in the division of labour, are distributed throughout the class structure, and do not constitute an exploited class; indeed, that the injustice they suffer is quintessentially a matter of recognition, thus making their struggles into a matter of cultural recognition, rather than that of material oppression. Although Fraser acknowledges that 'gender' is a basic structuring principle of the political economy, the reason she offers is that it structures unpaid reproductive work (1997: 17f.). Yet, as Judith Butler too points out, Fraser does not ask how the sphere of reproduction that guarantees the place of 'gender' within political economy is circumscribed by sexual regulation; that is, through mandatory exclusions the sphere of reproduction becomes delineated and naturalized (2008: 52). Butler questions the validity of analysing how normative heterosexuality and its 'genders' are produced within the sphere of reproduction without noting the compulsory ways in which homosexuality and bisexuality, as well as transgender, are *produced* as the sexually 'abject', and extending the mode of production to account for precisely this social mechanism of regulation. She radically submits that it would be a mistake to understand such productions as 'merely cultural' if they are essential to the functioning of the sexual order of political economy, that is, constituting a fundamental threat to its very workability.

Queer feminist claims and (im)possibilities of justice

Cock and Bernstein (2001) explain that, in South Africa, gender inequalities have been generally understood as epiphenomena – effects of the inequalities created and maintained by the apartheid state. The apartheid state was all-pervasive – extending even to prescriptions of legitimate sexual partners – and the sweep of apartheid totalitarianism made the personal political (2001: 144). The racial character of the apartheid state had obscured its gendered nature, and whereas women in the North originally identified the family as a site of women's oppression, black women in South Africa attempted to protect the family from the encroachments of capital and the state, and point to the weakening of black family life as one of the most grievous crimes of apartheid (ibid.). The feminist voice at the time was that of an elitist feminism, perceived to be more concerned with extending the power and privilege of middle-class women than with total social transformation to eliminate the source of that privilege. The outcome was that feminism in South Africa was widely viewed as divisive, reactionary or inappropriate; as a poison which spread infection, as concerned with exotic and distant issues such as sexual preference. Moreover, for many, the term 'feminist' was a stigmatized identity, partly because of its association with lesbianism (ibid.).

The post-colonial decentring of the state from feminist analyses of the condition of women was due in part to willingness of South African women's movements to embrace a more inclusive, coalition-based politics of social justice which, though based on difference, did not dislodge the heteronormative delimitations of gender and sexuality that had marked earlier discourses. The apartheid state's penetration of every sphere of 'private' life confounded traditional feminist critiques of the public/private divide as the gendered regulation of sexuality and womanhood was designed to serve specific social, political and economic interests of the white, racist apartheid project. The gender discourse was structured almost exclusively around the political economy of race relations during those dark years, while sexuality hardly featured in the public discourse.[12] What is observed at present is a deeper retreat of sexuality into a culturally defined discursive space, and a less nuanced association of gender and sexuality to the 'superstructure'. Nancy Fraser's contentions are again instructive here. While she acknowledges the bivalence of gender – its political-economy face as well as its cultural-valuational face – she nonetheless retains a separation between 'sexist and androcentric' cultural norms that institutionalize gender oppression in the state and the economy, and women's economic disadvantage that restricts women's 'voice' and impedes equal participation in the making of culture. In addition, while acknowledging 'cultural sexism' and the harms associated with it,[13] she insists that gender injustices are harms of recognition that are relatively independent of political economy (2008: 24). Fraser affirms a similar bivalence of sexuality, yet, contra Judith Butler's suggestion that sexuality is inextricable to gender, maintains that 'yoking gender and sexuality together too tightly covers over the important distinction between a group that occupies a distinct position in the division of labour, on the one hand, and one that occupies no such distinction on the other hand' (Fraser 2008: 21). This dichotomy is reflected in Nadia Sanger's analysis of the non-governmental organizational space in South Africa, in which she notes the split between 'those working to protect rights and interests of women as a particular group' and 'those focused on the interests of self-identified lesbian, bisexual, transgendered and intersexed women', explaining this to be in part an effect of the post-colonial focus on gender equality in South Africa, where 'gender' is most often understood as synonymous with women. Furthermore, deeply entrenched norms around heterosexuality often mean that the concerns of gender non-conforming women are rendered marginal and invisible (2010: 25).

Upon what basis, then, one might ask, do lesbians make claims to justice in an economic and political ideological environment that constructs them outside of the dominant framework of claims-making? For instance, how is one to

12 As Cock and Bernstein (2001: 144) point out, many of the social tensions that initially triggered feminist consciousness in women of the industrialized countries in the northern hemisphere were absent in South Africa. For many women, life was a daily struggle for physical survival, and the strains experienced by women as mothers and workers were initially understood to derive from the apartheid state rather than from patriarchal relations within the household or workplace. The racial character of the apartheid state had obscured its gendered nature.

13 These include the pervasive devaluation and disparagement of things coded as 'feminine', paradigmatically – but not only – women (Fraser 2008: 24). This devaluation, she notes, is expressed in a range of harms suffered by women, including sexual assault, sexual exploitation and pervasive domestic violence; trivializing, objectifying and demeaning stereotypical depictions in the media; harassment and disparagement in all spheres of everyday life; subjection to androcentric norms in relation to which women appear lesser or deviant and which work to disadvantage them, even in the absence of any intention to discriminate; attitudinal discrimination; exclusion or marginalization in public spheres and deliberative bodies; and denial of full legal rights and equal protections.

understand the 'corrective rape' discourse other than through a critical examination of its discursive limits? For one, as Matebeni (2013) shows, by framing black lesbians as 'special' victims of a form of rape, the language of 'corrective' rape locates black lesbians in the townships of South Africa outside the wider gender, class, sexuality and racial struggles of social justice in South Africa. Second, stating the actual intention and act of the perpetrator as 'curative' can mean or be misinterpreted to implicate the victim as 'deserving' of the crime. Such language positions her (all cases of such reported rapes are women) as being 'cleansed' of something that is 'unwanted', 'abnormal' and outlawed in society. Through 'corrective/curative' rape, lesbians then become cured and 'normalized'. Third, the use of such language (or the reading of violence as 'curative') suggests an elevated status of the perpetrator who is seen as 'curing' and 'correcting' for the good of dominant culture, while stigmatizing and branding the survivor (Matebeni 2013). Despite the guilty verdict, outside of the court system the perpetrator mediates a crucial space of public discourse within which lesbian sexuality is covertly exploited. This exploitation may be read as based upon a class-specific morality, which, Binnie argues in Chapter 8 of this volume, is significant in thinking through the morality of the market and the sexual politics of neoliberalism. By materially applying the said constructions of the black lesbian Other to mass media representations[14] of the rape incidences of black lesbians, could not an element of the fetishization of female sexuality that is intended to arouse heterosexual desire among both male and female consumers be made visible? Is this not a continuation of capitalism's moralistic project of societal regulation that relies on abjection to explain away its ills and failures of justice?[15] Is justice for queer women, especially given the current disparagement of the cultural within the South African neo-liberal context, even probable?

14 Both local and international media reports on the rape and murder of black lesbians in South Africa – many informed by reports from local civil society organizations – have tended to reproduce the 'exceptionalism' of sexual violence against black lesbians, delimiting analysis within a framework of cultural harms and delinking it from broader issues of economic survival in poor townships, along with generalized violence, including xenophobia and rape, that permeates South African society (for instance, see media reports: TIME, www.time.com/time/world/article/0,8599,2057744,00.html; Digital Journal, http://digitaljournal.com/article/313566; CNN, http://edition.cnn.com/video/?/video/international/2011/10/12/ex-world-untold-stories-corrective-rape.cnn, all accessed 12 January 2012). Highlighting media's apparent apathy, the Human Sciences Research Council (HSRC) reports that when a lesbian support organization approached a local television production company about its negative presentation of homosexuals in a drama series, the producers turned down any possibility of discussion with the organization. News media also tended to be insensitive to the need for lesbian rape survivors to protect their identity, to avoid attracting more attacks (HSRC 2007).

15 Rosemary Hennessy's (2000) argument, that it is ideology that generates what counts as socially made 'reality', is persuasive in this regard. In it she uses the theorization of the materiality of ideology to counter the idea of an objective reality outside discourse.

'Justice within capitalism'

Setting aside briefly the assumption that the law anticipates and is capable of satisfying the justice claims of queer groups, or indeed that it is its *application* that activism ought to focus upon,[16] it is worth considering the mediating space between the dispensers of justice and those who receive it. This space problematically places those ostensibly with the power to 'guarantee' justice on one end and those in need of some form of redress, whether redistribution or recognition, on the other, and assumes that this distribution takes place through the allocation of particular goods or services. However, a distributive understanding of power as a possession of particular individuals or groups misses the supporting and mediating function of third parties (Young 1990), and misses the structural phenomena of domination (Hartsock 1983). Critiquing distributive paradigms, Young (1990: 16) displaces talk of justice that regards persons as primarily possessors and consumers of goods to a wider context that also includes action, decisions about action, and provision of the means to develop and exercise capacities. She formulates a concept of social justice that includes all aspects of institutional rules and relations insofar as they are subject to potential collective decision, arguing that concepts of domination and oppression, rather than the concept of distribution, should be the starting point of a conception of social justice. In the context of a queer feminist politics of resistance, this means, for example, paying regard to the ways in which power is reproduced (by the powerful) through discourses such as 'corrective rape'. While queer feminists increasingly question the usefulness of this term, and insist on the need for an alternative term (Matebeni 2013) that describes the specific oppression being lived when black, economically marginalized lesbians are targeted on the basis of sexuality, this task in itself is impossible if it does not take into account the structure of oppression that is experienced not only by queer groups but by all the other social movements that are struggling at the margins of capitalism. These movements are densely spread across South Africa's urban and rural settlements, protesting the failure of the state in dispensing services such as water, electricity, decent housing and sanitation, demonstrating against police brutality and insecurity, and demanding jobs and better schools. These are the groups recognized by the capitalist, 'predatory' state as the *real* threat, the ones the state identifies with claims for social justice and (often with brutality) responds to. This recognition is in part due to the fact that these groups are highly critical of the African National Congress (ANC) government, and reject as a façade the idea that the current government is concerned with the welfare of the economically oppressed. These groups are struggling to insert new codes into their justice claims, and through this process can provide a critical space out of which the voice of the queer subaltern can also re-emerge. Such a politics of coalition requires blurring the distinction between cultural and

16 The latter view permeates the approach of activists campaigning around LGBTIQ issues in South Africa.

economic oppression, between 'primary' and 'secondary' oppression, but, most importantly, insisting, as Butler (2008) does, that difference remain constitutive of any struggle.

References

Bunch, C. (1997) 'Not for Lesbians Only', in R. Hennessy and C. Ingraham (eds) *Materialist Feminism: A Reader in Class, Difference, and Women's Lives*, New York: Routledge, pp. 54–8.

Butler, J. (2008) 'Merely Cultural', in K. Olson (ed.) *Adding Insult to Injury: Nancy Fraser Debates Her Critics*, London: Verso, pp. 42–56.

Cock, J. and Bernstein, A. (2001) 'Gender Differences: Struggles around "Needs" and "Rights" in South Africa', *NWSA Journal* 13(3): 138–52.

Ekine, S. (2010) *The LGBTI Movement and Social Media in Africa*, Heinrich Böll Stiftung. Available online at www.boell.de/worldwide/africa/africa-africa-LGBTI-social-media-9043.html (accessed 24 November 2014).

Fanon, F. (1965) *Wretched of the Earth*, New York: Grove Press.

Fraser, N. (1997) *Justice Interruptus: Critical Reflections on the 'Postsocialist' Condition*, New York: Routledge.

—— (2008) 'From Redistribution to Recognition? Dilemmas of Justice in a "Post-socialist" Age', in K. Olson (ed.) *Adding Insult to Injury: Nancy Fraser Debates Her Critics*, London: Verso, pp. 68–93.

Hall, S. (2001) 'When Was "the Post-Colonial"? Thinking at the Limit', in I. Chambers and L. Curtis (eds) *The Postcolonial Question: Common Skies, Divided Horizons*, London: Routledge, pp. 242–60.

Halperin, D. M. (1995) *Saint Foucault: Towards a Gay Hagiography*, New York: Oxford University Press.

Hartsock, N. (1983) *Money, Sex and Power*, New York: Longman.

Hennessy, R. (2000) *Profit and Pleasure: Sexual Identities in Late Capitalism*, New York: Routledge.

Hoad, N. (1999) 'Between the White Man's Burden and the White Man's Disease: Tracking Lesbian and Gay Human Rights in Southern Africa', *GLQ: A Journal of Lesbian and Gay Studies* 2(4): 559–84.

HSRC (2007) *Cloud over the Rainbow Nation* Vol. 5, No. 1. Available online at www.hsrc.ac.za/en/review/March-2007/rainbow-nation (accessed 10 December 2014).

Jagose, A. (1996) *Queer Theory: An Introduction*, New York: New York University Press.

Livermon, X. (2012) 'Queer(y)ing Freedom: Black Queer Visibilities in Postapartheid South Africa', *GLQ: A Journal of Lesbian and Gay Studies* 18(2–3): 297–323.

Matebeni, Z. (2011) *Exploring Black Lesbian Sexualities and Identities in Johannesburg*, unpublished PhD thesis, University of the Witwatersrand, Johannesburg. Available online at http://wiredspace.wits.ac.za/bitstream/handle/10539/10274/Matebeni%20PhD%20thesis%202011.pdf?sequence=2 (accessed 24 November 2014).

—— (2013) 'Deconstructing violence towards black lesbians in South Africa', in S. Ekine and H. Abbas (eds) *Queer African Reader*, London: Pambazuka Press.

Mauss, M. (2000) *The Gift: The Form and Reason for Exchange in Archaic Societies*, trans. W. D. Halls, New York: W. W. Norton.

Muholi, Z. (2004) 'Thinking through Lesbian Rape', *Agenda* 18(61): 116–25.

Nyong'o, T. (2012) 'Queer Africa and the Fantasy of Virtual Participation', *WSQ: Women's Studies Quarterly* 40(1–2): 40–63.

Ossome, L. (2013) 'Postcolonial Discourses of Queer Activism and Class in Africa', in S. Ekine and H. Abbas (eds) *Queer African Reader*, London: Pambazuka Press, pp. 32–47.

Pizzale, E. (2011) *A Tricky Debate on Hate Crime*. Available online at http://victimempowermentlaw.org.za/2011/03/30/a-tricky-debate-on-hate-crime (accessed 10 December 2014).

Posel, D. (2005) 'Sex, Death and the Fate of the Nation: Reflections on the Politicization of Sexuality in Post-Apartheid South Africa', *Journal of the International African Institute* 75(2): 125–53.

Rubin, G. (1975) 'The Traffic in Women', in R. R. Reiter (ed.) *Towards an Anthropology of Women*, New York: Monthly Review Press, pp. 157–210.

Saalfield, C. and Navarro, R. (1991) 'Shocking Pink Praxis: Race and Gender on the ACT UP Frontlines', in D. Fuss (ed.) *Inside/Out: Lesbian Theories, Gay Theories*, New York: Routledge, pp. 341–69.

Stychin, C. F. (1996) 'Constituting Sexuality: The Struggle for Sexual Orientation in the South African Bill of Rights', *Journal of Law and Society* 23(4): 455–83.

Walcott, R. (2007) 'Somewhere Out There: The New Black Queer Theory', in M. H. Wright and A. Schuhmann (eds) *Blackness and Sexuality*, Berlin: LIT Verlag, pp. 29–40.

Young, I. M. (1990) *Justice and the Politics of Difference*, Princeton, NJ: Princeton University Press.

—— (2008) 'Unruly Categories: A Critique of Nancy Fraser's Dual Systems Theory', in K. Olson (ed.) *Adding Insult to Injury: Nancy Fraser Debates Her Critics*, London: Verso, pp. 327–46.

Chapter 8

Classing Desire

Erotics, politics, value

Jon Binnie

> The marginalization of social class from sexualities research raises epistemological questions about whose experiences are being used to generalize understandings of sexual and intimate life.
>
> (Elizabeth McDermott 'The World *Some* Have Won')

Discussions of how distinctions are drawn between valued and unvalued (queer) lives have often overlooked questions of social class, despite the claim by Raffo (1997: 6) that 'Issues of class frame and run rampant through queer political issues'. Any attempt to produce more just economies of desire is therefore devalued to the extent that it neglects class. In this chapter, I critique the marginalization of class within sexuality studies and discuss how class analysis can contribute towards the imagination of more just economies of desire. I suggest that a class-sensitive critique of contemporary sexual politics would benefit from a holistic perspective that integrates both cultural and economic approaches to class. Critical work on homonormativity can sometimes reproduce classed perspectives and generalize about the social, economic conditions of sexual dissidents, based on the experiences of the economically privileged. In a similar vein, Heaphy (2011: 59) argues that '"Undifferentiated" accounts of gay life tend to narrate relatively well-resourced and privileged experience as gay experience, and normatively promote this as a script for how gay life should be conceived and lived'. I suggest that the erasure of working-class experience is notable even within work that has explicitly sought to address the class politics of eroticism, for instance on the phenomenon of so-called 'gay chavinism' in the UK, which Johnson (2008) and Brewis and Jack (2010) have framed as the consumption and commodification of working-class men by middle-class gay men. Finally, I argue that the emerging body of work on the class politics of sexuality in the UK would benefit from considering the relationship between class and sexuality in a transnational context, and engaging more directly with the politics of race and racism.

Class as an unsettling subject

Sayer (2005: 1) has argued that 'class is an embarrassing and unsettling subject'. Indeed, some queer scholars from working-class backgrounds have suggested that discussing class within some academic spaces can be more difficult and troubling than discussing sexuality (Oldfield and Johnson 2008: 3; see also Taylor 2012). As Taylor (2011: 42) reminds us, 'while we are all implicated in class and sexuality, these categories have more power, purchase and even pain for some more than others'. Some sexual identities are more marked in class terms than others, and writing about class often involves the exercise of moral judgment – for example, about the sexual politics of classed consumption practices. For instance, Jackson argues that:

> It seems that if a woman's stiletto heels are designed by Manolo Blahnik, rather than being white plastic discount store purchases, she is allowed considerably more moral latitude in the conduct of heterosexual encounters. Morality, of course, has always been class specific.
>
> (2011: 17)

It is this class-specific nature of morality that is significant in thinking through the morality of the market and the sexual politics of neoliberalism. This is particularly important as overt hatred of the working class is seen as legitimate in mainstream media in the UK: as Skeggs (2009: 37) argues, 'We are now in a period where outright contempt is freely expressed *against* the working class'. While such contempt of the working class may be a feature of contemporary British political life, it is important to note how judgmentalism regarding class can also operate within critical discussions of sexual politics. For instance, Gould has recently provided a thoughtful discussion of the relationship between class, gender and white privilege in relation to the politics of affect and solidarity in ACT UP (AIDS Coalition to Unleash Power). Discussing Cohen's (1998) examination of the classed dispositions of entitlement within gay, white, middle-class members of the organization, and how HIV/AIDS constituted a class dislocation, she seeks to interrogate these claims about the class and racial privilege of participants within ACT UP more closely. Whilst recognizing the partial validity of these claims, Gould suggests that there can sometimes be a judgmental and moralistic tone to the denigration of the privilege of these men:

> Politically, the claim that ACT UP members felt entitled to state assistance in a time of crisis sometimes contains a judgmental, moralizing stain that implies, in my view problematically, that being privileged is itself an irredeemably bad thing and a valid reason to disregard a person's political claims. The suggestion is that white, gay men should not have been fighting for their own lives, that to do so was somehow selfish.
>
> (2009: 144–5)

These concerns about judgment and representation mean that it can be difficult to explore the relationships between class and sexuality, and may partially explain why they remain under-discussed within sexuality studies. Moreover, some writers may feel more entitled, or compelled, to write about class in relation to sexuality because of their specific classed subjectivity in relation to sexual politics, while others may be more confident, or materially privileged, to speak about how class impacts upon their everyday negotiation of sexual practice and identity. Being able or empowered, or willing, to articulate a perspective on class within academic spaces can be intimately tied to the performative aspects of classed practices – for instance, in the UK where one's class position can be marked and placed by one's accent (Wilson 2008). Access to the authorization of representations is highly unequal, meaning that those who control the production of representations reveal classed positions. Having outlined what I perceive to be some of the difficulties faced by discussing class in relation to sexual politics, I proceed to provide a brief examination of the way in which class has been framed within debates on the relationship between economics and sexual politics.

Sexuality, class and economics

Sexuality has been routinely marginalized within class analysis, even the new class studies that have been more sensitive to the gender and cultural dimensions of class politics. Class is a contentious category, and conflicts over how to conceptualize class have centred on the relative analytical weight given to the economic and the cultural. Bottero (2009: 8) argues that '"class" also means different things to different people, and its exact meaning, in both academic and everyday use, is notoriously slippery'. Focusing on class as a purely economic construct, as opposed to a culturally mediated category, has consequences for how we can envisage a sexual politics of class. Despite recent valuable ground-breaking attempts to queer Marxism (Bassi 2006; Floyd 2009), Marxist-informed class analysis and politics have often been hostile towards sexual politics. Introducing sexuality into discussions of class in such a context constitutes a challenge to the neglect of sexuality within Marxism. Indeed, Floyd (2009: 2) has argued that 'A strong sense of Marxism's limits, of its tendency to elide questions of sexuality, was central to and even constitutive of what we might call queer theory's early stage'. Within recent sociological debates on class, there have been tensions between those who integrate culture and economy, or prioritize one over the other (see Crompton and Scott 2005 for a discussion of these alternative framings of class analysis). I maintain it is necessary to retain the integrity of culture and economy, and not prioritize one over the other. Analyses of class are limited to the extent that they neglect socio-economic inequalities or questions of identity and subjectivity. It is this tension between cultural and economic dimensions of class that has also permeated discussions of the sexual politics of contemporary capitalism.

On the Left there has been a long history of sexual politics being treated as an unwelcome distraction to class politics. Sexual politics has been seen as either complicit with the capitalist system, or irrelevant to an understanding of and struggle to transform that system. For instance, consider Žižek's (1997) argument that struggles for sexual rights are a diversion from the real political struggle against the capitalist mode of production. This tendency to construct the politics of sexuality as divisive, limited and a distraction from the real struggle against capitalism has been most notably taken to task by Butler. I do not want to restate the well-rehearsed arguments regarding the debate between Butler (1997) and Fraser (1997) regarding whether sexual and queer politics were 'merely cultural' (for discussion and critique, see Bell and Binnie 2000; Floyd 2009; Smith 2001). While Butler has criticized Fraser's framing of gay and lesbian politics as part of the politics of recognition as opposed to redistribution, there are a number of other writers including Patel (2006) who have criticized sexuality studies for lacking an economic component. Likewise, Robson (1997: 173) argues that 'Economic deprivation constricts choices, including the opportunity to create a life in which one's lesbianism can flourish', in the same way that McDermott (2010) argues that possession of greater amounts of social, economic and cultural capital may better enable middle-class lesbians to cope with psychological issues on coming out.

Bourdieu's work on class distinctions as the product of differential accumulation of social, cultural, economic and symbolic capital has been highly influential in recent attempts to theorize the relationships between class, gender and sexual politics beyond the recognition-versus-redistribution debate. Building on the work of Skeggs, McDermott (2011) argues for a queering of Bourdieu, suggesting that there are affinities between Bourdieu's theorization of social identities and queer theory in that both share a concern with binaries and how these are embodied. She argues that developing Bourdieu's insights on class with those of queer theory 'may overcome the material/cultural binary, which has proven problematic to the development of intersectional studies of class and sexuality' (2011: 76). Recent research examining the relationship between class and sexuality in the UK has often been informed by a Bourdieuian approach to class – for instance, work examining the class dimensions of working-class lesbian parents' negotiation of the education system (Nixon 2011) and the classing of LGBT people's post-compulsory school choices (McDermott 2011). This nuanced work articulates a class-informed queer critique that can interrogate and integrate the material and symbolic dimensions of classed sexualities. It also highlights the need for recognition of the complexity of the ways in which sexual lives and economies are classed.

The class politics of homonormativity and neoliberal sexualities

While recent work on the sexual politics of neoliberalism has focused critical attention on gay affluence and privilege (Brown 2009; Cossman 2007; Duggan 2003; Woltersdorff 2011) and the social and material inequalities between and within queer communities, I argue that there is not a singular logic that can define the relationship between sexuality and neoliberalism. Rather than presume that neoliberalism is generative of a more gay-friendly sexual politics (however narrowly defined in terms of the politics of consumer citizenship and the politics of individualization, responsibiliation and privatization), we need to recognize that there is a much more ambivalent relationship between sexual politics and neoliberalism. An awareness of the spatial and temporal politics of neoliberalism can help us understand that the relationship between sexuality and neoliberalism may take on different formations in different historical and geographical contexts. For instance, examining the authoritarian neoliberal sexual politics of Thatcherism in the UK in the 1980s, Hoggart (2005: 154) suggests that 'There is an obvious contradiction between on the one hand, the individualism and libertarianism fundamental to neoliberalism and on the other, the call for state intervention to regulate sexuality within private lives'. While certain regimes of accumulation may deploy a liberal, gay-friendly mode of regulation, others may deploy a more authoritarian, socially conservative mode of regulation that may be deeply hostile towards the interests of lesbians and gay men (see Binnie 2014 for a discussion of the gender and sexual politics of neoliberalism in contemporary Poland). We therefore need to recognize the ambivalence with regard to the sexual politics of neoliberalism, echoing May *et al.*'s (2008: 82) statement that 'Rather than searching for the either/or, we need to understand the contradictions inherent within neoliberalism'.

When I first read Duggan's (2002) pioneering and inspirational essay on the sexual politics of neoliberalism, I was drawn to the concept of 'homonormativity' because it drew attention to material inequalities within queer communities, and reinforced critiques of 'gay conservatism', the assimilationist agendas of mainstream gay and lesbian politics centred around gay marriage, and the role of the pink economy discourse in legitimating this assimilation. Duggan's notion of homonormativity has been immensely productive in generating research on the material inequalities within queer lives (as shown in the chapters by Gressgård and Kapur in this volume). Duggan's pioneering essay and her other writing on the sexual politics of neoliberalism (Duggan 2003) has helped to re-orientate critical attention within sexuality studies towards issues of social and economic justice (even if the relationship between economics and sexuality has a longer history – see, for instance, Evans' [1993] wide-ranging analysis of the material basis of sexual politics and sexual citizenship). But as Ossome's discussion of struggles against sexual violence towards black lesbians in South Africa demonstrates (in Chapter 7 of this volume), the broader and material and class dimensions of sexual politics are often rendered invisible in struggles for sexual justice.

However, I have been concerned by the way in which the term 'homonormativity' can sometimes be used and would like to question its place within the lexicon of queer social and political thought. For instance, Brown has argued that:

> there is a danger that the more we name 'homonormativity' and (un)critically apply it to all mainstream expressions of lesbian and gay culture, the more we stoke its discursive power and reinforce it as the dominant, unassailable

> expression of (an equally all-powerful and ubiquitous) neoliberalism in the realm of intimate life.
>
> (2009: 1497)

Brown (2009) is critical of the way in which the label of 'homonormativity' has sometimes been applied in an undifferentiated manner to the analysis of lesbian and gay male consumption practices. Like other commentators, he suggests that notions of lesbian and gay male affluence can reproduce and reinforce problematic stereotypes in this regard. Informed by Gibson-Graham's (2006) exploration of alternatives to capitalism, Brown argues that even the figure of the affluent lesbian and gay male consumer can be imagined differently as participating in ethical consumption and forms of exchange that are alternative or in opposition to the market economy. I am concerned with the politics of naming and labelling and who has the power to name and label same-sex consumption practices as 'homonormative', who traditionally is marked and labelled as undesirable and politically reactionary, and whose agency is seen as politically problematic. This focus on the deployment of the concept of 'normativity' resonates with Gressgård's statement (in Chapter 5 of this volume) regarding the importance of queer critique in 'politicizing the content of normative judgment'. On the issue of who has the power to label and make judgments about other people's behaviour, I note Kadi's (1997: 34–5) argument that 'Working-class/working-poor people claim the dubious honour of being dubbed more homophobic (and more racist, and more sexist) than rich people. This holds true in mainstream society, queer organizations, and other progressive movements.' Queer politics is itself also marked by classed distinctions, and in this context I am concerned who or what gets labelled as not queer enough, as homonormative, and who has the power to vocalize and judge. I prefer to recognize the ambivalent nature of gay and lesbian consumption in simultaneously offering opportunities for both resistance to and incorporation within late capitalism. For instance, in her study of the emergence of a British Asian gay club night within the context of shifts in the political economy of Birmingham's Hurst Street gay scene, Bassi (2006: 214) argues against simplistic constructions of commodified gay space as part of a 'wider strategy to simply contain sexual dissidence', arguing that 'Instead of posing gay political economy as a structure of control and despotic force to be sweepingly rejected (with radical counter-potential as somehow outside of this), perhaps we might consider how immanent within capitalism itself there is both capture and escape' (2006: 214) and noting that 'the monthly nights of the British Asian gay club scene have opened up channels within the capitalist leviathan for contestation and alternative ordering' (ibid.: 227). As Bassi has shown, there are dangers in the reductionism of some political economic approaches to the study of sexuality in which sexual dissidence is simply read as being unproblematically incorporated into or emblematic of late capitalism. Her work recognizes the ambivalence by many users of spaces of the pink economy. We need to articulate a vision of social justice that places sexual politics at the core of economic, social and political geographies, and does not treat them as merely cultural, superfluous and tangential. In the context of the recession in the UK in the early 1990s, I wrote about the dangers of the pink economy discourse in marking gay men as an affluent niche market and constituency (Binnie 1995). Likewise, in her discussion of the imperial geography of white gay tourism in the Caribbean, Alexander (1998: 285) argues that 'The myth of the gay consumer as a prosperous, perhaps undeserving elite, is now so prevalent as to be politically dangerous'. As Alexander suggests, the stereotype of gay affluence can be harmful and, unfortunately, radical queer scholarship can sometimes reproduce this stereotype. However, scholars such as Brown (2009) and Woltersdorff (2007) have sought to critique it.

Unjust desiring economies: the eroticization and commodification of the working-class body

In the UK, discussions of the representational politics of classed sexualities have crystallized in the figure of the 'chav' and what Brewis and Jack (2010) term 'gay chavinism'. By studying the representational politics of the 'chav', we can see how class matters to sexual politics. It also helps us to see how notions of judgment and value are deployed in analyses of class erotics. Studying the complex class erotics of the figure of the chav can therefore assist us in thinking through the relationships between eroticism and social and economic justice more broadly. 'Chav' is a highly pejorative term that connotes class hatred and the objectification and dehumanization of a specific typology of white working-class people, mocking, amongst other things, their accent, bodily deportment and penchant for designer labels and brands. In his study of representations of gay consumption of chav aesthetics, Johnson (2008) argues that while 'chav' bodies were devalued in the mainstream media, at the same time they became objects of desire for gay men and used to derive capital for entrepreneurs on the commercial gay scene. Johnson (2008) argues that the establishment of gay 'chav nights' on the gay scene fetishizes and objectifes working-class bodies that were objects of disgust in dominant media representations. Brewis and Jack use the term 'gay chavinism' to denote the commodity practices of 'gay men buying clothes in order to dress as chavs' (2010: 252). They go on to argue that:

> chavs, themselves depicted in popular discourse as avid, brand-aware consumers, have apparently become commodities for *others'* consumption; in this case, gay men who supposedly hail from the middle classes. It is this translation of a particular kind of sexual fascination into commodity form that constitutes our object of inquiry.
>
> (ibid.)

This statement is notable for the way in which gay men are presumed to be non-working-class, reproducing the equation of gay identity with a middle- or upper-class subject position. Working-class men figure here only as victims of a uni-directional middle-class gay gaze that objectifies them. 'Chavs' are commonly pathologized for their consumption practices that supposedly display a vulgar consumerism and lack of taste. It is therefore noteworthy that Brewis and Jack frame the consumption of 'chavs' by middle-class gay men as symbolically violent and tasteless.

Johnson's (2008) analysis also draws attention to the relationship between desire and disgust, arguing that representations of the chav reproduced through gay chav nights serve to fix the (heterosexualized) working-class body in place as a container of essentialized characteristics of an excess of masculinity and hardness. Such representations reveal and reflect middle-class anxieties and fears, but also desire for the working-class male body. Like Brewis and Jack, Johnson's argument tends to presume that gay consumers of such representations are middle-class, which can render invisible working-class subject positions, although, to be fair, Johnson does make it clear that his discussion of the gay chav is not concerned with how such representations are consumed by differently classed viewers. While Johnson argues that such representations draw a clear demarcation between gay and working-class subjectivities, it is important to consider multiple, alternative ways in which these particular representations of the gay chav could be interpreted differently. Part of the problem here resides in the difficulties of claiming positive working-class gay identities. For instance, Heaphy argues that:

> Access to the positive content of working-class identities is premised on being heterosexually male. This exclusion of gay men from positive working-class identities goes some way to explaining some men's reluctance to embrace these, as well as the minimal nature of many gay men's affirmation of working-class identity.
>
> (2011: 58)

In this context, assertions of working-class gay claims to class authenticity and masculinity are easily devalued by hegemonic assumptions in both academic and popular culture that gay men are uniformly middle-class. Heaphy argues that the exclusion of gay men from the positive and affirming characteristics of working-class identities, which can be difficult to claim, can reinforce dis-identification from working-class identity altogether. Alternatively, the gay chav could be conceptualized as a strong affirmation of and mobilization of working-class identity and class pride. It may also serve to maximize body and cultural capital within some parts of the gay scene. In a survey of 3,000 young people in Scotland that examined their identification with 'neds' (so-called 'non-educated delinquents', the Scottish equivalent term for 'chav'), Young found that self-identification with ned/chav identity was common by middle-class young people, arguing that 'many middle-class youth now emulate and adopt apparel and attributes associated with working and underclass youth' (2010: 1157). This suggests that ned/chav identity may have a broader class basis than evident from discussions of chav in media and academic commentary on the chav hitherto. It also suggests that chav aesthetics are valued much more widely than suggested in the discussions of gay chavinism by Brewis and Jack (2010) and Johnson (2008). Young (2010) suggests that the widespread adoption of the chav/ned identity demonstrated by his survey point towards 'a major divergence between the perceptions of social commentators and youth of every social class about the connections between social class and embracing a marginalized (Ned/Chav) identity which requires deeper sociological exploration' (2010: 1158). Young's findings should make us circumspect about drawing any conclusions about the exceptionality of middle-class gay men's 'commodification' of chav identity and aesthetics.

While supportive of Johnson's analysis of the symbolic violence afforded by the gay chav phenomenon, das Nair and Hansen (2012) argue that Johnson's analysis is limited by the failure to recognize the agency of working-class youths marked or self-identifying as 'chav': 'the assertion that this refers to "a largely voiceless group" denies the people who are referred to as, or who self-refer as, chav the agency they have' (2012: 144). Johnson's essay examines the representation of one gay chav club night, arguing that such representations fix working-class sexualities into place, for the benefit and consumption of the mobile, middle-class consumer, creating distinctions between the mobile, desirable neoliberal subject and the abject working-class object, which is fixed into place. This relational geography of class formation (Stenning 2008) also features in Alderson's (2011) analysis of the class and neoliberal sexual politics of the film *Billy Elliot* (2000), which was directed by Stephen Daldry. *Billy Elliot* focuses on the gender politics of working-class life in the North East of England at the time of 1984 miners' strike and features Billy Elliot, the son of a striking miner, and his process of becoming a ballet dancer. Alderson (2011: 2) argues that:

> In its account of the development of a striking miner's son into a successful ballet dancer, *Billy Elliot* presents the transition to neoliberalism as one from a repressive and repressed 'masculine' past to a more tolerant, expressive, cosmopolitan, and 'feminine' present.
>
> (2011: 2)

Alderson critiques the way in which working-class masculinities are represented in the film as backward and non-modern, reflecting the way in which Skeggs (2005) has argued that working-class life in Britain is commonly represented as being backward and an obstacle to the national economic progress. This argument resonates with Gressgård's critique of the spatial and temporal politics of discursive constructions of gay cosmopolitanism. It should be evident from the discussion of the class erotics of the 'gay chav' that while the classed nature of desire is a complex issue, cultural stereotypes have often framed class dynamics within gay male identities in terms of middle-class gay/working-class straight dichotomy. Furthermore, the relationship between class, erotics and desire can be subject to change across the life-course. This is evident in Bérubé's (1996) narration of how the classed nature of his same-sex desire and erotic attraction changed throughout his life-course. From a French–American, working-class background, Bérubé describes how his sexual desire changed when he obtained a scholarship to a private preparatory school:

> My desire to belong in an intellectual world – which in this school taught us to take whiteness, upper-class privilege, and maleness for granted – aroused a new but secret and often sexual desire for these smart, well-to-do, articulate men. I wanted to have them, I wanted to be them, and I wanted to be wanted by them. And so my homosexual desires began to split into two directions. They moved horizontally, toward working-class men like myself and the scholarship boys I worked with in the kitchen. Since childhood, I had eroticized such boys as brothers, and now I associated them with my past and my family. My homo desires also moved up vertically, toward my 'betters', who seemed to give me self-respect, verify my respectability, and offer me another escape route into a better, more secure future.
>
> (1996: 149)

Bérubé suggests that his erotic desires changed over time and that his erotic desire came to be focused on working-class men. He expresses anxiety about what lies behind this change, and whether this was due to his entry into the middle classes. Bérubé's thoughtful reflections on the changing nature of the class orientation of his erotic desires and Heaphy's (2011) discussion of the complex ways in which class difference was articulated by his respondents present a complex pattern of classed erotic desire that challenge pathologization of the working class in the representations of the chav critiqued by Johnson. In this context, I also recognize the complexities of class positioning within lesbian articulations of desire discussed by Taylor (2008) in her study of working-class lesbian perspectives on the commercial scene in Scotland and the North of England. Taylor argues that a number of women in her study articulated feelings of exclusion from the mainstream commercial scene. This exclusion was economic in that they did not have the economic resources to travel to distant lesbian commercial spaces. Some women articulated a desire to distance themselves from middle-class spaces, where they did not feel comfortable and did not have the resources to occupy a 'homonormative' space of entitlement, but also dis-identified with working-class scene spaces.

Conclusion

In this chapter, I have argued that an awareness of the cultural and economic dimensions of class is necessary in order to imagine more just economics of desire. By challenging the neglect of the material and subjective dimensions of class within sexuality studies, I have sought to draw critical attention to the limitations of the concept of homonormativity. I have argued that the term can sometimes be used uncritically to reproduce classed stereotypes about the universality of lesbian and gay affluence by overlooking the conditions and situations of working-class lesbians and gay men. We need to recognize the resilience of such stereotypes and the marginalization of working-class experiences within discussions of the sexual politics of neoliberalism. My discussion of critical work on the eroticization of the working class within 'gay chavinism' has questioned the way that homosexuality is equated with a middle-class subjectivities, while working-class sexual subjects are constructed as passive victims. To argue for a class analysis does not mean that other formations of difference should be downplayed. It means (re-)integrating class into intersectional perspectives on sexuality. In this context, Bottero (2009) argues that an emphasis on the whiteness of the working class renders invisible the classed dimensions of socio-economic inequalities pertaining to other ethnic groups. Noting that historically the lower classes in Britain were often marked in racialized terms with their bodies compared to African natives, Nayak (2009: 29) suggests that although 'working-class youth have long been held in a precarious and contingent relationship to whiteness', they are today marked as 'the authentic carriers of whiteness' (ibid.). Moreover, a class analysis that is bounded within the UK, for example, can occlude the transnational and intersectional politics of class. For instance, Alexander argues that white-dominated gay organizations in the US fail to recognize the transnational class politics of consumption and production:

> They refuse to see that 'First World' citizenship is linked to consumption and that the 'Third World' enables the standard of living and the unequal consumptive patterns of the 'First World' overall, providing cheapened labor that makes it possible for lesbian and gay consumers living in the U.S. and other 'First World' metropoles to enjoy a certain way of life.
>
> (1998: 285)

Failure to recognize the transnational dimensions of class politics thereby devalues class-informed analysis of sexual politics.

One recent example of work that has foregrounded agency and desire in the context of classed sexual labour in a transnational context is Collins' essay on the sexual politics of hospitality labour in Manila. Collins (2009: 541) argues that 'Transnational frameworks situate desire in the shifting social geographies of transnational experience and relations, shedding light on the differential mobilities, power, and resistance that constitute "identity"'. Her focus on the desiring subjectivity and agency of the host man and his labour means that he is not simply seen as a passive, objectified victim of globalizing economic processes. Collins places questions of agency and desire in the core of her analysis of the labour of hospitality, arguing that 'Through their performance of desire, [her respondents] assert agency over hospitality relationships, constructing them as a worthwhile exchange relationship' (ibid.: 549). Collins' work stresses the necessity of foregrounding working-class agency and desire within analyses of the sexual politics of contemporary capitalism. However, my earlier discussions of the gay chav, queer classed subjectivities, and dis-identifications with working-class identities suggest that articulating working-class agency in relation to the sexual politics of capitalism is not always straightforward.

References

Alderson, D. (2011) 'Making Electricity: Narrating Gender, Sexuality, and the Neoliberal Transition in *Billy Elliot*', *Camera Obscura* 25(3.75): 1–27.

Alexander, M. J. (1998) 'Imperial Desire/Sexual Utopias: White Gay Capital and Transnational Tourism', in E. Shohat (ed.) *Talking Visions: Multicultural Feminism in a Transnational Age*, Cambridge, MA: MIT Press, pp. 281–305.

Bassi, C. (2006) 'Riding the Dialectical Waves of Gay Political Economy: A Story from Birmingham's Commercial Gay Scene', *Antipode* 38(2): 213–35.

Bell, D. and Binnie, J. (2000) *The Sexual Citizen: Queer Politics and Beyond*, Cambridge: Polity Press.

Bérubé, A. (1996) 'Intellectual Desire', *GLQ: A Journal of Lesbian and Gay Studies* 3(1): 139–57.

Binnie, J. (1995) 'Trading Places: Consumption, Sexuality and the Production of Queer Space', in D. Bell and G. Valentine (eds) *Mapping Desire: Geographies of Sexualities*, London: Routledge, pp. 182–99.

—— (2014) 'Neoliberalism, Class, Gender and Lesbian, Gay, Bisexual, Transgender and Queer Politics in Poland', *International Journal of Politics, Culture and Society* 27: 241–57.

Bottero, W. (2009) 'Class in the 21st Century', in K. P. Sveinsson (ed.) *Who Cares about the White Working Class?* London: Runnymede Trust, pp. 7–15.

Brewis, J. and Jack, G. (2010) 'Consuming Chavs: The Ambiguous Politics of Gay Chavinism', *Sociology* 44(2): 1–18.

Brown, G. (2009) 'Thinking Beyond Homonormativity: Performative Explorations of Diverse Gay Economies', *Environment and Planning* A 41: 1496–510.

Butler, J. (1997) 'Merely Cultural', *Social Text* 52/53: 265–78.

Cohen, P. F. (1998) *Love and Anger: Essays on AIDS, Activism, and Politics*, New York: Harrington Press.

Collins, D. (2012) 'Gay Hospitality as Desiring Labor: Contextualizing Transnational Sexual Labor', *Sexualities* 15(5–6): 538–53.

Cossman, B. (2007) *Sexual Citizens: The Legal and Cultural Recognition of Sex and Belonging*, Stanford, CA: Stanford University Press.

Crompton, R. and Scott, J. (2005) 'Class Analysis: Beyond the Cultural Turn', in F. Devine, M. Savage, J. Scott and R. Crompton (eds) *Rethinking Class: Culture, Identities and Lifestyle*, Basingstoke: Palgrave Macmillan, pp. 186–203.

das Nair, R. and Hansen, S. (2011) 'Social Class', in R. das Nair and C. Butler (eds) *Intersectionality, Sexuality and Psychological Therapies: Working with Lesbian, Gay and Bisexual Diversity*, Chichester: Wiley-Blackwell, pp. 137–62.

Duggan, L. (2002) 'The New Homonormativity: The Sexual Politics of Neoliberalism', in R. Castronovo and D. Nelson (eds) *Materializing Democracy: Toward a Revitalized Cultural Politics*, Durham, NC/London: Duke University Press, pp. 175–94.

—— (2003) *The Twilight of Equality: Neoliberalism, Cultural Politics, and the Attack on Democracy*, Boston, MA: Beacon Press.

Evans, D. T. (1993) *Sexual Citizenship: The Material Construction of Sexualities*, London: Routledge.
Floyd, K. (2009) *The Reification of Desire: Toward a Queer Marxism*, Minneapolis: University of Minnesota Press.
Fraser, N. (1997) 'Heterosexism, Misrecognition, and Capitalism: A Response to Judith Butler', *Social Text* 52/53: 279–94.
Gibson-Graham, J. K. (2006) *A Post-Capitalist Politics*, Minneapolis: University of Minnesota Press.
Gould, D. (2009) *Moving Politics: Emotion and ACT-UP's Fight Against AIDS*, Chicago, IL: University of Chicago Press.
Heaphy, B. (2011) 'Gay Identities and the Culture of Class', *Sexualities* 14(1): 42–62.
Hoggart, L. (2005) 'Neoliberalism, the New Right and Sexual Rights', in A. Saad-Filho and D. Johnston (eds) *Neoliberalism: A Critical Reader*, London: Pluto, pp. 149–55.
Jackson, S. (2011) 'Heterosexual Hierarchies: A Commentary on Class and Sexuality', *Sexualities* 14(1): 12–20.
Johnson, P. (2008) 'Rude Boys: The Homosexual Eroticization of Class', *Sociology* 42(1): 65–82.
Kadi, J. (1997) 'Homophobic Workers or Elitist Queers?', in S. Raffo (ed.) *Queerly Classed: Gay Men and Lesbians Write About Class*, Boston, MA: South End Press, pp. 29–42.
May, J., Datta, K., Evans, Y., Herbert, J., McIlwaine, C. and Willis, J. (2008) *Travelling Neoliberalism: Polish and Ghanaian Migrant Workers in London*, in A. Smith, A. Stenning and K. Willis (eds) *Social Justice and Neoliberalism: Global Perspectives*, London: Zed Books, pp. 61–89.
McDermott, E. (2010) '"I Just Want to be Totally True to Myself": Class and the Making of the Sexual Self', in Y. Taylor (ed.) *Classed Intersections: Spaces, Selves, Knowledges*, Farnham: Ashgate, pp. 199–216.
—— (2011) 'The World *Some* Have Won: Sexuality, Class and Inequality', *Sexualities* 14(1): 63–78.
Nayak, A. (2009) 'Beyond the Pale: Chavs, Youth and Social Class', in K. P. Sveinsson (ed.) *Who Cares about the White Working Class?* London: Runnymede Trust, pp. 28–35.
Nixon, C. (2011) 'Working-Class Lesbian Parents' Emotional Engagement with Their Children's Education: Intersections of Class and Sexuality', *Sexualities* 14(1): 79–99.
Oldfield, K. and Johnson III, R. G. (2008) 'Introduction', in K. Oldfield and R. G. Johnson III (eds) *Resilience: Queer Professors from the Working Class*, Albany: State University of New York Press.
Patel, G. (2006) 'Risky Subjects: Insurance, Sexuality, and Capital', *Social Text* 89: 25–65.
Raffo, S. (1997) 'Introduction', in S. Raffo (ed.) *Queerly Classed*, Boston, MA: South End Press.
Robson, R. (1997) 'To Market, to Market: Considering Class in the Context of Lesbian Legal Theories and Reforms', in S. Raffo (ed.) *Queerly Classed: Gay Men and Lesbians Write about Class*, Boston, MA: South End Press, pp. 165–78.
Sayer, A. (2005) *The Moral Significance of Class*, Cambridge: Cambridge University Press.

Skeggs, B. (2005) 'The Re-Branding of Class: Propertising Culture', in F. Devine, M. Savage, J. Scott and R. Crompton (eds) *Rethinking Class: Culture, Identities and Lifestyle*, Basingstoke: Palgrave Macmillan, pp. 46–68.

—— (2009) 'Haunted by the Spectre of Judgment: Respectability, Value and Affect in Class Relations', in K. P. Sveinsson (ed.) *Who Cares about the White Working Class?* London: Runnymede Trust.

Smith, A. M. (2001) 'Missing Poststructuralism, Missing Foucault: Butler and Fraser on Capitalism and the Regulation of Sexuality', *Social Text* 67, 19(2): 103–25.

Stenning, A. (2008) 'For Working Class Geographies', *Antipode* 40: 9–14.

Taylor, Y. (2008) '"That's Not Really My Scene": Working-Class Lesbians in (and out of) Place', *Sexualities* 11(5): 523–46.

—— (2011) 'Complexities and Complications: Intersections of Class and Sexuality', in Y. Taylor, S. Hines and M. E. Casey (eds) *Theorizing Intersectionality and Sexuality*, London: Routledge, pp. 37–55.

—— (2012) 'Facts, Fictions, Identity Constrictions: Sexuality, Gender and Class in Higher Education', in Y. Taylor (ed.) *Educational Diversity: The Subject of Difference and Different Subjects*, Basingstoke: Palgrave-Macmillan, pp. 257–67.

Wilson, A. (2008) 'Possibilities', in K. Oldfield and R. G. Johnson III (eds) *Resilience: Queer Professors from the Working Class*, Albany: State University of New York Press, pp. 211–21.

Woltersdorff, V. (2007) 'Neoliberalism and its Homophobic Discontents', *Interalia* 2: 1–9.

—— (2011) 'Paradoxes of Precarious Sexualities', *Cultural Studies* 25(2): 164–82.

Young, R. (2010) 'Can Neds (or Chavs) Be Non-Delinquent, Educated or Even Middle Class? Contrasting Empirical Findings with Cultural Stereotypes', *Sociology* 46(6): 1140–60.

Žižek, S. (1997) 'Multiculturalism, or, the Cultural Logic of Late Capitalism', *New Left Review* 225: 28–52.

Part III

The political economy of queer embodiments

Chapter 9

Queer needs commons!

Transgressing the fiction of self-ownership, challenging westocentric proprietism

Christine M. Klapeer and Karin Schönpflug

More than ten years ago queer theorist Margaret Davies stated that 'queer as a theory and practice' has not yet 'managed to create a new understanding of property', even though some major issues of queer criticisms – modern ideas of a stable and fixed self, a coherent and autonomous subject/ivity – are fundamentally shaped by the (liberal/libertarian[1]) fiction of property in the person and/or[2] (self-)ownership (Davies 1999: 342). Davies argues that if queer theories' purpose is to re-conceptualize these very modes of 'being' on a foundational level, then modes of 'having' as well as the problematic interlinkages of ideas of 'having' and 'being' have to be radically re-thought as well (ibid.). Davies' (ibid.: 330) claim for an 'altered understanding and practice of property' (not only) in queer contexts correlates with an ongoing feminist, race-critical, anarchist and (post-)Marxist debate about the dangerous implications and effects of the liberal/libertarian 'myth' of property in the person and/or self-ownership, thereby discussing how these powerful legal and philosophical fiction(s) may or may not legitimate to 'sell' (all[3]) parts of oneself, one's own labor or – according to recent feminist and bioethical debates – parts of one's own body on the capitalist market on the basis

1 The term liberal/libertarian points to the multiple political and philosophical traditions which have been arising from classical liberal ideas (individual freedom, free will, private property), reaching from 'conservative' liberalism, to free-market liberalism, 'social liberal' liberalism, economic libertarianism, to anarchistic and leftist libertarianism. Even though there is no clear line between 'libertarianism' and 'liberalism', especially because the meaning widely depends on the geopolitical context, they can be differentiated by their opinion on the role of government and state power. For libertarians (from both political spectra) individual freedom is the most important entitlement in a society, which should be privileged over all other needs and rights, therefore arguing for no government or as little government intervention as possible. Liberalism argues that a state is needed to protect and guarantee these basic liberties.

2 Some authors use the terms 'self-ownership' and 'property in person' as interchangeable (see Richardson 2010); others – such as Carole Pateman, for instance – argue that it is more precise to use the term 'property in person' to describe the narration of free contracts in capitalist and patriarchal society. Only if property is perceived as 'alienable' can it be subject to a contract, but if the 'self' is completely 'owned', then it would be not possible to alienate parts (Pateman 2002).

3 Thus, the central crux for liberals/libertarians has been the question whether it is 'legitimate' to sell him/herself into 'slavery'.

of a 'free will' (see Cohen 1995; Pateman 2002; Phillips 2011; Richardson 2010; Taylor 2005). While some critical thinkers (Cohen 1995; Ingram 1994; Pateman 2002) argue that the idea of property in person serves to create and legitimate subordination and/or exploitation in capitalist economies by declaring aspects of one's own property as alienable (his/her labor, talents) and therefore subject to a 'freely' chosen 'contract', not only liberals/libertarians but also feminists or human rights defenders see emancipatory potentials in the concept of ('full') self-ownership (Richardson 2010; Cohen 1995). Self-ownership is therefore often linked with the idea of having 'full' control or a governing right over oneself (including one's own body) as well as with concepts of self-realization and self-determination. Thus, questions regarding the compatibility and constant tension of ('full') self-ownership with the requirements of capitalist economies ('selling' parts of one's own) are highly debated by critical thinkers who point particularly to the 'bourgeois', 'racialized' and 'androcentric' implications of the idea of fully 'owing oneself'.

Interestingly enough, even though there has been an increasing number of queer examinations of commodification practices in capitalist economies, as well as a growing body of research on neoliberalism and commodified forms of gender flexibilization, the powerful liberal/libertarian 'myth' of self-ownership and property in person has not yet been a fundamental subject in queer analyses. This seems to be even more surprising when looking at some critiques from feminist, leftist and postcolonial and race-critical thinkers which indicate a liberal/ist 'trend' in recent queer political moves, writings and self-perceptions by reproducing liberal conceptions of an abstract, dislocated and sovereign subject (Cohen 2005; McCluskey 2009; Morton 2001; Phelan 2000; Perez 2005; Samuels 1999).

This chapter therefore looks into some ambivalent implications and effects of the fiction of (self-)ownership and property in person in relation to the possibility of creating queer subject(s)/ivity and identities as 'positionalit[ies] vis-à-vis the normative [... at odds] with the normal, the legitimate, the dominant' (Halperin 1997: 62). Therefore the first part of this chapter is concerned with the danger of a 'silent' reception of 'established modes of "having" within some queer concepts of fluid identities, bodily autonomy and demands for the right to gender/sexual self-definition' (Davies 1999: 343). It analyses how the fictional idea of self-ownership shapes (certain) queer claims for self-determined/self-defined identities, genders and sexualities. Thus, the chapter follows to some extent the analytical distinction made by Carole Pateman (2002) between 'self-ownership' and 'property in person' when using the term 'self-ownership' mainly for examining queer claims of self-realization, self-determination and the freedom to control (or alter) one's own body.

By integrating class-sensitive and Marxist approaches, the second part of this chapter takes the critique of individualized versions of queer/ing based on a (liberal) notion of full self-ownership a step further by asking what these queer aspirations signify in relation to the commodification of labor within the 'working classes'. Referring to Marxist and post-Marxist critiques of self-ownership, we want to ask if a queer/ed version of 'full' self-ownership then (again) becomes a sign of the 'bourgeois' queer subject while 'working-class queerness' is perceived as less 'queer' because that 'queerness' might be the ambivalent outcome of capitalist requirements (e.g. Rosie the Riveter as gender-transgressing, hard-working 'butch') or economic deprivation (e.g. the figure of the 'promiscuitive welfare mother'). Drawing on some recent debates on the compatibility of capitalist logics and non-heteronormative identities, it will be argued that if 'queerness' is reduced to a non-materialist and individualized destabilization of gender/sexualities, then capitalist commodification processes are also able to produce 'queer' subjects. Hence, we will deal with the fundamental question of how and in what ways current struggles for (subversive) queer subjectivities are constantly caught in westocentric proprietism, thus pointing to the necessity of going beyond liberal concepts of (self-)ownership and property in person in order to imagine queer subjectivities beyond liberal/libertarian and capitalist logics. Thus, as a possible way out of this dialectical problem, we propose a radical epistemological and political reconceptualization of the relationship between 'having' and 'being' instituted in what we call a theory and practice of 'queer commons'.

John Locke as Jack-in-the-queer-box

> This is my body. I do what I want with it.
> This is my body. I make my own choices.
> This is my body. I use it as a canvas,
> tattoo it, decorate it, and pierce it.
> I take medicine if I want to and only undergo medical procedures I choose.
> I eat what I want, exercise for my health, and wear what I like.
> I fall in love with whomever,
> fuck/sleep with whomever and marry whomever I choose.
> I decide when and how to become a mother.
> This is my body, not yours.
>
> (From the film *This Is My Body*, co-created by Jason Stefaniak and Siobhan O'Loughlin, http://jasonstefaniak.com/news)

Queer as a critical theory, method(ology) of analysis and political practice has posed an incipient and significant challenge to essentialist models of sexuality and gender. Arguing for a fluid and performative understanding of gender and sexuality, queer theories and practices have been and are still interrogating the normalizing logics of heteronormativity and hetero/gendered assumptions about identities. Nonetheless, the question of how de/constructivist and performative conceptualizations of gender and sexuality can or might be linked to individual bodily agency and the material situatedness of gendered/racialized/sexed subjects subverting heteronormativity through (individual and/or political) acts of gender/sexual transgression continues to be a highly contested issue in queer, feminist and postcolonial discourse. Particularly relevant for our discussion of the ambivalent relationship between (liberal) notions of self-ownership, property and queer/ness are those postcolonial, feminist and race-critical interrogations that problematize the danger of re-appropriating liberal concepts of universality, autonomy and abstract individualism within queer approaches (Phelan 2000; Perez 2005; Samuels 1999; McCluskey 2009; Cohen 2005; Morton 2001). Jacinth Samuels (1999), for instance, argues that even though queer theory intends to be a postmodern critique of the liberal subject, certain versions of queer anti-essentialism and identity critiques – she analyses introductory articles to queer theory/politics from Steven Epstein and Donna Penn – show strong similarities with liberal humanist concepts of a dislocated and distanced subject/ivity. Samuels states parallels between the 'abstract' implications of queer concepts of fluidity and non-identity and the liberal idea of 'abstract, sovereign subjects without concern for their social location' (Samuels 1999: 91). According to Hiram Perez, queer approaches which pledge for a dislocated 'anti-identity' are therefore reproducing an 'imperial gaze', because it reproduces unmarked 'white' privileges while simultaneously claiming 'race-neutral objectivity' (Perez 2005: 172). The argumentation of Martha T. McCluskey takes a similar direction. She is especially critical of the work of Janet Halley who argues for a radical intimate autonomy and sexual freedom. Hence, McCluskey points to the problematic individualistic and anti-social implications of such queer perceptions of autonomy and freedom (e.g. by marginalizing human dependency). According to McCluskey, queer discourse is in danger of reciting a liberal 'myth of autonomy', which is also prominent in 'traditional liberalism' (McCluskey 2009: 116).

In this chapter we want to take the problem of potential parallels between liberalism and (certain) queer conceptualizations of identity, freedom and autonomy a step further. Therefore, we are linking the critical insights discussed above with a strand of feminist and (post-)Marxist analysis which argues that the idea of private property and self-ownership lies in the heart of every liberal conception of autonomy, freedom and agency (Christman 1991; Cohen 1995; Pateman 2002; Taylor 2005; Richardson 2010; Phillips 2011). As approaches critical of subordination and exploitation in capitalist economies and of individual freedom based on liberalism/libertarianism, those strands are grounded on the fundamental insight that ('modern') perceptions of subjectivity, identity and 'the self' are historically and philosophically intrinsically interlinked with the idea of self-ownership and 'the property in one's own person', therefore arguing that an anti-capitalist critique has to radically rethink or completely reject those liberal conceptions of 'being'.

Philosophically, the concept of self-ownership can be traced back to the works of John Locke who perceived the 'person' – in his theory only 'white' males were capable of being 'free' and political eligible 'persons' – as owner of his own body: 'Though the Earth, and all inferior Creatures be common to all Men, yet every Man has a *Property* in his own *Person*. This no Body had any Right to but himself' (Locke 1689: V-§§ 27). From the concept of self-ownership, liberals/libertarians therefore derived a so-called 'control right' based on the idea that one has 'final authority' over his properties (his/her body; his/her private property) and is 'free from interference in the exercise of that authority – unless [...] the [control] rights of others are being threatened' (Taylor 2005: 467; Christman 1991). 'Having and being oneself' thus defines an autonomous and free person in classical liberal/libertarian theory (Davies 1999: 344).

For John Locke, 'having property in his own person' was also the precondition for the appropriation of all 'private property' since only those persons who 'own themselves' and – according to the important race-critical work of Cheryl I. Harris (1993) – own 'whiteness'[4] are perceived as fully legible 'persons' to claim private property. Thus, the autonomy and right for non-interference of every individual is fundamentally linked to notions of having 'private property' and 'property in oneself' (Naffine 1998), whereas the 'self-possessing [white] subject' then becomes the 'foundation of all other property rights' (Frow 1995: 155). This implies that (free) individuals are self-owners in the sense that they have private property rights over themselves and their bodies and abilities in the same way that people can have private property rights over inanimate objects. They can 'use' private property as well as their property in themselves without interference (Naffine 1998; Harris 1993).

However, the liberal/libertarian fiction of self-ownership was and is still very much connected with ideas of (personal) autonomy, the right of non-interference (particularly with regard to one's own 'privacy'), freedom of 'choice' and 'self-determination' (Phillips 2011; Christman 1991). Since self-determination, freedom of 'choice' and autonomy over one's own body have been and still are central to feminist and human rights movements, the idea of property in the person has been functioning as 'a powerful political force' within a variety of 'progressive movements' (Pateman 2002: 21; Phillips 2011). Davina Cooper and Didi Herman therefore speak in their recent piece of a 'propertied conception of identity' with regard to current legal debates on sexual orientation/sexuality in the context of equal rights laws (Cooper and Herman 2013). Because if sexuality is perceived as 'chosen property', it must be acknowledged, since it is part of one's private property, the 'self' (ibid.).

Following this argumentation, we would also like to demonstrate how queer claims for self-determined/self-defined identities[5] and (sexual/gender) autonomy

4 This argumentation was also the basis for legitimizing slavery and colonial conquest, thereby only acknowledging the property claims of 'white' men. Cheryl I. Harris thus makes clear that 'the hyper-exploitation of Black labor was accomplished by treating Black people themselves as objects of property' (Harris 1993: 1716).

5 See for instance also the discussions and definitions for the word 'genderqueer' as some sort of self-defined gender/trans* identity beyond the heteronormative male/female binary within queer communities.

are very often articulated in a liberal self-ownership language that follows a liberal advocacy for property and/or self-control rights for (queer/s) bodies, thus complicating a more fundamental queer critique of (private) property and capitalist formations. As one example of this kind of discursive incorporation of a liberal self-ownership language, we want to use the website of the queer online community 'Queer Mutiny' which published a manifesto called 'This is your body' (Queer Mutiny 2011; see Figure 9.1). This manifesto can be seen as an ostensive and paradigmatic example for shaping queer claims in a self-ownership language. According to the manifesto, the 'queer' individual should perceive him/herself as rightful owner of his/her body, thus exercising full control over his/her own property in self. According to the comprehensive strand of critique, it can be argued that such a queer claim not only disregards the gendered, classist and racist genealogy of the ownership concept, but also implicates a queer claim to 'bourgeois' privileges – those of (rational) self-control and property in one's own person – thereby rejecting the notion of anyone being 'public property' (Cohen 1995; Pateman 2002). Ngaire Naffine has, for instance, convincingly argued that the concept of self-ownership relies on the idea of a 'divided self [...] with the body as the object of property, and something other [...] as the subject of property' which is in liberal theory the (rational) 'mind' (Naffine 1998: 201f.).

However, claiming one's own body as 'property of one's own (queer) mind' then also refers to the idea that one can (consciously) use or alter one's body 'by (political) choice' in order to transgress or subvert gender/sexual norms. 'Doing queer' is then reduced to some sort of a 'continuing and conscious decision' of 'defy[ing] and destabiliz[ing] gendered behaviors, sexes, and sexualities' (Mock 2003: 20). Referring back to Locke, this implies that the 'queer consciousness', with its notion of being a rightful owner and master of one's body who establishes 'rules' (rationally in a queer sense?) over this body, thus initiates a subversive gender/sexual performance and self-defined (gender/sexual) identity. Queerness or a 'queer consciousness' thus 'can be entered and/or exited at will' (Samuels 1999: 95). This not only indicates a Lockean subject but, according to Jacinth Samuels, also a 'neo-Kantian theoretical heritage' where 'freedom' is also 'the product' of a moral, and thus the 'rational choice' of an abstract, disembodied and dislocated individual who liberated him/herself from 'ascriptive or achieved characteristics' (ibid.). In this reading, the queer subject therefore resembles the liberal subject that is 'free to occupy the subject position of its choosing without regard for the exigencies of race, class, sexuality or gender' (Samuels 1999: 103). The perception of bodies as (queer) properties thus stays within a logic of westocentric proprieties and is therefore directly linked to the idea of unlimited commodification – if one can 'own' even the self as a 'commodity', then 'everything can become alienable private property' (Pateman 2002: 51). Hence, it can be argued that liberalism and such readings of queer have a great deal in common: the temptation of 'choice', evoking unlimited possibilities for the individual self-determination of the subject beyond material conditions and/or locations (see also Weber 2004; Engel 2009).

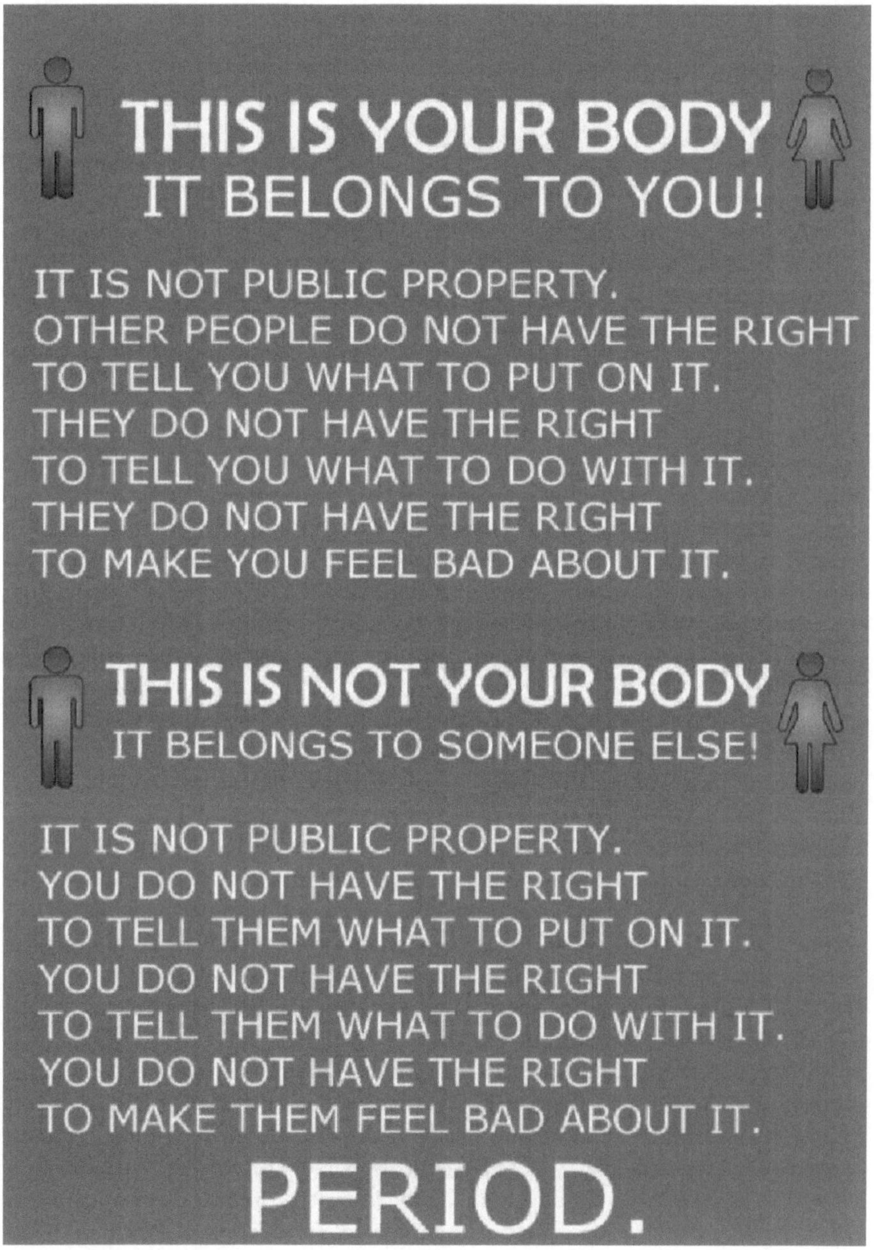

Figure 9.1 Queer Mutiny 'This is your body …'.
Source: http://queermutiny.tumblr.com (20 May 2011).

Classing queer/s – queer/ring commodification

> A commodity appears, at first sight, a very trivial thing, and easily understood. Its analysis shows that it is, in reality, a very queer thing, abounding in metaphysical subtleties and theological niceties.
>
> (Marx 1867)

> [A]s long as a cleavage exists between the particular and the common interest, as long, therefore, as activity is not voluntarily, but naturally, divided, man's own deed becomes an alien power opposed to him, which enslaves him instead of being controlled by him.
>
> (Marx 1845)

At this point it has to be asked whether the above discussed liberalist tendencies in queer theories as well as the general lack of engagement with questions of (private) property and concepts of self-ownership can be directly linked to the marginalization of 'class' in queer theories (Cohen 2005; Morton 2001; Hennessy 2000). Since it can be argued that class plays not only a fundamental role in the historical and present acknowledgment and eligibility of a (fictional) self-ownership, the relation between commodification processes and notions of 'property in the person' becomes an even more important issue when the economic status is constituted by the extent of commodification of (parts of) the self. Drawing on Marxist and post-Marxist analysis, it can be argued that the extent to which one is symbolically or materially commodified constitutes the class status and therefore maintains the basis of the 'class split' between the 'worker's class' and the 'bourgeois' (Cohen 1995). However, the concept of self-ownership seems to have acquired a 'curious duality of meaning', referring not only to autonomy and the right to maintain the 'sacred wholeness of one's person or body' but also to the opposite of this – that is, the capitalist constraint to deal with one's own body as a commodity (Halewood 2008: 134). Thus, (claims to) full self-ownership seem(s) to be connected with 'white' and 'bourgeois' privileges of 'having' (private property) and 'being' rightful owners of one's own body as well as not being forced to 'sell' parts of this body on the capitalist market.

With regard to this contradiction, one may also better understand the analytical distinction of Carole Pateman (2002) between 'self-ownership' and 'property in person' since only a concept of 'property in person' may legitimize capitalist 'exchange' of alienable parts of one's own property. The 'fiction is that what is offered in the labor market and what has been rented out is a piece of property (labor power, a service, a commodity, a factor of production)' (Pateman 2002: 47). So if one 'voluntarily' contracts for part of his property in person, 'his labor power [...] to be used on behalf of another [...] there is no question of injustice' (ibid.: 25). Consequently, claims for full self-ownership have also been articulated by leftist/Marxist movements and theories; they can also be found in the Marxian debate of the alienation (*Entfremdung*) of the worker from the products of his labor (Marx 1844).[6] But are, then, the queer claims for self-ownership as were discussed above implicating a class aspect, a struggle for a liberal, bourgeois subject who is a full owner of him/herself? What would that mean in terms of those critical approaches which are pointing to the ('unconscious') queerness of persons, who do not fulfill the requirements of white, middle-classed heteronormativity, such as the Black 'welfare queen' discussed by Cathy Cohen (2005)? How is the definition and emergence of 'queerness' then related to the commodification of one's labor force? Is 'queerness' rather the product of a 'self-defined' person who fully 'owns' him/herself or can it (also) be the product of capitalist economies, thus being an ambivalent phenomenon which subverts and reifies those structures at the same time? This argument might also resonate in Rosemary Hennessy's analysis of the emergence of new concepts of 'sexuality' and 'sexual orientations' with regard to capitalist logics, arguing that the 'choice' of the 'sexual object' became the determining factor of one's sexuality/sexual orientation, thus allowing homosexual identities to become visible and somehow recognized, but still being linked to the logic of 'consumption' (Hennessy 2000).

Hence, in this second part of our analysis we want to draw attention to the ambivalent relationship between the commodification of the 'working/welfare class' and a (classed) production of queer subjects in capitalist economies. Here we are in particular referring to some selected postcolonial, governmentalist and materialist analyses on the paradox of the interdependence of capitalism and queer/ness (Charusheela 2008; Hennessy 2000; Cohen 2005; Engel 2009). We are arguing that ('other') queer subjects can also appear as an effect of unequal power relations, uneven distribution, deprivileged access to property and a self-ownership that is situated within a hegemonic field of capitalist property relations. Developing those arguments further, we are pointing to the effects of capitalist commodification on the destabilization of gender/sexual norms and identities and to the aporia of queer claims to (full) self-ownership.

The commodification of the labor force in the Marxian sense is related to the objectification process inherent in producing exchange values, while the commodification process in queer liberalism is driven by strong accounts of individualism expressed – for example, in (personal) gender performance based on *consumption*, or appropriation, and finally ownership. The Marxian commodification of workers can be remodeled by government-driven economic gender/identity policies (such was the case with the famous example of Rosie the Riveter in WWII[7]) that may, if need be, queer or de-queer the labor force. In this

6 Workers themselves become commodities in the sense that they make use of their (fictional) self-ownership and sell their labor power on the labor market. As any other commodity, the commodification of the laborer does not express a 'thing', but a social relation.

7 Rosie the Riveter has become a U.S. nationalist and international feminist icon. The image of 'Rosie' was thought to encourage women to engage in heavy-duty war production, while the men were at war. In various depictions this character crosses from a classical feminine body to a tough, contemporary interpretation of a butch-looking gender variation, while she is

sense this chapter is a further contribution to analyzing the macroeconomy as a bearer of gender, not by looking at 'male' versus 'female' laborers or for 'male' versus 'female' productivities, but instead by theorizing the entire labor force as a gendered body of workers and as a 'bearer of gender' per se. Men and women become more or less arbitrary concepts of certain types of workers which can be dissolved or re-modeled when activating or deactivating the 'reserve army of labor'. This line of thinking is strongly inspired by S. Charusheela's observations of biopolitical mechanisms of discipline and sanction that shape a nation's constitution of private households, which are the basic units of all consumers and workers (Charusheela 2008).

Charusheela states that economic policy influences the way households are organized by promoting and enforcing a very specific version of heteronormativity. She argues this by drawing on Nayan Shah's and Kim Berry's historical studies of family policies, One is the San Francisco Chinatown population that transformed from a space of mostly single men during the late 1800s into 'a space of middle-class values with flats inhabited by nuclear families' after World War II. Her second example is the 'project of constituting home-makers who espoused middle-class norms' in the rural United States around 1900, where the U.S. government encouraged certain types of families via processes of commodification (Charusheela 2008). Adding to Charusheela's reasoning, we argue that government interventions in economic cycles may not only enforce ('white') middle-class and heteronormative gender performances, but may also be gateways for queer gender constructions – especially in certain dystopian circumstances such as wartime, when the working bodies become even more of a public property on a new level of commodification. The paradox that leaves the working/welfare class somehow differently 'queer' without full self-ownership can be the effect of a specific commodification process that may turn the working classes 'queer' (Cohen 1995) – for instance, in relation to gender.

Towards a theory and practice of 'queer commons'

> Indeed, if commoning has any meaning,
> it must be the production of ourselves as a common subject.
>
> (Federici 2010)

With respect to the discussed paradoxes and ambivalences for creating, being or acting as (anti-hegemonial) queer subjects within capitalist economies, the third part of this chapter tries to offer an alternative to westocentric proprietism by radically repulsing the idea of self-ownership and property in person on the level

still acceptable as a feminine wartime icon on the cover of the *Saturday Evening Post.* In this instance, gender conception has changed according to economic needs. The different images for Rosie the Riveter can be seen online at http://en.wikipedia.org/wiki/Rosie_the_Riveter (accessed 11 December 2014).

of subject and identity formation as well as on a material and economic level. Our critique is based on the insight that turning away from the westocentric notions of self-ownership poses an important precondition for destabilizing capitalist economies in its foundational structure, because 'if my relationship to myself is not simply one of self-referentiality, or self-ownership, then I can hardly be said to have an unidirectional, determining, sovereign relationship to any external which I am said to own' (Davies 1999: 347). Hence, queer theories de-centering the idea of fixed identities and unified, self-identical subjects would, according to Davies, at least have the epistemological potential of supporting a new understanding of property. 'If persons are never fully [...] individuated entities, then the justification for private ownership which relies upon property in the person begins to look decidedly shaky' (ibid.: 348).

But even though Davies sees these potentials, community-based, non-anthropocentric and interpersonal notions of identity and subjectivity (and therefore also of property) have been marginalized within queer contexts in favor of more individualistic conceptions of autonomy, bodily agency and gender/sexual subversion. There have also been no further discussions about the analytical and political potential of queer/feminist cyborg-theories, post/trans-human or 'fluid-border' approaches for rethinking westocentric concepts of property, self-ownership and questions of 'owning' nature or natural resources. Nonetheless, seriously considering queer and feminist approaches on the indefiniteness of identity and the lack of clear boundaries between the 'human' and 'non-human', between culture, nature and technology, poses a challenge to the entire anthropocentric, individualist and 'abstract' approaches which can also be found in queer theories, shifting the focus toward materialist, naturalist and post-humanist interactive, inter-nature and inter-personal practices and conditions of materializations and existence, creating conceptions beyond the notion that things, land or bodies can exist and thus be owned or subverted as/by separate non-related entities (Barad 2003; Sandilands 1997).

Giving up self-ownership as a fundamental referentiality for queer identity and subject formations would imply to accept that identity is not something that someone 'own[s] individually but [is] owned and developed in common with others', as private property 'itself relies on the myth of the separate person' (Davies 1999: 347). Every existence, non-human or human, then can only be considered in its materiality and connected to its relativity and indefiniteness, within a flux 'overflowing *jouissance*' of a comprehendible 'nature' (Sandilands 1997: 141). This rejection of individualized 'human' entities can also already be found in Donna Haraway's 'A Cyborg Manifesto':

> The self is the One who is not dominated, who knows that by the service of the other, the other is the one who holds the future, who knows that by the experience of domination, which gives the lie to the autonomy of the self. To be One is to be autonomous, to be powerful, to be God; but to be One is to be an illusion, and so to be involved in a dialectic of apocalypse with

> the other. Yet to be other is to be multiple, without clear boundary, frayed, insubstantial. One is too few, but two are too many.
>
> (Haraway 1991: 177)

This kind of fundamental critique of anthropocentric (and thus androcentric and colonial) implications of 'western' dualistic and individualistic paradigms has been particularly articulated in ecofeminist thought, thereby pointing to the interrelatedness of 'nature', 'society' and the 'self'. Due to the strong anti-essentialist and constructivist implications within queer approaches, it is reasonable that only a few of them would deal with ecofeminist thought, which promotes a naturalized, often heterosexual gender binary by essentializing the connection between 'woman' and nature. However, ecofeminist thought as well as feminist utopian writings from the 1970s and 1980s – being widely influenced by these ideas of creating a 'new', egalitarian and therefore often female-centered 'good' society – has been developing some thought-provoking new models for communal goods, property and/or 'natural resources'. Thus, when ecofeminist thought is queer/ed, it might offer a great potential for creating new imaginaries and understandings of interconnectedness and reciprocity, thereby subverting economic individualism and neo-/liberal capitalism (see Sandilands 1997, 2002, 2005; Gaard 1997). Within queer ecofeminism, to transgress heteronormative gender systems is intrinsically connected to the challenge of proprietism and the strong desire for creating new models for distributing or dealing with communal goods and nature. Queer ecofeminist writer Catriona Sandilands, for example, draws attention to the political, ecological and anti-capitalist potential of 'gender-bending physical experiences' and approaches developed within rural lesbian-feminist communities in the 1970s and 1980s (Sandilands 2002: 131). By 'experiencing nature as an erotic partner' rather than as a separate commodity, these communities transformed 'relations to [...] ownership' by 'crafting new cultures of nature against the dominant social and ecological relations of late capitalism' (Sandilands 2002: 132).

> The women take feminism into the landscape and, in turn, draw from an active landscape new ideas about gender. What many have managed to do is create a life world in which the boundaries between culture and nature are not experienced so sharply, in which the active agency of nature is vitally part of everyday physical and poetic awareness.
>
> (Sandilands 2002: 148)

This demand is playfully taken further by queer artists and eco-sexologists Annie Sprinkle and Elizabeth M. Stephens. In their *Love Art Lab* project they perform, among other things, their marriage to the earth, bringing desire into the concept of being connected or being 'one' with Earth. According to Sprinkle and Stephens, '[i]t would be better to think of the Earth as a "Lover" because we take care of our lovers instead of expecting them to take care of us' (loveartlab.

com). Not only do ecosexuals make love with the earth, they see themselves as interrelated community with the earth and its creatures, therefore pointing to the fluidity and permeability of borders between humans, animals and the earth.

This idea of 'one-ness' with 'the earth' and/or 'nature' can also strongly found in the teachings of the Tibetan Buddhist nun Tenzin Palmo (2007), whose thoughts we found not only inspiring but also mind-blowing from a queer perspective. Even though we might be criticized for not providing an adequate contextualization of the thoughts of Tenzin Palmo (and Tibetan Buddhism in general) or for just reading her 'queer' and thus very selectively, we are still very much convinced by the intellectual and epistemological potential of her Buddhist notion of 'oneness'. Just 'acknowledging' some epistemological parallels between several strands of feminist/queer critiques of an anthropocentric, decontextualized, individualistic and propertied concept of the 'subject' and Palmo's idea of the interrelatedness of the world not only points to the westocentric bias of most queer and feminist writings itself, but also makes us wonder whether there might exist a shared but not identical 'desire' of living in 'one-ness':

> [T]he main problem which obscures us from liberation is the fact of our identification with a false sense of an I or an ego. [...] this ego manifests itself through our thoughts, and our feelings, our emotions, our sense of time and our sense of duality, our sense of prejudices and concepts, [...] – which we think is me – [...] who I am. And so there is the understanding that, behind that, [...] there is that quality of knowing that we usually don't recognize because we're so caught up in the thinking [...] in the Tibetan tradition this is compared to being the sky. [...] the sky-space, it has no center, it has no circumference, it is infinite and you can't evaluate that and say that is my bit of space and that is your bit of space. I mean whether you are high caste or low caste you are all breathing the same air and that's something which we all share together and so this is therefore a very good simile of the nature of the mind which has no center and has no ending. [...] that sense of unborn awareness [which Palmo calls the Buddha nature] is that which unites us with all existence not just human beings but everything. Because as I say it has no boundaries, [...] there's no sense of I and other. That sense of duality simply doesn't exist. There is just the quality of knowing of being very aware and very open and spacious mind. So in that sense you could call that a state of oneness.
>
> (Palmo 2007; own transcription)

What Tenzin Palmo considers as an experiencing of one-ness and describes as a spiritual connection with all species that leaps over and transgresses but does not transcend or ignore constructions of race, class and gender or fundamental social inequalities, we would call a 'common subject/ivity'. (Concerning practicality: this notion should not simply be dismissed since it seems that a significant number of people reaching and enacting 'Buddha nature' is just as likely as the establishment of an international sky trust; it might even be quite clearly correlated with it.)

This idea of a common subjectivity or the 'commoning' of subjects can be found not only in Federici's materialist work but also in feminist utopian writings from the 1970s and 1980s. Feminist utopian literature linked ideas of trusts for the commons with the ideals of personal spiritual advancement. The clearest example we are aware of is in Starhawk's *Fifth Sacred Thing* (1995). The utopian novel's characters are engaged in spiritual practices interlinking them in one-ness, and in their village council people act as trust holders for animals and the environment. Also Marge Piercy's novels *Woman on the Edge of Time* (1997) and *He, She, It* (1993) link alterations of gender (roles) to a fundamental communalized re-organization of property and bodies. So, when considering community, rather than the fragmented person, Katherine Gibson (1999) refers to a definition by Iris Young who describes that 'the "ideal of community" presumes [that] subjects can understand one another as they understand themselves [...] it privileges unity over difference, immediacy over mediation, sympathy over recognition of the limits of one's understanding of others from their point of view' (Young 1990: 300f.). We would further argue that this definition is also in line with Gibson-Graham's later resistance of 'the pull of the sameness or commonness of economic being and instead focus on a notion of economic being-in-common' (Gibson-Graham 1996: 85f.). The being-in-common can be seen as a form of unity, where subjects can understand one another but not necessarily have to be like each other. This might, as Antke Engel writes, 'create space for difference, for a potentially conflictual heterogeneity defined by complex interdependencies' (Engel 2010).

Thus, a theory and practice of 'queer commons' means not only rejecting the individualized and abstract ownership of oneself (including gender identities), commodities and land, it also accepts that there is a general interrelatedness and connectedness, a one-ness or a world's 'commons'. When talking about 'commons', it is necessary therefore to distinguish between a common and the commons. A common is always a very specific place. A good example from the feminist collective memory pool is the women's peace and cruise missiles resistance camp at Greenham Common. In this case, that common is public land in Berkshire, Great Britain, where feminist peace activists camped out for nearly 20 years. The commons, on the other hand, is 'an abstract concept similar to the market or the state. It is the sum of thousands, perhaps millions, of individual commons' (Barnes 2003). Peter Barnes defines the characteristics of the commons. The commons are 'stuff' we share, inherit, and must pass on to future generations. The commons are large – they are spaces or systems and the commons are people's source of basic sustenance; the source of all natural resources; the ultimate waste sink; they hold humanities accumulation of science, art, customs and laws; they are the set of symbols and languages necessary for human communication; they are used whenever travelling from place to place and 'we rely on the commons for our sense of community' (Barnes 2003). Barnes describes the commons as the 'pond in which the fish of private property swim' (Barnes 2003); they are much more than any privately held company can ever absorb. In his book *Who Owns the Sky?* (2001), Barnes describes the commons as instances that can never be commodified as such, since they surpass what a single company can ever hold, because the commons are inclusive; ownership is shared as widely as possible. Barnes is concerned with how such a communal essential may be protected. He suggests market-like and money-based surroundings enabling a supply and demand system where established trusts will, for instance, guard the pollution of the sky by setting pollution prices according to scarcity of clean air. Solutions like this are probably practical and charming for mainstream economists, given that one must assume that international conventions will never install an organization like the Sky Trust that Barnes proposes. Nevertheless, from a more holistic perspective the idea of money-fixed, gradual pollution still seems rather inefficient and not very thorough.

However, creating a theory and practice of 'queer commons', transgressing concepts of individualized self-ownership and private property on a discursive and on a material level, is a path that could possibly lead to a fundamental re-vision and/or collapse of our globalized capitalist economy which is based on westocentric notions of proprietism. Hence, we are convinced that bringing together ideas and approaches from feminist utopian writings, from ecofeminist/ecosexual and cyborg theory, selected models on commons as well as some spiritual thoughts offered by Tibetan Buddhism – all somehow critical of an anthropocentric, decontextualized, individualistic and propertied concept of the 'subject' – could offer fruitful impulses for developing 'post-propertied' (Cooper and Herman 2013) conceptualization of queer subject(s)/ivities.

References

Barad, K. (2003) 'Posthumanist Performativity: Toward an Understanding of How Matter Comes to Matter', *Signs* 28(3): 801–30.

Barnes, P. (2001) *Who Owns the Sky? Our Common Assets and the Future of Capitalism*, Washington, DC: Island Press.

—— (2003) 'Schumacher Lecture I: Capitalism, the Commons, and Divine Right. October 2003, Stockbridge, Massachusetts'. Available online at http://peter-barnes.org/topics/business/schumacher-lecture-capitalism-the-commons-and-divine-right (accessed 11 December 2014).

Charusheela, S. (2010) 'Gender and the Stability of Consumption: A Feminist Contribution to Post-Keynesian Economics', *Cambridge Journal of Economics* 34(6): 1145–56.

Christman, J. (1991) 'Self-Ownership, Equality, and the Structure of Property Rights', *Political Theory* 19(1): 28–46.

Cohen, C. J. (2005) 'Punks, Bulldaggers, and Welfare Queens: The Radical Potential of Queer Politics', in P. E. Johnson and M. G. Henderson (eds) *Black Queer Studies: A Critical Anthology*, Durham, NC: Duke University Press, pp. 21–51.

Cohen, G. A. (1995) *Self-Ownership, Freedom, and Equality*, Cambridge: Cambridge University Press.

Cooper, D. and Herman, D. (2013) 'Up Against the Property Logic of Equality Law: Conservative Christian Accommodation Claims and Gay Rights', *Feminist Legal Studies* 21: 61–80.

Davies, M. (1999) 'Queer Property, Queer Persons: Self-Ownership and Beyond', *Social and Legal Studies* 8(3): 327–52.

Engel, A. (2009) *Bilder von Sexualität und Ökonomie: Queere kulturelle Politiken im Neoliberalismus*, Bielefeld: transcript.

—— (2010) 'Desire for/within Economic Transformation', *e-flux journal* 17. Available online at www.e-flux.com/journal/desire-forwithin-economic-transformation (accessed 8 October 2012).

Federici, S. (2010) *Feminism and the Politics of Commons.* Available online at www.mitchelcohen.com/?page_id=2111 (accessed 8 October 2012).

Frow, J. (1995) '"Elvis" Fame: The Commodity Form and the Form of the Person', *Cardozo Studies in Law and Literature* 7(2): 131–71.

Gaard, G. (1997) 'Toward a Queer Ecofeminism', *Hypatia* 12(1): 114–37.

Gibson, K. (1999) 'Community Economies: Economic Politics Outside the Binary Frame'. Unpublished paper presented at the Rethinking Economy Conference, ANU, August 1999. Available online at www.communityeconomies.org/site/assets/media/old%20website%20pdfs/Papers/word%20files/Community%20economies%20economic%20politics%20outside%20the%20binary%20frame.pdf (accessed 8 October 2012).

Gibson-Graham, J. K. (1996) *The End of Capitalism (As We Knew It): A Feminist Critique of Political Economy*, Cambridge, MA: Blackwell.

Halewood, P. (2008) 'On Commodification and Self-Ownership', *Yale Journal of Law and the Humanities* 20: 131–62.

Halperin, D. (1997) *Saint Foucault: Towards a Gay Hagiography*, Oxford: Oxford University Press.

Haraway, D. (1991) 'A Cyborg Manifesto: Science, Technology, and Socialist-Feminism in the Late Twentieth Century', in *Simians, Cyborgs and Women: The Reinvention of Nature*, New York: Routledge, pp. 149–81.

Harris, C. I. (1993) 'Whiteness as Property', *Public Law and Legal Theory Research Paper Series*, Research Paper No. 06-35. Available online at http://ssrn.com/abstract=927850 (accessed 2 March 2014).

Hennessy, R. (2000) *Profit and Pleasure: Sexual Identities in Late Capitalism*, New York: Routledge.

Ingram, A. (1994) *A Political Theory of Rights*, New York: Oxford University Press.

Locke, J. (1689) 'The Two Treatises of Civil Government', ed. Thomas Hollis, London: A Millar. Available online at http://oll.libertyfund.org/titles/222 (accessed 8 March 2012).

Loveartlab (n.d.) Available online at www.loveartlab.com (accessed 8 October 2012).

Marx, K. (1845) *The German Ideology.* Available online at www.marxists.org/archive/marx/works/1845/german-ideology/ch01a.htm (accessed 7 March 2012).

—— (1867) *Capital.* Available online at www.marxists.org/archive/marx/works/1867-c1/ch01.htm#S4 (accessed 7 March 2012).

—— (1844) *Economic and Philosophical Manuscripts of 1844.* Available online at www.marxists.org/archive/marx/works/1844/manuscripts/labour.htm (accessed 8 October 2012).

McCluskey, M. T. (2009) 'How Queer Theory Makes Neoliberalism Sexy', in M. Fineman, J. E. Jackson and A. P. Romero (eds) *Feminist and Queer Legal Theory: Intimate Encounters, Uncomfortable Conversations*, Farnham, Burlington: Ashgate, pp. 115–34.

Mock, R. (2003) 'Heteroqueer Ladies: Some Performative Transactions Between Gay Men and Heterosexual Women', *Feminist Review* 75: 20–37.

Morton, D. (2001) 'Global (Sexual) Politics, Class Struggle, and the Queer Left', in D. Altman (ed.) *Postcolonial, Queer: Theoretical Intersections*, Albany: State University of New York Press, pp. 207–38.

Naffine, N. (1998) 'The Legal Structure of Self-Ownership. Or the Self-Possessed Man and the Woman Possessed', *Journal of Law and Society* 25(2): 193–212.

Palmo, T. (2007) 'The Nature of the Mind'. Uploaded by Global Oneness Project on 22 June 2007. Available online at www.youtube.com/watch?v=sOsQa7sf6FE&feature=relmfu (accessed 8 October 2012).

Pateman, C. (2002) 'Self-Ownership and Property in the Person: Democratization and a Tale of Two Concepts', *Journal of Political Philosophy* 10(1): 20–53.

Perez, H. (2005) 'You Can Have My Brown Body and Eat It, Too!', *Social Text* 23(3–4): 171–91.

Phelan, S. (2000) 'Queer Liberalism', *American Political Review* 94(2): 431–41.

Phillips, A. (2011) 'It's My Body and I'll Do What I Like With It: Bodies as Objects and Property', *Political Theory* 20(10): 1–25.

Piercy, M. (1993) *He, She and It*, New York: Ballantine Books.

—— (1997 [1976]) *Woman on the Edge of Time*, New York: Ballantine Books.

Queer Mutiny (2012) 'This is your body …' Available online at http://queermutiny.tumblr.com/post/4932028824/this-is-your-body-it-belongs-to-you-it-is-not (accessed 8 October 2012).

Richardson, J. (2010) 'Feminism, Property in the Person and Concepts of the Self', *British Journal of Politics and International Relations* 12(1): 56–71.

Samuels, J. (1999) 'Dangerous Liaisons: Queer Subjectivity, Liberalism and Race', *Cultural Studies* 13(1): 91–109.

Sandilands, C. (1997) 'Wild Democracy: Ecofeminism, Politics, and the Desire Beyond', *Frontiers – A Journal of Women Studies* 18(2): 135–56.

—— (2002) 'Lesbian Separatist Communities and the Experience of Nature: Toward a Queer Ecology', *Organization and Environment* 15(2): 131–63.

—— (2005) 'Unnatural Passions? Notes Toward a Queer Ecology', *Invisible Culture: An Electronic Journal for Visual Culture*, 9. Available online at www.rochester.edu/in_visible_culture/Issue_9/sandilands.html (accessed 8 October 2012).

Starhawk (1995) *The Fifth Sacred Thing*, New York: Bentham.

Taylor, R. (2005) 'Self-Ownership and the Limits of Libertarianism', *Social Theory and Practice* 31(4): 465–82.

Weber, J. (2004) 'Performing Post/Trans/Techno/Queer. Pluralisierung als Selbst- und Machttechnologie', in C. Rosenthal, T. Frey Steffen and A. Vaeth (eds) *Gender Studies: Wissenschaftstheorien und Gesellschaftskritik*, Würzburg: Königshausen & Neumann, pp. 111–21.

Young, I. (1990) 'The Ideal of Community and the Politics of Difference', in L. Nicholson (ed.) *Feminism/Postmodernism*, New York: Routledge, pp. 300–23.

Chapter 10

The ruse of sexual freedom

Neoliberalism, self-ownership and commercial sex

Leticia Sabsay

In recent years I have received several letters from the London Metropolitan Police updating me about the progress made regarding the expulsion of street sex workers from the neighbourhood in their commitment to increase neighbours' safety through the implementation of Anti-Social Behaviour Orders (ASBOs). I live in East London, a five-minute walk away from Brick Lane – nowadays a key tourist spot – between Whitechapel, Bethnal Green and Shoreditch, where Terence Conran's hotel stands out as one of the many markers of the apparent gentrification of the area. From the Borough of Tower Hamlets to Hackney, it seems that the removal of the sex industry is seen as essential for an area to advance up the urban social hierarchy. But not only here: more ten years ago, thousands of miles across the Atlantic Ocean to the south, I was living in Palermo, a neighbourhood of Buenos Aires, Argentina, when it was being gentrified. These days, Palermo is a place where tourists from around the world hang out, searching for the coolest shops, bars and restaurants, gay-friendly boutique hotels and classy B&Bs. But during the time I lived there, and for many years after, Palermo was the site of one of the most protracted battles over the expulsion of trans street sex workers in an effort to convert this informal red-light trans district into the residential middle/upper-class fancy area that it has become today. And the story doesn't stop there. In between Buenos Aires and London, I spent the first decade of the twenty-first century living in Spain, where I witnessed yet another campaign for the expulsion of street sex workers, in the Market of La Boquería, one of the hottest tourist spots of Barcelona's emblematic Ramblas. Unfortunately, these are far from exceptional urban scenes; indeed, the list could continue endlessly. The controversy around sex work tends to be repeated in a broadly applicable and familiar logic that is easily recognizable by different publics in different cities, currently shaped by the requirements of neoliberal economic tendencies upon urban politics. The pervasive reluctance to meet sex workers' demands and definitively decriminalize sex work in so many different geo-political contexts goes hand in hand with the controversy over the clampdown on red-light districts following the modernization, gentrification or internationalization of renovated urban environments across the globe.

This policy has become even more overtly implemented in parallel with the steady empowerment of militarized security forces in the context of a renewed worldwide trend for criminalizing social protest, and the concomitant spread of paranoid discourses linking 'safety' to 'social order'. As Laurie Penny reminded us, citing Emma Goldman, it is not surprising that in the midst of the current economic crisis, where conditions of life are systematically undermined under the auspices of austerity policies, 'moral crusades' provoking intense and passionate debates such as the sex-work controversy have become good, diverting political goals to promote (Penny 2013). It was in this adverse context, in December 2013, that we witnessed the Soho raids in downtown London, in which at least 18 safe sex-work places were closed down, and where, by the way, a new mixed-use property development has been underway since 2012.[1] This news was broadcast at the same time as the media coverage of the systematic raids being carried out in France and Ireland.[2] Certainly, the situation had intensified, with the European Union planning a reform of the legislation on sex work to criminalize the purchase of sexual services at that time. On 24 February 2014, the European Parliament finally passed the resolution which, following the so-called Swedish model, criminalizes clients instead of sellers.[3] This conservative move regarding the sex industry comes as no surprise, and does not augur well for sex workers. The measure, as sex workers have repeatedly denounced, will not improve their situation, but will further precarize their work conditions and, furthermore, will reinforce the rejection of sex workers' demands for the decriminalization of commercial sex both at local and international levels.[4]

If we consider the articulation between desire and economy, the polemic over the sex industry opens up a wide range of issues to consider. However, it is not this that I am interested in pursuing here. Rather, I am bringing it into the discussion because it is an extreme case that exposes the regulatory dimension of sexual freedom enacted by liberal, and later neoliberal, discourses, with which this chapter takes issue. Indeed, one of the central questions that has established the terms of the vexed debates over the legal status that sex work should hold, is whether those who make a living from commercial sex were *really* free to choose to do so. This question has acquired new shades of complexity since the prosecution of sex work was reshaped under the trafficking paradigm (Anderson and Andrijasevic 2008). Underpinning this shift, the question still remains as

1 Development Managers Limited is in charge of the development of the Walker's Court project for Soho Estates. Walker's Court is a development for commercial, business and entertainment purposes, and will include offices, restaurants and a theatre. See: www.dml-group.com/project/walkers-court (accessed 30 April 2014).

2 www.sexworkeropenuniversity.com/2/post/2013/12/press-release-swou-responds-to-the-soho-raids.html; and www.thejournal.ie/sex-workers-concerned-over-indiscriminate-nature-of-brothel-raids-468800-May2012 (both accessed 12 December 2013).

3 www.europarl.europa.eu/news/en/news-room/content/20140221IPR36644/html/Punish-the-client-not-the-prostitute (accessed 4 March 2014).

4 www.sexworkeurope.org/news/general-news/560-ngos-and-94-researchers-demand-members-european-parliament-reject-ms-honeyball (accessed 26 February 2014).

to whether or not *selling* sexual services could count as the expression of sexual freedom understood as an autonomous choice.

Taking sex work as an illustrative case in point, in this chapter I critically examine the epistemic frameworks that have facilitated the association of sexual freedom, in turn characterized as autonomy, with liberal, and later neoliberal, economic imaginaries. In particular, I explore how the (ideal of) sexual freedom that current global discourse compels us to nourish, use, expand and defend is cast by both possessive individualism and the model of self-owned subjects for whom their relationship to their bodies, desires and sexuality becomes one of ownership. There is perhaps no other case where the intricate connection between self-ownership, possessive individualism and sexual freedom is revealed more clearly than within the intractable controversies around sex work. These disputes are crucially underpinned by the assumption that one's own body is a property that one *owns*. It is only by departing from this ingrained assumption that we can begin to understand the question of whether or not one can legitimately use the sexual capacities of one's own body for commercial purposes.

What uses of the body might count as the expression of sexual freedom? How does the neoliberal idea of autonomy and choice affect the way in which bodies and sexual desires are conceived? How do bodies, conceived as a property, become our own? In order to tackle these questions, I will begin by tracing the relationship between sexuality, desire and freedom in contemporary neoliberal governmentality, which I characterize as dependent on self-ownership understood as a paradigm (Davies 1999; Skeggs 2004; Bhandar 2011; Klapeer and Schönpflug, Chapter 9 in this volume). As I will show, this paradigm is at the same time intimately linked to the legacies of colonial relations. I then turn my attention, therefore, to questions of sexuality and racial logics, or, more specifically, to the racial inscription of the emergence of the self-ownership paradigm. Having established the emergent entanglement of freedom and self-ownership, which is central to the colonial enterprise and the development of racism, I will move on to consider how this entanglement is currently working in neoliberal and postcolonial contexts. This will finally lead me to ask how sexual freedom can be articulated in such a way that it disrupts the paradigm of neoliberalism instead of offering itself to its subjugation.

Sex work, sexual freedom, self-ownership

The case of sex work is interesting because while it offers a way into the regulatory dimension of neoliberal ideals of sexual freedom, it also shows how sexual freedom, when reduced to free choice, may lead to the conception of autonomy as self-ownership in contradictory ways. For instance, the contempt shown towards sex workers' demands for the decriminalization of commercial sex is based on an imaginary, well-established opposition between sexual desire and economic trade. But the evident operative links between desire, economy and sexuality are crucial to our understanding of the historical and current functions of marriage and the family unit, and are likewise omnipresent within current key business areas, such as advertisements, fashion, showbiz, beauty and creative industries, where normative sexualized ideas of success and fulfilment function as aspirational triggers. And yet it seems that in order to qualify as the expression of sexual autonomy, desire should be de-linked – or at least set at a prudent distance – from economy.

If, according to this (moral) imaginary, desire cannot be so directly linked to economic trade in order to be the expression of sexual autonomy, it follows that selling sexual services cannot be the expression of free choice of desire. This is where abolitionist liberal feminist arguments, perhaps unwittingly, become allies of conservative moralistic positions. In contrast to anti-sex conservatism, however, these feminists consider sex work as a form of 'sex-slavery', retrieving a long tradition of feminist scholarship concerned with the ways in which women's bodies have historically been objectified, reduced to their sexual value, and subsequently sexually exploited or abused under the guise of societal hetero-patriarchal patterns and sexist imaginaries (Barry 1984; Jeffreys 1997; MacKinnon 1993). Yet they share with anti-sex conservatism the assumption that people selling sex cannot really be freely choosing to do so, because nobody would freely choose this.

Clearly, at stake here are the conditions in which one can actually 'choose', and the fact that there is no such thing as an absolute 'free choice' that would not be delineated by the conditions that both restrain and enable it – and even more so when such a choice involves strategies for survival, and is made under conditions of great inequality and constraint. But this latter line of reasoning would lead to other kinds of questions involving how to improve the conditions in which sex work might actually be chosen and exercised, rather than simply abolishing it. It is this line of reasoning that shapes the demands of sex-worker organizations and the sex workers' rights movement, along with the commitments and projects they are embarked on.[5] In spite of the claims of sex workers, the 'sex-slavery' framework has been reinforced in recent years by reframing the battle against the sex industry within the trafficking paradigm, to which I will come later (Agustín 2007; Andrijasevic 2010). In this context, when sex workers contend that they were not forced to enter the industry and have engaged in commercial sex of their own will, abolitionists of different strands systematically refuse to recognize the voices of those they claim to speak for (see, for example, McKinnon 2011).

These discourses, which actually deny sexual freedom in the name of sexual freedom, involve profound beliefs regarding the relationship between freedom, sexual desire, bodies and economy within current neoliberal logics. In what follows, I examine some of the grounds for these beliefs.

Let us start with the premise that the deployment and further globalization of capital is closely related to the colonization of 'desire' as the *locus* of 'individual

5 See the mission and campaigns of the International Committee on the Rights of Sex Workers in Europe (ICRSE): www.sexworkeurope.org/about; and the Global Network of Sex Work Projects (NSWP): www.nswp.org/page/our-work (both accessed 26 February 2014)

freedom' (Jameson 2005: 182–210; Žižek 2009). Put in these condensed terms, this point of departure might sound too obvious to some, while unacceptable to others, and in any case presumably too abstract to let the reader determine what it actually implies. Let me expand. The argument that I would like to develop here is that the imaginary of individual freedom has been not only central to the deployment of liberal and later neoliberal governmentality, but also modelled by the paradigm of private property proper to the capital form, understood in Marxist terms as a social relation, and the colonial enterprise that shaped it. It is in part a product of the inheritance of these three entangled historical developments that desire surfaces as a pivotal locus where this ideal of freedom is both enabled and enacted (D'Emilio and Freedman 1997; Hennessy 2000; Duggan 2003; Ferguson 2004; Thomas 2007). But what do I mean by 'individual freedom' and 'desire' in this specific context? 'Individual freedom' refers in this context to the liberal imaginary of freedom by which freedom becomes not only individualized but also, and more crucially, understood as an ontological condition that defines the Western modern subject. Even when it distances itself from the idea of freedom as an original condition and is recast as a condition to be achieved, individual freedom, since the post-Enlightenment, has acquired an ontological character and is understood as the inevitable counterpart of the innate faculty of reason (Foucault 1987, 1996). This foundational character of individual freedom, linked to the capacity for reasoning (that is, the capacity to think – and make decisions – for ourselves without constraints) by which 'moral autonomy' is achieved, continues to be central to late-modern (and for some, post-modern) investments on subjectivity alike (Brown 2006). This is the first idea of freedom that is implied in sex-work debates, when the capacity to make a reasoned and autonomous choice on the part of those who have decided to engage in commercial sex is doubted or questioned.

I have placed 'desire' between inverted comas to indicate the widely held view that locates desire at the centre of either a deliberate or an aspirational subject. As a starting point, it may suffice to limit this reference to its conventional definition: a 'strong feeling of wanting to have something or wishing for something to happen' (*Oxford English Dictionary*). However, desire is also directly linked to the sexual realm, both in Freudian terms and within capitalist symbolic logics of consumption. In what follows, taking the sexualized forms that desire takes as the focus of my reflection, I trace plausible connections between the grammars of neoliberal economies and the imaginary of sexual freedom as one of the emblematic discourses where desire is called upon.

I have argued elsewhere that the subject of sexuality, for whom current liberal sexual liberties and rights are claimed and bestowed, is a sovereign subject that emerged as the effect of the liberal reason of government, understood in Foucaultian terms as a regime whose goal is to produce both freedom and a subject who desires to be free (Sabsay 2012). Considered in these terms, the freedom of this liberal subject becomes the means by which subjects are governed rather than something that is opposed to government (Foucault 2008). It is through the enticement of the desire for freedom that productive forms of power take full shape. Significantly, it was in relation to sexuality that Foucault explicitly developed his argument about the productivity of power as against a conception of power as exclusively repressive (Foucault 1990). According to Foucault, modern Western sexuality emerges as a new regime of truth by which sexuality produces a range of sexual types (today maybe re-enacted as identities); along with this, it becomes, as well, the *locus* where the subject's most inner and fundamental desires and truths are to be found. This understanding of sexuality as the key entry point to personal identity would entice this new sexual subject to search for and discover its deepest (and presumably repressed) sexual desires, producing a new field of knowledge and potential freedoms. It would be precisely through the negotiation of these desires and sexual freedoms produced by the regime of truth of sexuality that the sexual subject would, then, become regulated. I will come back to the question of sexual freedom and regulation in relation to the case of sex work in the next section, but first let us focus on the body of this sexual subject of liberalism, as it is described by Foucault.

The reflexive move towards the self and its own desires suggests that the liberal self of sexuality and freedom also corresponds with the imaginary that conceives the body as an objectified property of such a self. This subject is conceived as an entity that possesses and masters a body, rather than being a body, taking for granted that sexuality is located within this body that such a subject is said to have. This leads us to the relationship between freedom and possessive individualism, self-ownership, and the capitalist and colonial logics that form its basis. As Beverly Skeggs indicates, the 'possessive individual' is a person who is defined not only 'through *his* capacity to own property in *his* person', hence its masculinist and colonial evocations, as it has been constituted against its gendered and colonial others, but also through 'the capacity to "separate" from "his body"'. This latter aspect indicates that he then has 'a proprietal relation to him/self as bodily property (Pateman 1988)' (Skeggs 2004: 75–6; emphasis in the original).

While the capacity to own our body surfaces here is a crucial indicator of self-ownership, reading Locke, Margaret Davies also reminds us that self-ownership was a symbol for personal autonomy and rights that historically entitled the European colonial man to own property, including the lands and the bodies of others who were considered to lack these capacities (Davies 1999). In this regard, Brenna Bhandar points out that the attributes or capacities that constitute this self-owned subject ontologically as prior to what *he* might possess were co-constituted with relations of property in the colonial context, highlighting that this 'propertied subject' is always already a racialized one (Bhandar 2011). This gendered and racialized paradigm of self-ownership over-determines the body of the Foucaultian sexual subject. Constitutively entangled with relations of property, this paradigm will also come into view – albeit in a different guise – with regard to the body of labour within capitalism.

Marx showed that capital was not a thing but a social relation accounting for a particular organization of the means of production. Paraphrasing Marx, the particularity of capital was that those who do not own the means of production are compelled to sell themselves *of their own free will* (1990[1867]). In other words, what characterizes capitalism is that workers, as free subjects who have been deprived of the means of production, are bound to sell the labour-power that their bodies can provide.[6] What interests me here is that, under capitalist conditions, bodies become the only means of production that workers have *as sovereign owners of their bodies.* This gives us an important insight into the imaginaries of the modern objectification of the body. First, the detachment between bodies and labour: it is not their bodies that 'free workers' – 'liberated' from other means of production than their own bodies – are going to sell, but the labour-power produced by their bodies. Second, insofar as they can sell their labour-power as self-owned 'free workers', their bodies, conceived as property, become the representatives of their freedom.

This logic, whereby ownership becomes, in economic terms, a representative of freedom, informs the rationale of the Western liberal, and later neoliberal, self-owned subject. The objectified body of labour, the racialized body that carries the legacies of colonialism and the gendered body all define self-ownership just as self-ownership affects the body of sexuality. In effect, according to this entangled logic, sexuality, as an attribute of the body, becomes an objectified property that the subject is said to possess (see Hennessy 2000; Alexander 2005; Floyd 2009; Cooper and Herman 2013). This possessive modality, in which the subject is currently compelled to relate to her sexual practices, orientations, preferences and identifications, forms the basis of neoliberal ideals of sexual freedom, ideals that also conjoin the sexualized body-object with the fantasy of a transparent sexual identity.

The legacies of the notion of sexual freedom that I have traced, either as the innate faculty to make autonomous choices on the basis of unconditioned reason or the faculty that links freedom to the possession of our own body based on notions of self-ownership, shape the current controversies over sex work, and also define their limits. Why is it so difficult to consider commercial sex as a form of labour worthy of exchange value? Why is it that, by a metonymic displacement of sorts, selling sexual services almost immediately leads to the naturalized idea that when one sells sexual services, one is selling one's own body, or even oneself?

The stigma borne by sex workers mirrors, to some degree, the work of the metonymic chain that conflates sexual labour and identity, displacing the commercial uses of the body on to the property status of the body itself as a matter of identity. Leaving aside the question of sex trafficking for the moment – as Rutvica Andrijasevic rightly points out, there is a constant slippage between forced prostitution and sex trafficking (everyone is of course against sex trafficking and sex exploitation) (2008: 138) – this metonymic chain is also mobilized when it

6 According to Marxist economic theory, insofar as in capitalist relations labour becomes a commodity to be sold by the worker with abstract exchange value, it materializes as labour-power.

is claimed that 'prostitution' is always enforced. In effect, the paradigm of sex slavery that underpins the claim that sex work can never be chosen (and is therefore ultimately enforced in one way or another) confuses sexual labour with the dispossession of the body. And it does so in spite of the complexity of the sex industry, which ranges from sex tourism, escort agencies, private cooperatives and private apartments and brothels, massage houses, saunas, lap-dancing and stripper clubs, online virtual sex, chats and hot lines, from phone sex to street sex work, some of which are more or less organized, more or less casual, or independent.

As the stigma of sex work suggests, the overinvestment in all that is sexual, as well as the force of sexuality to define who we are – particularly apparent in the case of sex work – demands that we look at the Western imaginary of the sexual subject more closely. I will do so in the next section, examining the intersection of sexuality with processes of racialization.

Colonial legacies: racialization and sexuality

In her seminal book, *Race and the Education of Desire* (1995), Ann Laura Stoler discusses Foucault's notion of biopower. Drawing on Michel Foucault's *History of Sexuality* (1990[1976]), Stoler argues that Foucault's theory of the emergence of sexuality as a *dispositif* – that is, both as a discursive field and a technique of government – in the West is complicit with the widespread tendency to create immanent histories of Western modernity. In other words, Stoler contests Foucault's failure to take fully into account the crucial role of the colonial context in which Western sexuality developed. Rather than just highlighting the Euro-centrism of Foucault's perspective, Stoler aims to show how the emergence of sexuality as a scientific discourse of truth parallels what Foucault understood as the 'birth of state racism'. Stoler's contention is that a conjoint reading of Foucault's *History of Sexuality* and his Lectures at the Collège de France of 1976 and published as *Society Must be Defended* (2003[1997]) would allow us to see that he actually 'analyses how a discourse of sexuality articulates and eventually incorporates a racist logic' (Stoler 1995: 22). Even though Stoler goes on to challenge Foucault's understanding of the history of racisms, she concedes that he pointed out 'the ways in which a prior technology of sexuality provided a cultural susceptibility and discursive field for them' (Stoler 1995: 22). In the light of this reading, it would be within Foucault's concept of biopower that we might bear witness to the intersections of these technologies (of sexuality and race) by which bodies become the core of individual government and population regulation.

Foucault described the *dispositif* of sexuality as a technique of government that appeared in the context of the development of biopolitics. For the purpose of this limited argument, the emergence of biopolitics, or biopolitical power, can be broadly characterized as the move by which government techniques started to focus on the regulation of human-life processes and be justified through biosocial discourses of difference and the scientific regimes of truth attached to them.

In the context of biopolitics, sexuality becomes one of the realms where regulative power takes centre stage, constituting a key vector of the 'normalization of society'. Sexuality becomes a key means for the control of populations by effectuating two key epistemological moves: namely, the configuration of sexuality as a bio-scientific discourse of truth and the demarcation of sexual species according to the different sexual practices individuals might stand for. Through this epistemic shift, sexuality becomes a technique of subjectivation: it will become a discourse where the subject might find its ultimate inner truth, and, based on manifold desires described as sexual, the discourse of sexuality will define the subject's belonging to a specific type (Foucault 1990, 2003).

While in *The History of Sexuality* race is described as one of the realms in which the discourse of sexuality, as a biologized form of constructing internal differences, might be displayed, in *Society Must be Defended* one of the main arguments is that 'the emergence of biopower inscribed modern racism in the mechanisms of the normalizing state' – that is, a state that normalizes individuals according to naturalized norms justified by 'biologized' standards (Stoler 1995: 55). Notwithstanding their differences in focus, both *The History of Sexuality* and *Society Must be Defended* provide us with an analysis of these two technologies, the discursive fields that built biological truths about sexuality and race, showing how they are at the core of the normalizing society. In effect, according to Foucault, both technologies provide the grounds for the creation 'of "biologized" enemies, *against whom society must defend itself*' (Stoler 1995: 59; my emphasis). According to Stoler, reading both works together could allow us to pinpoint how both technologies might recast each other vis-à-vis the biological underpinnings of their common epistemological framework and their mutual exchanges within the governing logics of biopower.

Foucault's depiction of the Western epistemic field opened up by the discourse of sexuality and its racial inscription reveals itself to be key for understanding contemporary grids of intelligibility concerning sexual freedom. On the one hand, it defines the terms of a long-standing debate over the tensions posed by the divergence between a focus on sexual practices and a focus on sexual identities. The subsuming of practice into identity underlies the stickiness of the stigma that sex workers carry in relation to their commercial sexual acts – evident in the displacement, for instance, from the description of sex work as a profession or a job to the word 'prostitute' as indicative of a social identity. On the other hand, it resonates with another long-standing dynamic, by which racialized and later cultural differences are sexualized. There is a sound body of scholarship accounting for this, to which I cannot do justice in the context of this chapter. Suffice it to say that the history of Western projections of hyper-sexuality onto a colonial and racialized other defined against the ideal of a European white respectable and reproductive sexuality has been extensively elucidated along with the key interventions of most influential authors such as Frantz Fanon (1986[1952]) or Edward Said (1995[1978]). More recently, a growing body of literature has attested to the reversal of this schema, accounting for the current civilizational imagination that finds in the postcolonial racialized other all the signs of a retrograde and repressive sexuality, this time projected as the inverted image of an idealized sexually liberated West (Massad 2007; Puar 2007; Butler 2008; El-Tayeb 2011; Bracke 2012).

The entanglement of processes of sexualization and racialization in processes of border building highlights the case of different kinds of sex work – notably sex work prosecution under the trafficking paradigm and sex tourism (Alexander 1997; Altman 2001) – in manifold ways. Given the scope of this chapter, I will limit myself to indicating two ways in which anti-trafficking rhetoric and practices point to the legacies of colonialism in neoliberal postcolonial contexts, while also working as a form of sexual regulation.

Departing from the understanding of criminalization as a technique of control, one can arguably consider how the prosecution of sex work operates not so much in favour of the effective eradication of 'prostitution' but rather as a form of regulation and control of those populations against whom society must defend itself. It has been amply argued that this is particularly the case in the context of anti-trafficking discourses (Agustín 2007; Andrijasevic 2010; Aradau *et al.* 2010; Mai 2013). Assessing the history of the conflation of sex work and sex trafficking, the report of the Global Network of Sex Work Projects situates as one of its landmarks the UN Protocol to Prevent, Suppress and Punish Trafficking in Persons, Especially Women and Children (2000). The Network states that, on the one hand, this Protocol was progressive insofar as it did not single out sex work and included trafficking for any form of labour (2011: 2). On the other hand, the report continues, it positioned the Protocol as a supplement to the UN Convention against Transnational Crime, allowing for trafficking to be 'tackled as a crime with the main focus on law enforcement and prosecution, not on the protection of human rights'. This unfortunate marriage, the report concludes, contributed to the conflation of the prevention of trafficking with the prosecution of sex work where sex work is illegal, criminalizing all the parties involved (2). In this context, the report denounces that it is migrant sex workers who are especially targeted (3). Along the same lines, the International Committee on the Rights of Sex Workers in Europe (ICRSE) demands that the debate on trafficking should be changed to a debate on labour, migration and human rights.[7] As these documents and other sex-worker organizations have systematically denounced, the prosecution of sex workers under the anti-trafficking framework works through racial profiling, and actually functions as a mechanism for border patrol and migration control, in particular, as a way to prevent the migration of postcolonial sex workers (Andrijasevic 2010; Aradau *et al.* 2010).

This leads us to another way in which the anti-trafficking paradigm works at a regulatory level. As Nick Mai has rightly pointed out, the rhetoric of sex

7 www.sexworkeurope.org/resources/recommendations-brussels-2005-conference (accessed 3 December 2014).

trafficking erases the complexities of the industry, and reinforces the stereotype of the dominant free Western man on the one hand, and, on the other, the postcolonial victimized woman who, according to this stereotype, is deprived of any agency and left unable to speak for herself (Mai 2013). Furthermore, it does not account for the differentiated dynamics of sex work with regard to whether it involves cis-women, cis-men, trans-women, trans-men or gender queers, nor does it consider whether sex work takes place in contexts that could be defined as heterosexual, gay or other, reinforcing heteronormative patterns (Mai 2012) – or take into account the multiplicity of meanings and value that sex has across different social-cultural landscapes (Altman 2001: 103–16). In these ways, the rhetoric of sex trafficking both Westernizes and heterosexualizes the image of sex work, while it also re-enacts the legacy of colonialist views according to which the colonized other is subject to subjective destitution.

Sexual freedom as dispossession?

Unexpectedly very much in line with Foucault's remarks, David Harvey reminds us that the neoliberal turn, which invested in the idea that 'human well-being can be best advanced by liberating individual entrepreneurial freedoms and skills within an institutional framework characterized by strong private property rights', exceeds the economic sphere, to become 'an ethic in itself, capable of acting as a guide to all human action' (Harvey 2005: 2–3). It is in this context that we can clearly see how the notion of freedom has become reduced to 'freedom of choice'. Seen in this light, with freedom being conceived mainly as autonomy, this notion is less connected to self-determination than to the individualistic abstract self that corresponds to neoliberal economic ideals. Within this framework, desire as the expression of sexual freedom becomes not only privatized but also commodified with a new sign. And it is through these neoliberal investments in sexuality as the site of freedom as choice – leading, for example, to the normalization of sexuality through dominant forms of identity politics, binding sexuality to patterns of consumption, or to the exclusionary enactments of homonormativity – that desire is called upon as exclusively one's own, and subsequently exploited.

It is in this context as well that we bear witness to the exclusion of those kinds of sexual dissidence that oblige us to look again at the intimate link between sexuality and economy, as is the case with sex workers. The model of self-ownership and freedom of choice that sustains the arguments in favour of the prosecution of sex work, but also lends itself to its neoliberal exploitation, tends to overlook the differential conditioning of choices in a global economy, which, in the case of the sex industry, may translate into racialized and disenfranchised postcolonial others putting their sexual labour at the service of white European respectable classes (Agathangelou 2004). The conditions of exploitation of our needs, as well as the ways in which our choices are conditioned by the opportunities for survival we have available, are indeed occluded by the self-ownership model. A set of questions then arises: What would sexual freedom look like if it ceased to be defined by the equation of self-ownership to freedom of choice, which ends up negating 'choices' that are considered unacceptable and even assumed to be the sign of the lack of autonomy altogether, as becomes clear in the case of sex workers' claims? What would sexuality look like beyond the ontology of a self-owned individual by which we constantly run the risk of being exploited?

If the paradigm that poses desire and sexuality as the locus of freedom under the guise of a self-owned subject functions as the means by which we are constantly dispossessed, Judith Butler and Athena Athanasiou may be right in trying to reframe dispossession against such terms. In *Dispossession: The Performative in the Political* (2013), Butler and Athanasiou depart from the idea that dispossession has a double valence. On the one hand, dispossession accounts for the ways in which we are already dispossessed by the norms and frames of intelligibility that constitute us as subjects, as well as by our constitutive interdependence – that is, that we are interdependent beings who depend on social conditions, institutions and other beings to survive and live well. Key here for the question of sexuality is that this first sense of dispossession does evoke our 'bodily exposure' to others as well (13). On the other hand, within neoliberal logics, dispossession refers to the specific ways in which people are denied these conditions of survival. In this sense, either by 'declaring' people's lives disposable under the logics of precarization, rendering whole populations disposable, who are dispossessed of their lands, basic rights and basic conditions of survival, or simply left to die either in war contexts or under the indifference of neoliberal calculations of risks and costs, once human lives are reconsidered as human capital (1–29).

Butler and Athansiou set themselves the task of considering the challenges faced by these latter forms of dispossession 'beyond the logics of possession' (126). The central issue for them is to affirm freedom and justice by relying on the constitutive dispossessed character of our selves rather than on claims for the enhancement of self-ownership. Of course, there are no straightforward or easy answers to this. However, they propose that our concepts of freedom and justice, or the terms in which they are defined and subsequently claimed and denied, need to be completely rethought. Taking up the question of sexual freedom, it might be the case that rather than trying to expand all-known and differential sexual freedoms for preconceived self-owned selves, it would be better to continue questioning, again and again, the presuppositions that deny the primary ways in which we are always already dispossessed, and restrict how the sexual dimension of bodies' exposure to other bodies can be imagined.

Acknowledgments

The research leading to these results has received funding from the European Research Council under the European Union's Seventh Framework Programme (FP7/2007–2013)/ERC grant agreement no. 249379. I would like to thank the editors of this volume for their insightful comments on previous versions of this chapter, and the reviewers who also offered many significant suggestions for improvement.

References

Agathangelou, A. M. (2004) *The Global Economy of Sex: Desire, Violence, and Insecurity in Mediterranean Nation States*, London: Palgrave.

Agustín, L. (2007) *Sex at the Margins: Migration, Labour Markets and the Rescue Industry*, London: Zed Books.

Alexander, J. (1997) 'Erotic Autonomy as a Politics of Decolonisation', in J. Alexander and C. T. Mohanty (eds) *Feminist Genealogies, Colonial Legacies, Democratic Futures*, New York: Routledge, pp. 63–100.

—— (2005) *Pedagogies of Crossing: Meditations on Feminism, Sexual Politics, Memory, and the Sacred*, Durham, NC: Duke University Press.

Altman, D. (2001) *Global Sex*, Chicago, IL: Chicago University Press.

Anderson, B. and Andrijasevic, R. (2008) 'Sex, Slaves, and Citizens: The Politics of Anti-Trafficking', *Soundings* 40: 135–45.

Andrijasevic, R. (2010) *Migration, Agency and Citizenship in Sex Trafficking*, London: Palgrave.

Aradau, C., Huysmans, J. and Squire, V. (2010) 'Acts of European Citizenship: A Political Sociology of Mobility', *Journal of Common Market Studies* 48(4): 947–67.

Barry, K. (1984) *Female Sexual Slavery*, New York: New York University Press.

Bhandar, B. (2011) 'Plasticity and Post-Colonial Recognition: "Owning, Knowing and Being"', *Law Critique* 22: 227–49.

Bracke, S. (2012) 'From "Saving Women" to "Saving Gays": Rescue Narratives and Their Dis/continuities', *European Journal of Women's Studies* 19(2): 237–52.

Brown, W. (2006) *Regulating Aversion: Tolerance in the Age of Identity and Empire*, Princeton, NJ: Princeton University Press.

Butler, J, (2008) 'Sexual Politics, Torture and Secular Time', *British Journal of Sociology* 59(1): 59–77.

Butler, J. and Athanasiou, A. (2013) *Dispossession: The Performative in the Political*, Cambridge: Polity Press.

Cooper, D. and Herman, D. (2013) 'Up Against the Property Logic of Equality Law: Conservative Christian Accommodation Claims and Gay Rights', *Feminist Legal Studies* 21: 61–80.

Davies, M. (1999) 'Queer Property, Queer Persons: Self-Ownership and Beyond', *Social and Legal Studies* 8(3): 327–52.

D'Emilio, J. and Freedman, E. B. (1997) *Intimate Matters: A History of Sexuality in America*, Chicago, IL: University of Chicago Press (originally published 1988).

Duggan, L. (2003) *The Twilight of Equality? Neoliberalism, Cultural Politics and the Attack on Democracy*, Boston, MA: Beacon Press.

El-Tayeb, F. (2011) *European Others: Queering Ethnicity in Postnational Europe*, Minneapolis: University of Minnesota Press.

Fanon, F. (1986) *Black Skins, White Masks*, London: Pluto Press (originally published 1952).

Ferguson, R. (2004) *Aberrations in Black: Toward a Queer of Colour Critique*, Minneapolis: University of Minnesota Press.
Floyd, K. (2009) *The Reification of Desire: Toward a Queer Marxism*, Minneapolis: University of Minnesota Press.
Foucault, M. (1987) 'What is Enlightenment?', in P. Rabinow and W. M. Sullivan (eds) *Interpretive Social Science: A Second Look*, Berkeley: University of California Press, pp. 157–74 (originally published 1979).
—— (1990) *The History of Sexuality Vol. I: An Introduction*, New York: Vintage Books (originally published 1976).
—— (1996) 'What is Critique', in J. Schmidt (ed.) *What is Enlightenment? Eighteenth-Century Answers and Twentieth-Century Questions*, Berkeley: University of California Press, pp. 382–98 (originally published 1978).
—— (2003) *Society Must Be Defended: Lectures at The Collège de France 1975–1976*, London: Penguin Books (originally published 1997).
—— (2008) *The Birth of Biopolitics: Lectures at the Collège de France 1978–1979*, London: Palgrave.
Global Network of Sex Work Projects (2011) 'Sex Work is not Trafficking', Briefing Paper 03. Available online at www.nswp.org/resource/sex-work-not-trafficking (accessed 7 December 2013).
Harvey, D. (2005) *A Brief History of Neoliberalism*, New York: Oxford University Press.
Hennessy, R. (2000) *Profit and Pleasure: Sexual Identities in Late Capitalism*, London: Routledge.
Jameson, F. (2005) *Archaeologies of the Future: The Desire Called Utopia and Other Science Fictions*, London: Verso.
Jeffreys, S. (1997) *The Idea of Prostitution*, Melbourne: Spinifex.
MacKinnon, C. (1993) 'Prostitution and Civil Rights', *Michigan Journal of Gender and Law* 1: 13–31.
—— (2011) 'Trafficking, Prostitution and Inequality', talk given on 14 November 2011, at the Sawyer Seminar on Women's Human Rights: Paradigms, Paradoxes and Possibilities. Available online at www.law.uchicago.edu/audio/mackinnon11411 (accessed 12 December 2013).
Mai, N. (2012) 'The Fractal Queerness of Non-Heteronormative Migrants Working in the UK Sex Industry', *Sexualities* 15(5/6): 570–85.
—— (2013) 'Embodied Cosmopolitanisms: The Subjective Mobility of Migrants Working in the Global Sex Industry', *Gender, Place and Culture* 20(1): 107–24.
Marx, K. (1990) *Capital: A Critique of Political Economy, Volume I*, London: Penguin Books (originally published 1867).
Massad, J. (2007) *Desiring Arabs*, Chicago, IL: University of Chicago Press.
Penny, L. (2013) 'Laurie Penny on Sex Work: The Soho Raids Show Us the Real Problem with Sex Work Isn't the Sex – It's Low-Waged Work Itself', *New Statesman*, 11 December. Available online at www.newstatesman.com/2013/12/real-problem-sex-work-is-low-waged-work-itself (accessed 11 December 2014).
Puar, J. (2007) *Terrorist Assemblages: Homonationalism in Queer Times*, Durham, NC: Duke University Press.
Sabsay, L. (2012) 'The Emergence of the Other Sexual Citizen: Orientalism and the Modernisation of Sexuality', *Citizenship Studies* 16(5–6): 605–23.

Said, E. (1995) *Orientalism*, London: Penguin (originally published 1978).
Skeggs, B. (2004) 'Exchange, Value and Affect: Bourdieu and "the Self"', *Sociological Review* 52: 75–95.
Stoler, A. L. (1995) *Race and the Education of Desire: Foucault's 'History of Sexuality' and the Colonial Order of Things*, Durham, NC: Duke University Press.
Thomas, G. (2007) *The Sexual Demon of Colonial Power: Pan-African Embodiment and the Erotic Schemes of Empire*, Bloomington: University of Indiana Press.
Žižek, S. (2009) *The Ticklish Subject: The Absent Centre of Political Ontology*, London: Verso.

Chapter 11

Queer economies

Possibilities of queer desires and economic bodies (because 'the economy' is not enough)

Evangeline Heiliger

'Please, sir, I want some more.'

(*Oliver Twist*)

Queer desires

My mother has an incredible eye for design. Long before AMC's *Mad Men* repopularized modern furniture, she could spot a Herman Miller knockoff from a block away. 'Oh!' she would say, slowing the mint green '76 Pacer for a rolling drive-by. 'One moment, children. I just want to see what's in there.' To this, I would groan and slouch into the seat, knowing what was coming. Praying the neighbors weren't home to watch my mother digging in a pile of trash. Again.

'Why, Mom?' My three siblings and I would protest. 'It's broken! We don't need it!' And she would laugh, shrugging her shoulders and spreading her hands wide as if to ward off responsibility before loading discarded treasures of half-formed chairs, scrap wood, and lamps with shaggy, torn shades into the trunk.

'I just think it's so neat. It has possibility.'

Those drive-bys mingled hope and shame for all of us. Hope not only for basic needs but also for beautiful furniture, art, and possibility. My single mother, raising four kids in poverty, dared to have such queer desires in the United States during the Reagan era. Trickle-down economics meant being hungry and wearing ill-fitting, worn-out shoes and underwear. I was taught to feel shame for taking other people's castoffs, called 'scrub' for the dirt presumed to be fused to my skin because we dared to be poor in a stratified society. My mother, a schoolteacher working more than fulltime hours in Ohio, heard warnings about 'welfare queens' and checked her own behavior against white middle-class norms of propriety. She received regular paychecks. Paid taxes. Yet the income she earned wasn't enough to cover basic needs in those early eighties years. We – my family and other poor folks in my community – survived through creative repurposing, charity, bartering, trading, gardening, solidarity, food stamps, luck, and white privilege, as well as work for pay. My mother regularly scavenged trashcans and curbside leavings, browsed discount groceries, secondhand shops, and church sales. My family repurposed her take-home treasures in a variety of ways: some practical, some pleasurable, some downright embarrassing. This practice has been documented at length elsewhere by Jeff Ferrell, who spent nine months scrounging in Texas as part-fieldwork/part-survival. What Ferrell has found in trashpicking is 'an economy at the margins – literally – of society' (2006). In my own experience, while trashpicking might be 'at the margins' of mainstream social exchanges, the activities were central to my family and many of those we interacted with. Additionally, we all moved in and through more 'mainstream' middle-class spaces such as school, work, and church, often posing or passing as middle-class rather than as poor. As Binnie attests in Chapter 8 of this volume, to be 'able or empowered, or willing, to articulate a perspective on class within academic spaces can be intimately tied to the performative aspects of classed practices'. My family's complicated class identity required middle-class performances in particular material and social spaces, despite our material and social entrenchment in poverty. Yet, even as we gained partial upward mobility, there was never any attempt to leave behind trashpicking or other alternative or noncapitalist economic activities that we engaged in during those difficult Reagan years and beyond.[1]

Working in 'the economy' alone couldn't satisfy our needs. It still cannot. Trashpicking is just one example of an economic innovation by poor, queer, and working-class people in response to laws and policies that ignore the needs of marginalized folks. Yet rarely are these innovations acknowledged in traditional economic study; they become visible only as 'alternatives to' capitalism, and only if economic gains are quantifiable. In development studies, such activities are denigrated as 'economies of affection', viewed within that framework as a cause for poverty and a hindrance to progress (Escobar 1995; Scott 1996). The full range of economic activities enacted by poor, queer, and working-class people is missing from economic analysis. As noted by Binnie, class is an analytic of power by which people are differentiated from one another on the basis of differential access to material inequalities. Binnie argues for the integration of class into an intersectional analysis of sexuality, and an integration of sexuality into an intersectional analysis of class. This chapter answers Binnie's call by utilizing an intersectional sexuality–class analysis of different economic innovations by poor, queer, and working-class folks.

I have a queer desire. I want to convince you that there are worlds of economic activities that go unnoticed in traditional economic study. My goal is to explain the benefits of those 'other activities' – the alternative capitalist and noncapitalist activities – despite their being marked as 'outside' wage-earning capitalism. I want you to value them because they matter to people's survival. To do this, I have

1 The decision(s) to continue to trashpick, barter, trade, repurpose, and otherwise engage in alternative capitalist and noncapitalist activities was due both to the precariousness of my family's financial resources and the pleasures those activities provided for creating possibility and access using imagination, time, and repurposed goods.

to blend some strangely personal queer, poor, and working-class stories with a scholarly attempt to dethrone 'the economy' as a unified, closed system.

Economic bodies: multiplying vulnerable desires

I argue that queer desires inspire people to engage in clusters of nonnormative economic arrangements. These clusters of economic activity can best be understood metaphorically as 'economic bodies'. I imagine these economic bodies engaging the world much like living and nonliving bodies interacting with other living and nonliving bodies. They take in nutrients and excrete waste. They create and destroy, mimic and hide, hibernate, reproduce, and die (although not necessarily in that order).[2] One could consider capitalism as one type of economic body, although certainly not the only type. Economic bodies consist of people, tools, equipment, technical devices, algorithms, as well as non-human substances (e.g. food, plants, minerals, currencies), and actions such as labor, exchanges, and gifting. Economic bodies can exist at a large scale, similarly to how 'capitalism' is conceived, or at smaller scales such as micro-economies, families, groups, and individuals.[3] The relationships of and between economic bodies can be understood only through engaging a radical analysis that incorporates intersectional analytics of power, including but not limited to gender, race/ethnicity, class, sexuality, nationality, embodiment, and other structural forms of power.[4]

2 The porous boundaries of economic bodies hold promise for the queer commons called for by Klapeer and Schönpflug in Chapter 10 of this volume. My insistence that queer economic bodies are inherently relational aligns with their call to de-center the individual in economic policy discussions. Like my colleagues and the queer eco-feminists and eco-sexualists they cite, I envision that more just economies may be possible through recognizing an interconnectedness between living beings. The metaphor of queer economic bodies helps to visualize how 'being' rather than 'having' a queer identity could play out in practice.

3 While a single person's activities can be an economic body, there can never be only one economic body – bodies always exist in relation to other bodies, both human and non-human. See Callon and Latour 1981; Callon 1986, 2005; Latour 1987, 2005 for a discussion of human and non-human actors. See also eco-feminist theorists such as Gaard 1997 and Sandilands 2002 for a discussion of the non-boundary between humans, non-human animals, and nature.

4 While concept of 'actor' described by Actor Network Theory (ANT) would allow me to pluralize and multiply economic systems, the ANT method has been critiqued by scholars of feminist science studies for not adequately engaging analytics of power associated with structural inequalities, including but not limited to gender, race, class, sexuality, nation, and embodiment. See Quinlan 2012 for a larger discussion of these debates. Like feminist science studies scholar Sandra Harding (2008), I see the potential for ANT (via science and technology studies) and feminist science studies to inform one another's methods and epistemology. However, it would first be necessary to trace the scholarly arguments in favor of utilizing ANT for queer/feminist research on economics and political economy. This task is beyond the scope and purview of this short chapter, but one I hope to take up in a future project for the possibilities that a feminist ANT could bring to the political economic study of green/queer alternative economies, aka queer economies.

Why not then use the term 'actor' as developed by Callon and Latour in actor-network theory (also known as ANT)[5] (Callon and Latour 1981; Callon 1986, 2005; Latour 1987, 2005)? Latour's 'actor' calls to mind a human being who acts in relation to others, and whose actions can only be understood in connection to others, similarly to how I describe economic bodies functioning relationally to other bodies. Callon describes 'actors' as being made up of 'human bodies but also of prostheses, tools, equipment, technical devices, algorithms, etc.' (Callon 2005: 4). My description of economic bodies again aligns, although it elaborates further.

My observations of green, queer, and alternative economies (Heiliger 2011, 2012, 2013) leads me to articulate three reasons to use the metaphor of 'bodies' in this chapter – rather than 'actor', 'economy', or 'economic actor' – to describe an assemblage of people, parts, relationships, and actions that make up economic activities: (1) to pluralize and multiply economic systems; (2) to emphasize the vulnerability of the human bodies living and working under conditions of structural inequality;[6] and (3) to utilize the power of metaphor to insert images of vulnerable economies in the minds of readers. While ANT allows for a multiplying and plurality of economies via its concept of 'networks', in which multiple 'actors' can (inter)act, ANT does not meet the other two characteristics of green/queer/alternative economies.[7] My purpose in using 'bodies' as a metaphor is to call to mind both the *humans* included in economic activities and their *vulnerability*, a vulnerability mirrored in economic bodies. In *Precarious Life*, feminist and queer scholar Judith Butler writes that the vulnerability of our bodies is what connects us to one another. Our bodies signal 'dependency, vulnerability, agency: the skin and flesh expose us to the gaze of others, but also to touch and to violence' (2004: 26). This vulnerability of bodies is also what creates porousness: a body's capacity to help and to harm, to be assisted and to be hurt is interwoven with the dependency of bodies (Butler 2004). Economic bodies are equally vulnerable, a point which I address later in this section.

5 Actor-network theory (ANT) is a method of observing the social that explicitly allows for the inclusion of the material-semiotic. Through close observation, a researcher writes thick descriptions, from which analysis might later be drawn. ANT has been taken up primarily in science and technology studies (STS), but also by feminist studies (Quinlan 2012), economic sociology, and the anthropology of markets (Hardie and Mackenzie 2006).

6 Although here I emphasize human bodies, both economic bodies and queer economies include human and non-human animals as well as other non-human actors. See Callon and Latour 1981; Callon 1986, 2005; Latour 1987, 2005 for a discussion of human and non-human actors. See also eco-feminist theorists such as Gaard (1997) and Sandilands (2002) for a discussion of the non-boundary between humans, non-human animals, and nature.

7 Importantly, this project does not engage in the intense level of thick description that ANT calls for. I sketch details of multiple queer economies according to what was easily determined via internet sources and emailing with participants of the queer economies. For my purposes here, this is adequate to articulate the possibilities of queer economies for conceiving of economics and economic policy in more just ways. ANT, however, would ask a researcher to engage more fully in observation, a task best left for a future project.

I pluralize the metaphor of body, using 'economic bodies' (rather than economic body) to counter powerful existing metaphors that promote the idea of a singular, unified, economic totality such as 'the body of Capitalism' and 'the Market'. In making this argument, I align with Gibson-Graham (1996, 2006) in recognizing multiple forms of capitalism and the need to partially dis-unify the powerful ideology of 'the economy' or 'Capitalism' as a closed system. I also draw on embodiment theorists in recognizing the porousness of bodies, and on queer theorists to articulate how queer desires are pursued through economic bodies. The communal, polymorphous, intersubjective components of queer, feminist, and embodiment theories amplify the metaphor of 'bodies'. The communal, polymorphous, and intersubjective components also diffuse the idea of a monolithic economic process such as 'the market' or 'capitalism' into easily recognizable clusters of activity. It becomes possible to see my mother's teaching job, neighborhood foodsharing, charity clothing donations, and trashpicking as a connected cluster of economic activity that enabled my family's survival, rather than as a capitalist economic activity (teaching job) and several alternative capitalist and noncapitalist activities. Therefore, reading this metaphor of economic bodies through recent scholarship allows a more complex picture of multiple economic processes, particularly those utilized by poor and other marginalized people as survival strategies.

It may appear that the difference between 'body' and 'bodies' as an economic metaphor is so slight as to be insignificant. Yet recent studies by cognitive scientists Thibodeau and Boroditsky (2011, 2013) demonstrate that even slight, one-word differences in the metaphor used to describe a social or political issue can have profound impacts upon decision-making processes by individuals. Metaphors influence the kinds of solutions we think of and also direct us towards solutions that are consistent with the metaphor (Thibodeau and Boroditsky 2011). Furthermore, metaphors influence our thinking whether or not we are explicitly aware of the metaphor's role in our decision-making process (Thibodeau and Boroditsky 2013). Therefore, I argue that those who consider all economic activities part of a singular, unified entity such as 'the economy' will seek out economic solutions for a singular, unified economy, convinced these are the best solutions regardless of data. If the same people are willing to think of economies as bodies – as lots of different kinds of 'people' moving through the world interacting with other 'people' – they will look for economic solutions that meet the needs of diverse people who will function best by interacting with others to meet their needs.[8]

8 Thibodeau and Boroditsky (2013) have noted that in their (US-based) studies of metaphors and decision making about crime, participants' gender, race/ethnicity, and age do not influence results. However, political affiliation does have some bearing on how one is influenced by metaphors. Thibodeau and Boroditsky found that Republicans are more likely to generate enforcement and punishment for crime-related problems and are less swayed by metaphor than Democrats and independents. It is unknown whether Republicans are similarly less influenced by metaphors about economic or other social issues. This may or may not have implications for economic metaphors such as bodies and 'people'.

I propose *bodies* as a metaphor for economies because human bodies are not closed systems; they have complex interactions with other bodies and their environments via border crossings of flesh and consciousness 'more porous than previously imagined' (Grosz 2001). My family's intimate engagement with other people's refuse is one example of blurred boundaries: between us and other families; between work-for-pay and nonmarket activity; and between what no longer has possibility (trash) and what newly has possibility (trash-turned-treasure). Klapeer and Schönpflug concept of 'queer commons' in Chapter 9 of this volume illustrates the porous boundaries of human bodies more fully. If one considers identity as something formed in relation to others, rather than owned by one's individual self – as argued by Klapeer and Schönpflug – then my family's class identity and my mother's queer desires formed in relation to multiple others, both within and adjacent to our class. Human contact is porous in its overlaps: fingerprints left on trash meet fingerprints on trash-turned-treasure,[9] creating liminal spaces where my family's queerly classed identity was formed and re-formed. We interacted with one another as family members sharing the same material and social resources, and we brushed up against those whose trash became a means to my family's desires and survival.

Moira Gatens (1996) argues that the permeability and transitivity of human bodies is possible with any 'body' with which we have an affective relation, including corporate social bodies. Pushing out from Gatens, I suggest that economic bodies, as a form of social body, are controlled through human forces, behave in human ways, actively engage with other economic bodies, and utilize forms of social control and power. Bodies are vulnerable to racism, sexism, homophobia, xenophobia, and ableism (Butler 2004), which serve neoliberal aims through their visual and discursive association both with certain human bodies and with nonnormative economic bodies. Nonnormative economic bodies include intelligent, deliberate, and relationship-making processes such as bartering, gifting, trading, careshift collectives, trashpicking, and repurposing. However, these economic activities are frequently racialized, feminized, eroticized, and colonized, imagined in economic discourse as geographically located in the global south or in 'inferior' areas of the global north (e.g. inner-city urban or lower-class rural) (Escobar 1995). What we imagine about bodies interrelates with the socio-historic formations of economic realities and current understandings of economic 'truth'. Thus stereotypes about human bodies are transferred onto what we imagine about economic bodies, and imaginings about economic bodies cross the borders of 'social bodies' and become soaked up by the sponginess of the diverse human bodies that labor in the environments of that particular economic body. The bodies of the people in an economy – in an economic

9 Taking this concept of porous bodies in relation to a different economic activity, this could also be the liminal moment in which skin cells and scent left on charity clothing meets that produced by our own bodies when we put them on.

body – create meaning for that economy. What we imagine about bodies, our own and others', has powerful effects on how we relate to those bodies. This transitivity of bodies from material to imagined and back again in simultaneous time, combined with the spongelike ability of bodies to hold multiple meanings, is what I refer to here as the porousness of bodies, both human and economic.

How then might we use this porousness of bodies to imagine and engage in productively promiscuous economies? I take up this question in this chapter, offering five examples of porously queer economies that function like human bodies:[10] a single-mother desiring beautiful furniture, art, and possibility despite living in poverty; a homeless person making a livelihood on their own terms; medically altering one's body to better match one's gender regardless of age or ability to pay; moving cross-country despite being told that persons with disabilities ought to be satisfied with their current living situations; and creating social healing through cultivating queer black intergenerational community across state lines and in the absence of legal ties. I demonstrate that these queer desires inspire complex weavings of market, alternative market, and nonmarket economic activities. These blended activities in pursuit of queer desires are what I call 'queer economies'.

Queer economies

I define *queer economies* as economic bodies animated by queer desires. J. Jack Halberstam defines queerness as referring 'to nonnormative logics and organizations of community, sexual identity, embodiment, and activity in space and time' (2005: 6). The 'queer' part of queer desires, in this chapter, signals desires shaped by nonnormative logics of community, sexual identity, embodiment, and activity – including economic processes – in space and time. When queer desires motivate economic bodies, we can see that queer economies are shaped and moved by human bodies pursuing queer desires. Because queer economies blend economic activities, these kinds of economic bodies have radical potential for transformation, extending options to survive and thrive through deliberately relational activities such as bartering, trading, careshift collectives, and trashpicking.

Another feature of queer economies is their engagement with the erotic. In her seminal essay 'Toward a Queer Ecofeminism' (1997), Greta Gaard articulates how Western culture's devaluing of women, nature, and colonized peoples

10 I offer the first two examples of queer economies from personal experiences and observation in Ohio and California, USA; the remaining three were brought to my attention through queer internet networks. I have included only information easily found via internet resources. These five are not meant to be a complete list of queer economies, but merely to hint at the range of possibilities for queer economies. Members of both TTOSOD and MBHC saw drafts of this essay and were asked to provide input and edits on the portions of the text written about their economic bodies. T*FC did not respond to my email inquiries.

parallels a devaluation of both queerness and the erotic. Scholars such as Arturo Escobar (1995) and Catherine Scott (1996) have made similar claims that economic development discourse conceptually connects nature, women, indigenous people, and colonized nations. Given Gaard's eco-feminist theorization that colonization projects attempting to stamp out queer expressions of gender and sexuality simultaneously created a fear of the erotic (1997), I am intrigued by the idea that erotophobia might be preventing us from valuing a range of economic bodies. Can we conceive of nonnormative economies as queerly erotic bodies, sparking and enflaming queer desires? I can imagine them flaming, butch, dyke, crip, leather, trans*, closeted, polyamorous – even dandy! Yet I wish also to include 'punks' and 'welfare queens' amongst these queerly defined and imagined economic bodies that inspire queer desire (Cohen 1997: 438). For Cathy J. Cohen, using 'queer' politically allows for an expansive definition of identities linked to sexuality, labor, and visibility, a definition that includes those who blur gender/sexual boundaries as well as unmarried mothers or youth who reject capitalism in favor of anarchy. When our queer economies rub up against the skin of other queer economies, there lies powerful potential for desire and economy outside the (re)productive. I suspect many forms of queer economy go unnoticed because they represent refusals to 'sleep with' or 'be faithful to' a white hetero-male-capitalism. Thus, just as lesbians and queer women may be punished for refusing sexual availability to heteronormative demands, so too are queer economies deplored, ignored, and decimated for cheeky 'failures' to live up to capitalist expectations of profit, efficiency, and progress.

One example of a 'failure' to properly engage capitalism is that of contemporary trashpickers in LA County. They are typecast as homeless, male, dirty, and incapable of making rational decisions for their own well-being.[11] Yet evidence about scavenging demonstrates that at least some of those assumptions are false: collecting recyclables is a consistent means to make money. It requires skill and awareness, planning and follow-through. Trashpicking also requires patience and a certain amount of strength and mobility, although it doesn't have to be one's own legs or arms – wheelchairs and grabber-sticks are useful tools (Farrell 2006). Scavenging can be effective in teams or solo, or by collaborating with someone for company while collecting for oneself. Trashpicking allows for making a livelihood on one's own terms outside of or in addition to work for pay.

I list trashpicking as evidence of queer economy, partly because my own queer survival has depended upon it. I see it in action in every place I have

11 For examples of these debates in popular media, see Holguin 1993; Carpenter 2010; and Elekes 2012. See also Tapper90020 (2010) 'Garbage Scavenger – Stealing From Trash Cans in Los Angeles, California' and associated user comments, video uploaded to YouTube on 9 August 2010: www.youtube.com/watch?v=mTNkTwoZQjQ; and Gus Ugalde (2013) 'Opinion: Los Angeles needs better system to avoid trash, recyclables scavenging' at Boyle Heights Beats/Pulso de Boyle Heights, 8 March 2013: www.boyleheightsbeat.com/opinion-los-angeles-needs-better-system-to-avoid-trash-recyclables-scavenging-2217.

ever traveled or lived. Trash also brushes uncomfortably against the erotic, frequently cast in moral terms as a judgment: as dirty, unclean, something to be discarded and not thought about again. Those who engage in close, embodied contact with trash are categorized in the same way as the trash itself: disposable, unclean, and certainly not compatible with a middle- or upper-class status. At the same time, the embrace of 'trashiness' in popular culture – understood as a gendered and sexualized cultural performance – leaves me loath to romanticize trashpicking. It is dirty work, but hardly immoral: one might even argue that repurposing keeps valuable resources out of landfills and reduces greenhouse gasses, thereby improving local environments. This is where feminist, queer, and antiracist theories help us to see the language and practices used to denigrate particular human bodies. I propose that when we hear sexist, racist, ableist, classist, homophobic, or trans*phobic comments, there is an opportunity to observe queer economies that challenge the unity, singularity, and totality of 'capitalism'.

Why do I suggest that economies function like bodies? Contemporary English-language economic discourse frequently touts both the singularity of economy – '*the* economy is sick' – and economy's presumed human qualities – 'the economy is *sick*'. Existing descriptions of economies as gendered, racialized, disabled, and otherwise anthropomorphized in human terms bolster my claim that economies are *already* conceived at least partially in embodied terms. The anthropomorphized terms rely on a Western framework that values certain 'masculine-affiliated' qualities over 'feminine-affiliated' others. Catherine Scott illuminates that the gendered nature of economic discourse is fundamental to imbuing imperial and capitalist regimes with unearned power (1995: 4). Yet within this gendered, anthropomorphized language is 'the economy's' Achilles heel. The tendency to anthropomorphize 'the economy' also serves to break down an image of the economy as singular: 'the' economy is variously described as masculine, feminine, hard, soft, sick, dying, racialized, reproducing, and lazy. In paying attention to such discourses, one can only conclude that 'the economy' consistently changes genders, has multiple personalities, or is not as singular in form as dominant hegemonic discourse would lead us to think. Each of these scenarios holds promise for imagining multiple, diverse economic bodies.

Those invested in racism, sexism, ableism, erotophobia, heteronormativity, nationalisms, and colonial power are likely to take my suggestion that there are as many kinds of economies as there are types of human bodies as proof of the superiority of capital 'c' Capitalism (Gibson-Graham 1996), much as they take for granted the privileges and power granted to bodies upholding whiteness, maleness, wholeness, productivity, reason, heterosexism, the nation-state, and imperialism. My argument is not for them. I suggest thinking of economies as bodies so that those invested in valuing a range of diverse human bodies and relationships can claim our queer economies – our labors in service of queer desires – with the same ferocity that we claim our diverse, queer selves.

Benefits of economic bodies

The need for an 'economies as bodies' framework grew out of my research on two brands from so-called 'ethical trade': Café Femenino® and Product (Red)™ (Heiliger 2011, 2012, 2013). These brands and their campaigns are examples of a larger 'ethical consumerism' trend in the late twentieth and early twenty-first centuries, which is a social and economic phenomenon encouraging shoppers, primarily in the global North, to buy products that claim to make the world a better place for all. Gibson-Graham's dismantling of monolithic 'Capitalism' into 'capitalisms' (1996) proved critical for describing ways Café Femenino's Fair Trade economic processes differed from Product (Red)'s version of shopping for a social justice cause. However, once I began to analyse economic activities that blended market, alternative market, and nonmarket transactions, Gibson-Graham's (1996, 2006) framework of diverse economies no longer effectively described what I observed. One flaw in Gibson-Graham's description of diverse economies is its limited framing of diverse economies as consisting of transactions/labor/enterprise, which are conceived as taking place in one of three places: (1) markets, (2) alternative markets, or (3) nonmarkets. Depending upon how economic exchanges are compensated, Gibson-Graham categorize economic activities as either (1) capitalist, (2) alternative capitalist, or (3) noncapitalist. Yet economic bodies do not fit neatly into any one of these categories as strictly capitalist, alternative capitalist, or noncapitalist. Instead, diverse economic bodies – including queer economies – overlap different areas of Gibson-Graham's framework. The actions of economic bodies may include a combination of capitalist, alternative capitalist, and noncapitalist activities. Here, the metaphor of porousness is useful for understanding the ways that queer economies do not have defined boundaries around market, alternative market, and nonmarket activities. Rather, all three of these activities intermingle in queer economies to support nonnormative people as they pursue queer desires for surviving, thriving, and justice. Gibson-Graham's framework of diverse economies may not preclude the matrix of queer economies. However, it does not adequately theorize the ways queer economies mix economic activities in pursuit of specific queer desires.

Contemporary forms of trade such as ethical consumerism are a merger of capitalisms and alternatives such as Fair Trade (Heiliger 2011; Barnett *et al.* 2008). Instead of describing Café Femenino as functioning under a 'subsystem of capitalism' or Product (Red) as 'a more ethical capitalism', the framework of economic bodies catalogues each as its own economic body. Both are new economic bodies formed through an economic marriage. These are two different economies that have adapted quickly in response to critiques of globalization, and which play with one another on a global scale, as well as in local markets. In the coffee world, certified Fair Trade became more entrenched in legal documentation, a result that some considered a hindrance to the transformative possibilities of Fair Trade. In response, other forms of 'ethical' trade such as transparent contracts and direct trade spun off from Fair Trade and formed their own economic bodies, some of which continue to engage with formal, certified Fair Trade. Other economic bodies previously considered alternative have modified to more closely resemble conventional trade (e.g. Silk brand soy products). Economic offspring form just as human ones do: through unions sometimes clandestine, occasionally sexy, possibly expensive, but generally without much of note to alert the media.

This merger of ideological interests (if not actual practices) and social justice concerns is strange. It strikes me that current bodies of ethical economies operate a bit like idealized liberal American upwardly mobile heterosexual couples: practical, yet kind. When I am asked to comment on Fair Trade's radical potential, I can only say that I am in favor of Fair Trade in the same way that I am in favor of same-sex marriage. Whereas same-sex marriage allows increased legal benefits, protections, and responsibilities to those who participate, certified Fair Trade provides increased access to global markets, some financial protection, and responsibilities to a cooperative or group of farmers. Yet it must be noted that both same-sex marriage and certified Fair Trade provide benefits only to those who fit a limited profile. To participate in same-sex marriage in the United States, one must have a recognized citizenship and a legally recognized gender, only one adult partner who consents to marry you, money for a marriage license, and access to a state government that permits same-sex marriage. Fair Trade is similarly limited to those who are privileged. To participate in Fair Trade, one must have certification of Fair Trade practices, ownership of or access to land to grow crops, membership in a cooperative, and access to income or assets. Fair Trade provides major social and economic benefits to farmers and producers who participate, yet Fair Trade does not intervene in the lives of the very poorest farmers in most cases (Jaffee 2007). Certainly there are social, legal, emotional, and economic benefits of both Fair Trade and gay marriage to those who participate. However, both are solutions that work within existing legal and economic structures, systems designed to privilege heterosexuality, whiteness, existing wealth, able-bodiedness, and the nation-state. It is undeniable that some people – some bodies – will never be qualified to participate in either project, whereas others will not want to. As Lyn Ossome argues in Chapter 7 of this volume, a teleological view of economic justice can blind observers to those who cannot 'move forward' in the prescribed way. Ossome additionally questions whether justice can possibly be held within the embrace of capitalism. I want to focus primarily on Ossome's critique of attempting to locate justice *within* capitalism, for this leaves room to consider how justice might be struggled for across, through, and around capitalism by those who deliberately engage in queer economies – that is, a variety of capitalist, alternative capitalist, and noncapitalist activities motivated by queer desires – in order to survive and thrive. Therefore, I wish to stipulate that while a framework of economic bodies could chart progressive and liberal economies not usually visible within conventional economic discourse, more is needed to develop this concept in order to locate and describe radical, transformative, queer economies of desire. The next section elaborates on what I mean by queer economic bodies, and articulates ways these economies make queer survival possible.

Queer desires multiply economic possibilities

As I gather evidence of multiple, interrelated, queer economies through a process of witnessing, storytelling, and internet 'eavesdropping' (Facebook), it is obvious that queer people – using Cohen's radical political potential to include a wide range of individuals – co-create communities and economies blending capitalist, alternative capitalist, and noncapitalist activities into economic bodies. These economic bodies become queer economies if the blended activities are used to pursue queer desires shaped by (as Halberstam describes 'queer' to indicate) nonnormative logics of community, sexual identity, embodiment, and activity – including economic processes – in space and time.

One example of this blending for queer desires is the Trans*ition Fund Collective (T*FC), a Tumblr begun in January, 2012 to 'highlight the projects of trans* individuals fundraising for their transition while sharing some awesome trans*-friendly products and resources. Submissions are always welcome!' (T*FC; see website in notes at the end of the chapter). More than 15 individuals posted fundraising efforts and personal stories on T*FC during the first month, primarily for surgery and follow-up care for themselves or a loved one. Some fundraisers sell pre-made items such as video games, sex toys, or books, while others offer their skills in trade or to personalize a special gift. Most create art such as t-shirts, screen prints, jewelry, and paintings to fund medical costs. The remaining Tumblr posts include resources, information about moderators Ariel and Codi, binder giveaways, and general encouragement of trans* individuals. I classify the Trans*ition Fund Collective as a queer economy because it is prompted by the nonnormative desire to medically change one's body to better match one's self-identified gender, and it blends capitalist (the medical-industrial complex), alternative capitalist (fundraising via Tumblr), and noncapitalist (bartering, trading, and gifting) economic activities. The T*FC additionally manifests queer desires by not focusing solely on profit; its features include strengthening ties between individuals and their supporters via Tumblr. Its use of multiple economic processes (art, bartering, trade, gifting, collaborating, fundraising) alongside an engagement in the medical-industrial complex is an unconventional kind of economic arrangement, an economic body neither fully inside nor wholly outside a conventional profit-making capitalism. Additionally, its relationship-building (supporting, connecting, communicating, promoting) across in-person and internet interactions provides a model of community engagement and transformation for other trans* people.

Porously queer economies

One reason for the intermingling of various economic activities in a porous queer economy may be that the politically queer humans laboring in queer economies are themselves diverse and experience intersecting forms of systemic oppression that must be met with multiple forms of resistance. Engaging in different forms of economic activity – in different kinds of enterprise – is one strategy for resistance and survival. So, too, is engaging in a variety of relationships and forms of community. An example of a queer economy pursuing 'nonnormative logics and community' is a Tumblr called To the Other Side of Dreaming (TTOSOD; see website in notes at the end of the chapter). TTOSOD documents the journey of disability justice/transformative justice activists Mia Mingus and Stacey 'Cripchick' Milbern to move together from the US south to the Bay Area of California, despite immense economic and social limitations to mobility faced by people with disabilities. In pursuing this endeavor, they said to their communities in the blogosphere:

> [We] have decided to live together and create/cultivate interdependent queer disabled korean diasporic radical women of color home together. We are embarking on a journey together to put pieces of disability justice into practice, love each other and live on the other side of dreaming. A huge part of this is our need, as crips, as queers, and women of color, as korean (and all) diasporic people; we need each other and we need you.
>
> (TTOSOD)

Mingus and Milbern ask for assistance finding affordable, accessible housing and creating a community care collective in Berkeley, California, to assist with Milbern's needs until the state of CA approves her application and provides home assistive care. They transgress complicated state regulations and social norms that make it difficult for persons with disabilities to move. They explicitly name love and healing a variety of inter-related traumas as part of their relationship-building.

The response towards To the Other Side of Dreaming in the first two weeks was remarkable: members of their online and in-person community offered advice and connections to affordable housing and began creating a schedule for a care-shift collective. Some online community members sold books, while another friend organized an Etsy shop to raise money for their move and transition.

The kinds of support To the Other Side of Dreaming required to prepare to move across the United States differs from the kinds of day-to-day support needed after moving and settling in. Questions of quantity of assistance as well as quality of relationships are critical. Enough people have to be involved to avoid burnout – and those who commit to assisting need to be honest about what they can contribute and for how long. Some 'allies' stuck around to provide access for less than six months, perhaps not knowing or caring how their absence can shift a situation of thriving to one of surviving. TTOSOD, as queer economy, relies particularly on creativity, flexibility, and interdependence, as well as access to money, able-bodied persons with access, and state services. In Chapter 7 of this volume, Lyn Ossome challenges the teleological view of most discussions of economic justice, and her arguments apply here: that TTOSOD remains a functioning queer economy, but one that defies the linear narrative of progress and invites the question whether rubbing queer economies against other queer economies is always or necessarily pleasurable, particularly when some economies operate from greater privileges.

Queer economies, queer relationships

Like other economic bodies, queer economies engage in relationship-making and a variety of economic processes for survival of nonnormative human bodies. Some of these processes may look like a poor imitation of capitalisms – for example, so-called 'economies of affection' with activities such as gifting, trading, bartering, trashpicking, and repurposing. However, I would argue they no more mock capitalisms than a dildo mocks a penis. Each of these noncapitalist exchanges offers relational pleasures and responsibilities. Profit-making is not the sole point of these economic activities. Relationships and tool-usage matter as much as form and purpose. Gibson-Graham (1999) and Escobar (1995) reveal that a Western ideological framework invisibilizes some economic activities, while denigrating and calling for the destruction of others. Success and survival within this context become linked to one's ability to perform as an ideal 'rational' economic actor for capitalism. As Escobar has argued, 'through economic sciences (classical political economy) and broader philosophical conceptions (derived from the Enlightenment, utilitarianism, empiricism), this system produced a certain subjectivity, namely, that embodied in the modern producing subject' (2005: 142). Cultivating a sense of the profit motive was seen as a crucial component of becoming an ideal producer for the global market, while gift-giving, charity, bartering, and other forms of noncapitalist exchange were ridiculed as being non-rational and non-productive (Escobar 1995; Harvey 2005; Scott 1995).

My fifth example of a queer economy embraces many 'nonrational' economic activities. Mobile Homecoming (MBHC) is designed by Dr. Alexis Pauline Gumbs, black queer feminist poet and revolutionary, and her partner, Julia Wallace, revolutionary black queer filmmaker, to record the stories of queer black elders in the US. They reached out to online and in-person communities to raise funds for a mobile home to travel to the homes of queer black elders to conduct interviews. Gumbs and Wallace build relationships and raise money through holding freedom schools, selling poetry and books, creating films and teaching resources available online for free and for sale, sharing meals, asking for donations of money, love, and support, and connecting with other queer radicals in North Carolina, USA, and around the globe.

According to Gumbs and Wallace's MBHC (see website in notes at the end of the chapter), the point of their work is to heal, love, and honor black queers, and to support other revolutionary relationships. MBHC is explicitly not a nonprofit. They write:

> We understand that the modes of survival in our black queer communities which include:
>
> – social support organizing
> – artistic creativity
> – spiritual transformation
> – revolutionary interpersonal relationships
>
> are our key resources as we transform the meaning of life.
>
> (MBHC website)

MBHC is queer economy for its intentional mixing of monetary exchange, creative resourcefulness, and deliberate community-building meant to generate love and structural healing. Celebrating the full range of black queerness fundamentally shapes MBHC and affiliated projects. 'Community' is defined not by geographic boundaries, nor by boundaries around race or gender, but by reaching out to like-minded social revolutionaries working for justice. There are thousands of people who belong to Gumbs and Wallace's community – their project of celebrating black queer love and honoring queer intergenerational connection through listening projects and recording history clearly speaks to many. This is one example of how queer economies function – through connections, networks of respect and mutuality, and by speaking truth to power.

Because 'the economy' is never enough: desiring (more) queer economic bodies

In this chapter, I analyse five examples of queer economies to begin to think through what makes queer economies *queer*, and what makes queer economies *valuable*. In considering what makes queer economies queer, first, they are a type of economic body animated by queer desires. Economic bodies are inherently relational. Second, queer economies differ conceptually from 'the economy', because they are not a singular, unified entity like 'Capitalism' – they are multiple and allow us to 'have some more'. Third, queer economies differ from Gibson-Graham's framing of multiple economies (as capitalisms, alternative capitalisms, or noncapitalisms) because queer economies – like many economic bodies – weave together two or more kinds of economic activities in pursuit of queer desires. Finally, queer economies function differently from other economic bodies because they focus on nonnormative arrangements of community and relationship-building while pursuing queer desires.

The value of queer economies comes from this bundle of characteristics. The relationship-making aspects of queer economies are as important as their plurality and their blending of economic activities. Relationship-making – between people and between economies – enables queer economies to sidestep larger structural forces that disenfranchise queer people and thwart queer desires. Specifically, TTOSOD and MBHC name desires such as *love* and *healing personal and structural wounds* as key goals motivating the activities of their economic bodies. Attempting to diffuse or heal structural harms is also clear in T*FC's use of Tumblr to provide emotional support for trans* youth who experience social pressure to pretend to be the sex/gender assigned to them at birth. Scavengers like my family and trashpickers in Los Angeles have a nonnormative relationship with trash, which pushes back against structural norms that insist 'nice people' spend money to pursue their desires or that those who don't have money don't deserve to thrive. One reason queer economies might be difficult to identify and describe is that many are utilizing forms of alternative and noncapitalist exchange that are typically categorized as non-economic. Queer economies work differently from how we have been taught that capitalisms function, even as queer economies operate through, within, and outside them. Therefore, queer economies have the potential to create justice through desires for nonnormative logics of community, sexual identity, embodiment, and activity – including economic processes – in space and time.[12] This requires flexibility and creativity, as well as the pleasurable and often-difficult work of building relationships and being accountable for our actions.

Re-theorizing economies as bodies is not merely an intellectual exercise – I mean to multiply our options for engaging in economic activities. Naming and describing queer economies makes clear the unconscious links between economies-as-bodies and the embodied persons laboring within them in service of queer desires. So I ask: what queer desires move your economic bodies? What relationships must you engage in to manifest your desires? With whom will your economic bodies collaborate, flirt, merge, avoid, fight, make up, bargain, or trade? What – or who – will your queer economies long for? Applying our ideas about human bodies leads to greater recognition of – and perhaps participation in – economies *already* animated by queer desires and justice. What will your queer economies do? Because 'the economy' simply isn't enough to hold all your queer possibilities.

Acknowledgments

I wish to thank the editors and co-contributors of this volume, as well as the participants of the Desiring Just Economies/Just Economies of Desire conference for their feedback and intellectual engagement, and thank you to Chris Littleton and the UCLA Women's Studies (now Gender Studies) Department for financial support to attend the DJE/JED conference in Berlin in 2010. Thank you especially to Antke Engel, Carole Browner, Katie Oliviero, and J. Jack Halberstam for seeing the promise of this chapter during its embryonic stages. My gratitude goes to my writing accountability community: NCFDD, Kayla D. Hales, Jennifer Freeman Marshall, David Perez II, Kerry Ann Rockquemore, and Jessica Millward. Thank you to Stacy Milbern, Mia Mingus, Alexis Pauline Gumbs, and Julia Wallace for their willingness to correspond with me about their queer economies. My thanks always to Van Nguyen for making the world outside my head even more pleasurable than my lengthy romps through the fields of feminist/queer studies.

References

Barnett, C., Cloke, P., Clarke, N. and Malpass, A. (2005) 'Consuming Ethics: Articulating the Subjects and Spaces of Ethical Consumption', *Antipode* 37: 23–45.

Butler, J. (2004) *Precarious Life: The Powers of Mourning and Violence*, London/New York: Verso Press.

12 This definition of queer is borrowed from J. Jack Halberstam 2005.

Callon, M. (1986) 'Some Elements of a Sociology of Translation: Domestication of the Scallops and the Fishermen of St. Brieuc Bay', in J. Law (ed.) *Power, Action, Belief: A New Sociology of Knowledge?*, Boston: Routledge and Kegan Paul, pp. 196–233.

—— (2005) 'Why Virtualism Paves the Way to Political Impotence: A Reply to Daniel Miller's Critique of *The Laws of the Markets*', *Economic Sociology: European Electronic Newsletter* 6(2): 3–20.

Callon, M. and Latour, B. (1981) 'Unscrewing the Big Leviathan: How Actors Macro-Structure Reality and How Sociologists Help Them Do So', in K. Knorr Cetina and A.V. Cicourel (eds) *Advances in Social Theory and Methodology: Toward an Integration of Micro- and Macro- Sociologies*, Boston: Routledge and Kegan Paul, pp. 277–303.

Carpenter, S. (2010) 'Los Angeles is Banking on Recycling', *Los Angeles Times*, 10 March 2012. Available online at http://latimesblogs.latimes.com/greenspace/2010/03/los-angeles-banking-on-recycling.html (accessed 27 November 2014).

Cohen, C. J. (1997) 'Punks, Bulldaggers, and Welfare Queens: The Radical Potential of Queer Politics?', *GLQ: A Journal of Lesbian and Gay Studies* 3(4): 437–65.

Elekes, G. (2012) 'The Blue Bin Scavengers – Recycling and L.A.'s Lost Treasure', *North Hollywood-Toluca Lake Patch*, 18 April 2012. Available online at http://northhollywood.patch.com/groups/gerald-elekess-blog/p/bp--the-blue-bin-scavengers-recycling-and-las-lost-treasure (accessed 27 November 2014).

Escobar, A. (1995) *Encountering Development: The Making and Unmaking of the Third World*, Princeton, NJ: Princeton University Press.

—— (2005) 'Economics and the Space of Modernity: Tales of Market, Production and Labour', *Cultural Studies* 19(2): 139–75.

Farrell, J. (2006) *Empire of Scrounge: Inside the Urban Underground of Dumpster Diving, Trash Picking, and Street Scavenging*, London/New York: New York University Press.

Gaard, G. (1997) 'Toward a Queer Ecofeminism', *Hypatia* 12(1):114–37.

Gatens, M. (1996) *Imaginary Bodies: Ethics, Power and Corporeality*, London: Routledge.

Gibson-Graham, J. K. (1996, 2006) *The End of Capitalism (As We Knew It): A Feminist Critique of Political Economy*, London/Minneapolis: University of Minnesota Press.

Grosz, E. A. (2001) *Architecture from the Outside: Essays on Virtual and Real Space*, Boston: Massachusetts Institute of Technology.

Halberstam, J. J. (2005) *In a Queer Time and Place: Transgender Bodies, Subcultural Lives*, New York/London: New York University Press.

Hardie, I. and MacKenzie, D. (2007) 'Assembling an Economic Actor: The *Agencement* of a Hedge Fund', *Sociological Review* 55(1): 57–80.

Harding, S. (2008) *Sciences From Below: Feminisms, Postcolonialities, and Modernities*, Durham, NC/London: Duke University Press.

Harvey, D. (2005) *A Brief History of Neoliberalism*, Oxford/New York: Oxford University Press.

Heiliger, E. (2011) *Shopping Our Way to a Better World? Redefining Gender, Sexuality and Moral Citizenship Under Ethical Consumerism* (Doctoral dissertation). Available from ProQuest Dissertations and Theses database.

—— (2012) 'Ado(red), Abhor(red), Disappea(red): Fashioning Race, Poverty, and Morality Under Product (Red)™', in S. Tarrant and M. Jolles (eds) *Fashion Talks: Undressing the Power of Style*, Albany: State University of New York Press, pp. 149–64.

—— (2013) 'Coffee "Tied With a Pink Ribbon": Transgender Phenomena and Transnational Feminisms in Twenty-First Century Ethical Consumer Movements', *Reconstruction: Studies in Contemporary Culture* 13(2). Available online at http://reconstruction.eserver.org/Issues/132/Heiliger.shtml (accessed 2 April 2015).

Holguin, R. (1993) 'Walking Off With Trash for Cash', *Los Angeles Times*, 9 September 1993. Available online at http://articles.latimes.com/1993-09-09/news/hl-33157_1_scavengers-new-recycling-recycling-program (accessed 27 November 2014).

Jaffee, D. (2007) *Brewing Justice: Fair Trade Coffee, Sustainability and Survival*, Berkeley/Los Angeles/London: University of California Press.

Latour, B. (1987) *Science in Action*, Cambridge, MA: Harvard University Press.

—— (2005) *Reassembling the Social: An Introduction to Actor-Network Theory*, Oxford: Oxford University Press.

Quinlan, A. (2012) 'Imagining a Feminist Actor-Network Theory', *International Journal of Actor-Network Theory and Technological Innovation* 4(2): 1–9.

Sandilands, C. (2002) 'Lesbian Separatist Communities and the Experience of Nature: Toward a Queer Ecology', *Organization and Environment* 15(2): 131–63.

Scott, C. V. (1996) *Gender and Development: Rethinking Modernization and Dependency Theory*, Boulder and London: Lynne Rienner Publishers.

Thibodeau, P. H. and Boroditsky, L. (2011) 'Metaphors We Think With: The Role of Metaphor in Reasoning', *PLoS ONE* 6(2): e16782.

—— (2013) 'Natural Language Metaphors Covertly Influence Reasoning', *PLoS ONE* 8(1): e52961.

Websites

Café Femenino Coffee Project: www.cafefemenino.com

Mobile Homecoming (MBHC) Project: www.mobilehomecoming.org

Product (Red)™: www.joinred.com/red

To the Other Side of Dreaming: https://digitalsisterhood.wordpress.com/2011/05/19/congratulations-to-the-2011-digital-sisters-of-the-year-stacey-milbern-and-mia-mingus

Trans*ition Fund Collective: The Self Made Men: http://trans-itionfundcollective.tumblr.com

Index